Fifty Foods

That Changed the Course of

History

written by Bill Price

A FIREFLY BOOK

Published by Firefly Books Ltd. 2014

First printing

Publisher Cataloging-in-Publication Data (U.S.)

A CIP record for this title is available from the
Library of Congress

**Library and Archives Canada Cataloging in
Publication**

Price, Bill, author
Fifty foods that changed the course of history /
Bill Price.
Includes bibliographical references and index.
ISBN 978-1-77085-427-7 (bound)
1. Food—History. 2. Food—Social aspects—
History. I. Title.
TX353.P75 2014   641.309   C2014-
900629-2

Published in the United States by
Firefly Books (U.S.) Inc.
P.O. Box 1338, Ellicott Station
Buffalo, New York 14205

Published in Canada by
Firefly Books Ltd.
50 Staples Avenue, Unit 1
Richmond Hill, Ontario L4B 0A7

Cover and interior design: Lindsey Johns

Printed in China

Conceived, designed, and produced by
Quid Publishing
Level 4, Sheridan House
114 Western Road
Hove BN3 1DD
England

Fifty Foods

That Changed the Course of

History

written by Bill Price

FIREFLY BOOKS

Contents

Introduction

The fate of nations hangs on their choice of food.

Jean Anthelme Brillat-Savarin
(1755–1826)

The shelves of supermarkets are today stacked high with foods from all over the world, an astonishing variety that many of us may take for granted because the sight has become so familiar. If we were to stop for a moment to consider where all of these foods have come from and how they have arrived on the shelves in conveniently packaged forms, then the connection between the food we eat and the way we live our lives would become apparent. Delve a little deeper still and what begins to emerge is the history of the interaction between people and their food, which shows how close these connections have always been and gives us an indication of the influence food has had on the nature of society.

THE STUFF OF LIFE

Food plays a central role in our lives: it is a necessity for all of us, a pleasure for many and an obsession for a few. It can bring us together and on occasion drive us apart, but there can be no getting away from the simple fact that we have to eat to live. The way in which people have provided for themselves through time and across cultures may be very different, but nevertheless the essential nature of sustenance remains much the same. From our hunting and gathering ancestors to the industrial agriculture and food manufacturing processes of today, food has been a common factor throughout our existence and wherever we live in the world.

To begin at the beginning, this survey of the role of food in history starts with the foods of early hunters and gatherers before moving on to look at the adoption of agriculture and those foodstuffs eaten by the first farmers. From there we move on to the rise of cities and civilizations, while also taking in food cultures from around the world, and then carry on into the medieval period. Food provided the impetus for the Age of Exploration, when the Portuguese and Spanish began to open up trade routes around the world and were then joined by the

EGYPTIAN FARMER
A mural from the tomb of Sennedjem (c.1200 BCE) showing a farmer ploughing his fields, most likely to grow wheat to make bread.

Dutch and British. It would lead to the development of commercial networks and global financial systems as well as establishing the European empires that would come to dominate world history. European colonization of the New World would have a devastating impact on the indigenous cultures of the region and the foods they relied on, while, in the 20th century, it would be behind the rise of America to global pre-eminence. In this way, we arrive at the industrial and post-industrial world of today, with its convenience foods and the brand names we find on those supermarket shelves.

THE COURSE OF HISTORY

Some foods have had an enormous impact on history, such as bread or the potato, while the influence of others has been rather more subtle. Anzac biscuits, for instance, continue to connect the people of Australia and New Zealand with the experiences of their soldiers in the First World War and, in South Korea, kimchi bridges the gap between the traditional and modern in a rapidly changing society. A few drinks have also been included, which, strictly speaking, might be stretching the definition of food a little, but, at the same time, the histories of some foods and drinks are so intertwined that it can become difficult to discuss one without the other. To give just one example, the connections between the trade networks supplying tea and sugar to Europe, which developed during the 18th century, mean that it would be difficult to grasp one without understanding the other. It is also true to say that the enormous impact tea has had on history, however it is classified, makes it impossible to ignore in a book such as this one.

SACK OF SPUDS
Some foods have had an enormous impact on history, such as the humble potato.

The book is arranged by date to bring a little order to what might otherwise tend toward chaos, but this is only a rough guide and, as some of the discussions span thousands of years, it is probably best to take the chronology with a pinch of salt. But what we can say with confidence is that food has not only sustained us throughout our history, it has also played a crucial role in the way we live our lives, as it will no doubt continue to do in the future. If it is true to say that we are what we eat, then the examples described here show us that it is equally the case that what we eat makes us who we are.

A Book of Verses underneath the Bough,
A Jug of Wine, a Loaf of Bread — and Thou
Beside me singing in the Wilderness —
Oh, Wilderness were Paradise enow.
Rubaiyat of Omar Khayyam, *trans.*
Edward Fitzgerald

Woolly Mammoth

Origin: Northern Europe and Siberia

Date: From about 40,000 BP until the end of the Ice Age

Type: Large extinct mammal

✦ **CULTURAL**

✦ **SOCIAL**

✦ COMMERCIAL

✦ POLITICAL

✦ MILITARY

For most of our history, stretching back for something like 200,000 years, people have found sustenance from the natural environment in which they have lived by means of hunting, fishing, and gathering. It is perhaps fitting, then, to begin this survey of foods that have changed the course of history by looking at an example of an important food source taken from this long period of hunting and gathering, even if the mammoth, which has been extinct for thousands of years, may not be anybody's idea of food today. Nevertheless, it played a role in the spread of anatomically modern humans into Europe, Central Asia, and Siberia, and possibly into the Americas as well, as can be seen in the artifacts and cave paintings our ancient ancestors left behind.

THE MAMMOTH STEPPE

During the Pleistocene, the geological epoch lasting from 2.5 million years ago to about 12,000 BP, the climate in the northern regions oscillated between being extremely cold and relatively warm, resulting in the expansion and contraction of ice sheets across northern Europe and Siberia. The environment immediately to the south of the ice sheets consisted of an enormous expanse of open tundra and grassland, together with a few low-growing shrubs and small trees in sheltered places. It is sometimes known as the mammoth steppe because it supported a distinctive array of large grazing mammals and their predators, many of which died out during the transition between the

PLEISTOCENE ENVIRONMENT
An artistic reconstruction of mammoths in the tundra landscape that covered much of Europe during the Pleistocene.

Pleistocene and Holocene in what is known as the Quaternary extinction event. As well as woolly mammoths, there were woolly rhinoceros, wild cattle and horses, giant elk, steppe bison, cave lions, and saber-toothed cats, together with a number of others that did not become extinct, like the European bison and reindeer.

One explanation for the disappearance of so many animal species at the same time was that they failed to adapt to the changing climatic conditions and the subsequent encroachment of forests into the grasslands. A variation of this theory suggests that the extinction of the mammoths resulted in a large-scale change in the environment because, like elephants in the African savannah today, their presence limited the number of trees in the region. Once the mammoths had gone, forests began to grow and the other species, adapted to open grassland, began to die out as well. An entirely different theory places the blame on increased hunting pressure from human beings, who had begun to migrate into the mammoth steppe about 40,000 years ago and, if comparisons with other human migrations in different parts of the world are valid, then these people would have had a dramatic impact on their environment.

No consensus currently exists among scientists over the causes of the Quaternary extinctions, but there can be no such doubts about the importance of these animal species to those people who first migrated into the region. Limited opportunities existed for gathering wild plants because of the short summers and cold weather conditions, so people had to rely more on hunting and fishing there than they did in regions with more temperate climates. There is also evidence of people scavenging for food from kills made by lions and, at least according to one theory, of adopting a hunting strategy involving a degree of cooperation with wolf packs, which, if correct, would mark the beginning of the domestication of dogs.

Whatever else they may have done to survive, the earliest inhabitants of northern Europe and Siberia were certainly mammoth hunters. It must have been extremely difficult and dangerous given that their

PIT ROASTING

✦

We don't know how people cooked their food during the Pleistocene, but roasting meat in a pit was a common method used before the invention of the oven and it would not be unreasonable to suggest that our distant ancestors cooked mammoth in this way. The first stage is to light a fire on some suitable rocks and then, once they are really hot, use them to line the pit. The meat is then put in, covered over with more hot rocks, and the pit is sealed using branches, leaves, moss, soil, or anything else available. After several hours the meat should be ready, slow roasted so that it remains succulent.

Barbecue is a guy thing, a throwback to the spit-roast woolly mammoth.
Molly O'Neill, American Food Writing *(2007)*

weapons were made from stone and wood, but the rewards of a successful hunt were enormous. A single mammoth kill could provide 3 or 4 tons of meat, much of which would presumably have been preserved by smoking and air-drying, or possibly by making use of the cold conditions to freeze it. All the other parts of the animal would also have been put to good use, including its thick hide and double layer of fur, which, together with a layer of subcutaneous fat, were adaptations of the mammoth to the cold. The bones were made into a huge variety of tools, a few of which have survived. Archaeologists in Russia have also found in the steppe (where there are few trees) the remains of huts dating from 15,000 BP in which mammoth bones and tusks, some 15 feet (4.5 m) in length, had been used to build the basic structure, which were then presumably covered in animal skins.

THE RED LADY AND LION MAN

According to DNA studies, anatomically modern humans, or Cro-Magnons as they are sometimes called, only began to migrate northward long after they had spread eastward through Asia. People first occupied Australia about 60,000 years ago, fully 20,000 years earlier than the migration into Europe had begun. This comparatively slow movement into Europe could have been a consequence of modern humans not being sufficiently adapted to the cold or perhaps because the northern regions were already inhabited by another human species, the Neanderthals, who were occupying all of the suitable territory. Archaeological research has shown that Neanderthals lived largely on a diet of meat, hunting a range of animals that included mammoth, and that they used a distinctive set of stone tools that hardly changed over the entire period of their existence. The first modern humans to migrate into Europe used an

CAVE MAMMOTH
Cave paintings of a mammoth and aurochs dating to c. 25,000 BP from the caves of Pech Merle in southern France.

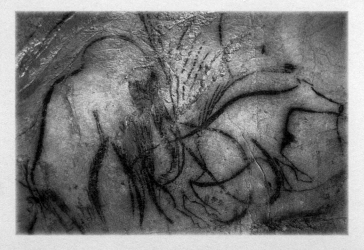

entirely different style of tool and, over the course of time, these tools changed as new styles were introduced. These differences have allowed us to distinguish between sites occupied by the two human species; they also suggest that modern humans may have been able to adapt more quickly to changing climatic conditions.

One of the earliest known skeletons of a modern human in Europe was found in 1823 by Reverend William Buckland, who conducted an archaeological excavation in Paviland Cave on the coast of South Wales and found an almost intact fossilized human skeleton that had been painted all over with red ocher and laid to rest next to the skull of a mammoth. Buckland thought the skeleton was of a woman from the Roman period and called it the Red Lady of Paviland, but more recent research has shown that it was actually a young man who was about 21 years old when he died. The bones have been dated to 32000 BP, placing him within the Aurignacian culture, named after the archaeological site in France where it was first described, which existed from the first human migration into Europe until the Last Glacial Maximum at about 25,000 BP, when the extreme cold forced humans to move to the south to live in warmer conditions.

A feature of the Aurignacian culture was the use of symbolic imagery, visible today in the extraordinary wall paintings in Chauvet Cave in France. More than 60 representations of mammoths have been found in the cave, together with numerous examples of other animals, particularly bison and horses, indicating a close relationship between people and their environment and, more than likely, some form of religious or ritual connection. Another beautiful example of the artistic capacity of these people is the so-called Lion Man found in Hohlenstein-Stadel in southern Germany, a strangely anthropomorphized representation of a standing lion carved from a mammoth tusk. It is, of course, impossible to know now what was on the mind of the individual who made this object, but the material used may well have been as important as the carved image. In depicting a person in the form of a lion, the supreme predator, the carver may have been attempting to transfer its hunting prowess to themselves to ensure success on future hunting expeditions.

LION MAN
The 40,000-year-old carved mammoth tusk found in Hohlenstein-Stadel, Germany. It depicts a figure with both human and lion characteristics.

© Dagmar Hollmann | Wikimedia Commons

In the hunting and gathering societies of today, people invariably display a remarkable and intimate knowledge of their environment, no doubt because they need such knowledge in order to survive. But they also exhibit a deeply held reverence for the animals they hunt that appears to go far beyond necessity alone. The evidence left behind by past hunting societies, in the cave paintings and carved mammoth tusks, suggests that they shared a similar set of beliefs, perhaps also engaging in the same sort of shamanic rituals as their modern counterparts. We don't know how the people of the Aurignacian culture hunted large mammals like mammoths, but presumably it would have been a collective effort and may have been similar in some cases to the way in which Native Americans would sometimes hunt buffalo by driving a herd over a cliff. However it was achieved, the provision of such a large resource of food in what was otherwise a challenging environment in which to live must surely have been an occasion of celebration as people feasted on mammoth meat after a successful hunt.

Another indication of the significance of the mammoth to the Aurignacian people can be seen in the burial of the young man found in Paviland. The gesture of placing his body next to a mammoth skull suggests that these animals were held in sufficiently high regard for it to be thought fitting for one to accompany him in his final resting place. Perhaps he had been killed in a mammoth hunt or was in some other way connected with mammoths in life, as shamanic hunters are often associated with particular animals today. But, whatever the reason, the bond between the two was marked by the people who buried him, demonstrating to us thousands of years later that mammoths probably meant more to our ancient ancestors than simply being a source of food alone.

CROSSING BERINGIA

Humans and mammoths shared the Pleistocene environment for more than 20,000 years before these Ice Age giants died out. Our ancestors must have followed the seasonal movements of the mammoth herds, traveling northward in the spring as the mammoths migrated to graze on the fresh grass of the steppe as the snow melted and then returning to the south as the hard winters set in. It is possible that the first people who crossed the land bridge that connected Siberia with Alaska were nomadic hunters following mammoths, traveling through an ice-free corridor in Beringia, the name given to the region later inundated by rising water levels at the end of the last Ice Age to form the Bering Strait.

Marks on mammoth bones found in the Bluefish Caves, an archaeological site in Yukon, Canada, have been interpreted as signs that the animal was butchered by humans and, as the bones have been dated to 28,000 BP, if this is correct, then it would show that humans were present in North America more than 10,000 years before the generally accepted date for the first migration into the continent. The presence of butchery marks on these bones does not necessarily mean that they were made at the time that the mammoths died. It could have occurred at a much later date, the marks being made by people who had found a frozen mammoth carcass, so it is impossible to say for certain if these finds represent some of the earliest signs of the peopling of the Americas.

The warmer summers experienced in Siberia in recent years have had the effect of releasing frozen mammoth carcasses that had been entombed in ice for thousands of years, allowing scientists to study them in much greater detail than had previously been possible. By examining the tusks, which grew constantly throughout the lives of the animals, it is possible not only to age the individuals concerned but also to gain an insight into the climate conditions prevalent during their lifetimes. Recent research has also established that small populations of mammoths existed on islands off the coast of Siberia and Alaska long after the mainland population had become extinct, the last ones continuing to live on Wrangel Island in the Arctic Ocean until only 4,000 years ago.

TUSK SECTION
A cross section of a mammoth tusk found in Siberia showing concentric annual growth rings.

The discovery of well-preserved frozen carcasses has allowed the recovery of undamaged strands of DNA, which under normal conditions degrades quickly, leading to the possibility of cloning mammoths. There are numerous technical issues to overcome before this could happen, and the ethics of recreating an extinct species will have to be addressed, but it has nevertheless raised the potential prospect of seeing live mammoths roaming across Siberia. It is certainly an intriguing thought, but, whatever happens, it would appear unlikely that mammoth will feature in our diet anytime soon.

Bread

Origin: Wherever people
have lived

Date: At least 30,000
years ago

Type: Cooked dough
of flour and water

+ **CULTURAL**
+ **SOCIAL**
+ **COMMERCIAL**
+ **POLITICAL**
+ MILITARY

If one food can be said to have been more closely involved with human history than any other, then it must surely be bread. It has been a staple of our diet for thousands of years and is now eaten in almost every culture. Considering that the starting point is much the same everywhere, a dough of flour and water, breads from around the world come in a truly astonishing variety of shapes and sizes, from nans and chapattis to baguettes and brioche, not to mention the sliced white bread sold in the local store or the organic whole-grain spelt loaf from the farmers' market. And where would we be without a few slices for a lunchtime sandwich or a bun for our burgers and hot dogs?

THE STAFF OF LIFE

Human beings are not adapted to eat grass; our stomachs are too small to digest it properly and, in any case, our large brains require more energy than we can derive from it. Paradoxically, various types of grass provide us with the staple foods many of us eat every day. Wheat, rice, and corn, to name only the most common, are all grasses and the reason why these have become so important to us as foodstuffs, despite all being largely indigestible in their raw state, is, of course, because we have developed methods of processing and cooking the most nutritious parts, the seed grains, to unlock the store of energy contained within.

The biologist Richard Wrangham has developed a theory that cooking was one of the main driving forces behind human evolution, allowing for an increase in brain size because of the greater amount of energy made available to us in food when it is cooked compared to when it is raw. Cooking has, he suggests, been with us right from the beginning, a defining characteristic of humanity, and, while he does not mention it directly, this also implies that food processing has come along with us as well because it is often an essential preliminary stage in the cooking process. In all cultures where cereals are eaten, the hard outer cover of grains must first be broken down by some form of grinding to expose the stored starch; otherwise they remain indigestible. And one of the earliest forms of processed food is bread, made from grinding and cooking grains.

Guide me, O thou great Redeemer,
Pilgrim through this barren land;
I am weak, but thou art mighty;
Hold me with thy powerful hand:
Bread of heaven, bread of heaven
Feed me till I want no more.
Feed me till I want no more.
William Williams Pantycelyn (1717–91)

Evidence of the processing required to make bread has been found in archaeological excavations of ancient sites in the form of the stones used to grind the grains, known as querns. Chemical analysis of the worn surfaces of some querns excavated in a number of different sites across Europe has revealed microscopic traces of the flour that was produced and this has been carbon dated to 30,000 BP, providing us with the earliest direct evidence we have for bread-making, even if there can be little doubt that it is actually very much older. If Richard Wrangham's theory about cooking is correct, then the chances are that our ability to make bread goes all the way back to our distant ancestor, *Homo erectus*, who emerged about two million years ago in Africa.

When anatomically modern humans first began to migrate out of Africa about 70,000 years ago, they most probably continued to gather the grains of the grasses they encountered in their new environments, no doubt grinding them up and making bread. The hunting and gathering lifestyle continued for tens of thousands of years as people spread out through Asia and into Europe before what has been described as the greatest social change in the history of humanity, the adoption of agriculture, began to emerge about 12,000 years ago in the Fertile Crescent. This arc of land straddles the arid Syrian desert and extends from the Zagros Mountains of Iran in the east to modern-day Israel and Jordan in the west.

The consensus of opinion in archaeological circles used to be that people remained as nomadic hunter-gatherers until they adopted a more sedentary lifestyle with the invention of agriculture, but, more recently, archaeological discoveries in the Fertile Crescent have suggested that, where conditions were conducive to sedentism, people lived in permanent settlements long before they began to grow their own food. In this scenario, the adoption of agriculture occurred as a gradual transition over the course of many generations. Archaeological studies of the Natufian culture, which existed from about 14,000 BP along the Levantine coastline of the eastern Mediterranean, in what is now Lebanon and Israel, provide this theory with some support. The favorable conditions in the Levant at that time allowed the Natufians to live in villages for much of the year even though they did not practice any form of agriculture, apparently only moving away for short periods to exploit seasonally available food sources. For the rest of the time, they lived on what was locally available and stored the surplus grains they gathered in stone granaries so they could make bread throughout the year.

GRINDING STONES
Three examples of Natufian querns used to grind grains, now in the Dagon Museum in Haifa, Israel.

The remains of some of these stone granaries have been found in excavations of Natufian villages, together with querns and stone sickles, used for harvesting grasses, indicating that much of the technology needed for the adoption of farming was already in place while people still lived as hunter-gatherers and suggesting that the shift between the two could well have been relatively easy to make. We don't know what prompted this shift, but it appears to have first happened in the region of the Fertile Crescent to the northeast of the Levant, in what is now southern Turkey, Iraq, and Iran. One theory suggests that a sudden cooling in climate, beginning in about 12,800 BP and known as the Younger Dryas, caused a dramatic reduction in food availability, forcing people to adopt a more reliable system of providing food than hunting and gathering by cultivating cereals for themselves. The increase in labor that this change would have entailed may have been a trade-off worth making to ensure a constant food supply in a more challenging environment than had previously been the case and, once farming had begun, going back to hunting and gathering even when the climate improved was not possible because the increased amount of food produced by farming had led to an increase in the population.

The wild ancestors of modern wheat varieties, einkorn and emmer, both grow naturally in this region of the Fertile Crescent, and, as people began to cultivate them, they must have selected the seeds from those plants that demonstrated the characteristics they wanted to retain to plant again in the following year. One of the characteristics they bred into their crops by selecting seed in this way was for ears of wheat that did not shed grains before being harvested. Wild wheat drops its seed when it is ripe, but it is much better for the farmer if a cultivated plant retains its seeds so it can be harvested. Presumably, a natural mutation occurred in the wheat plants being grown, which was recognized as being a useful trait for the future. Farmers would also have selected the plants with larger grains to keep for seed, together with those showing variations that led to an improvement in the quality of the resulting bread, and in doing so they began to separate domesticated wheat from its wild ancestors.

The type of bread being made by these first farmers was probably similar to the flatbreads made in the Middle East today. It is also possible that leavened breads were being baked, an innovation that may have occurred as a consequence of naturally occurring yeast spores getting into the dough so that, when it was cooked, it would have risen, producing bread with a lighter texture. No evidence has ever been found to support such a scenario so it is only possible to speculate at the moment, but leavened bread was being made 6,000 years ago in the Mesopotamian and Egyptian civilizations so it would not be unreasonable to suggest that it could have been made at an earlier date in the same region.

The surpluses produced by farming allowed people to specialize in different trades and made the development of cities possible. In the Sumerian city of Uruk, located in the southern region of Mesopotamia, scribes developed a system of accounting for this surplus produce by impressing marks on clay tablets, including a symbol for bushels of wheat, which developed into the earliest known form of writing. One of the first types of specialized tradesmen in Uruk and other cities were bakers, particularly those making leavened bread, which, as anybody who has attempted to bake at home without using a bread-making machine will know, is something of an art form that requires an intimate knowledge of the process and plenty of practice to master.

SOURDOUGH

✦

Rather than the alcoholic fermentation which occurs when yeast is used in bread-making to make the dough rise, the sourdough method involves a lactic fermentation. A starter containing bacteria is used, which gives the resulting bread a slightly sour taste. The starter is made by simply mixing flour with water and leaving it to become infected with naturally occurring lactobacilli and this is used to inoculate the dough with the bacteria. Once the starter culture has got going, it can then be fed with more flour and water to keep it active so that it can be used over and over again, for a period of months or even years.

It appears likely that ancient bakers were adding a small piece of the previous day's bread dough to the new mix in order to inoculate it with yeast in a method similar to the starters used in the sourdough method of baking today; or, they were using yeast from the brewing of beer and adding that to their dough. The relationship between bread-making and brewing is a very long one, persisting up to the 19th century when cultivated bread yeast became available for the first time, and it remained typical throughout the history of bread-making up until then for bakeries to be located next to breweries in order to make use of the brewer's yeast.

BREAD OF HEAVEN

When Moses led the Children of Israel out of slavery in Egypt, the Book of Exodus tells us, they left in such a hurry that there was no time to wait for bread to bake and they left without the leaven they used to make it rise. They existed on unleavened bread during their flight. This is the origin of the Jewish tradition of eating matzo, made only from flour and water, during the festival of Passover and, before the seven days of the festival has begun, of cleansing the house of any trace of chametz, food containing leavening. According to one interpretation of the biblical story, unleavened bread was eaten during the Israelites' journey into the wilderness because, unlike leavened bread, it could be kept for much longer without going stale, much as hardtack was used to provision military campaigns and long sea journeys in more recent times.

MATZOS
A stack of matzos, the traditional unleavened bread made for the festival of the Passover.

Matzos are made in the weeks leading up to Passover and are usually pricked with a fork before being cooked and then baked quickly in order to prevent any chance of them rising. At the Seder, the ritual feast held on the first evening of Passover, three matzos are placed in the center of the table along with a plate displaying six foods that have a special resonance during the traditional telling of the story of the Exodus. The first of these is karpas, a green vegetable, often parsley or celery, to symbolize the hopes of the Israelites in Egypt; it is dipped in salty water before being eaten to stand for the tears they shed after becoming enslaved. Haroset is a brown paste made of chopped fruit and nuts to make it look like the mortar the Israelites used in the building work they were forced to do in Egypt, while the two types of bitter herbs (maror and hazeret), often horseradish and romaine lettuce, are used to signify the bitterness of slavery in Egypt. The roasted shank bone of a lamb or goat (*z'roa*) stands for the sacrifice the Israelites were commanded to make on the night they left Egypt and at the Temple of Jerusalem after they had arrived in the Promised Land; the final component, a roasted hard-boiled egg, also symbolizes this sacrifice. In this way, the telling of the story of the Exodus is accompanied by the tastes, smells, and feelings experienced by the Israelites, making the Seder a ritual of the senses as well as a feast.

And as they were eating, Jesus took bread, and blessed it, and brake it, and gave it to the disciples, and said, Take, eat; this is my body.

Matthew 26:26

Bread also plays a central role in the Christian ritual of the Eucharist, representing the body of Christ and relating to the moment during the Last Supper when Jesus broke bread and shared it with the disciples. The exact nature of the observation of this sacrament was one of the sources of the Great Schism of 1054 in which the Roman Catholic and Eastern Orthodox Churches failed to agree on the use of either unleavened or leavened bread during the Eucharist. The dispute arose because the accounts given in the New Testament of the Bible do not make it clear what sort of bread was being eaten by Christ during the Last Supper. The tradition that developed in the Eastern Church in Constantinople was to use leavened bread, thereby

BREAKING BREAD
The Last Supper by the Spanish painter Juan de Juanes (c.1523–79) showing Jesus sharing bread with the disciples.

BREAD PROTEST
A Tunisian man holds a loaf of bread above his head during a protest in Tunis on December 27th, 2010, against the spiraling costs of living.

distinguishing Christianity from Judaism, whereas in the Western tradition either sort of bread was considered to be acceptable. At the heart of the matter were differences between the Patriarch of Constantinople and the Pope in Rome, and these led to a series of mutual excommunications, only finally lifted in 1965, after almost a thousand years.

THE PRICE OF BREAD

In "Them Belly Full (But We Hungry)," Bob Marley sang, "A hungry mob is an angry mob," summing up in one line the potential for civil unrest that has accompanied shortages of food or a sudden rise in the price of staple foods such as bread. One of the most famous instances of this phenomenon occurred in the late 1780s in France, where, after a series of poor harvests, the price of wheat rocketed and people began to go hungry, even if the revolution that began in 1789 was as much a consequence of middle-class dissatisfaction and the spread of enlightenment ideals of equality and republicanism as it had to do with the hungry mob in the street.

Having looked to government for bread, on the very first scarcity they will turn and bite the hand that fed them.

Edmund Burke, Thoughts and Details on Scarcity *(1800)*

A more recent example is the Arab Spring, which began in Tunisia in 2011 before spreading to Egypt and to other countries in the region. Extreme weather in Australia, Russia, and Pakistan over the course of the year had dramatically reduced the wheat harvest in those countries, pushing the price up on the commodity markets around the world, which was then increased even further by the activities of commodity traders out to make a fast buck from the crisis. The rising prices were felt particularly in the countries of North Africa and the Middle East, which import much of their bread-making wheat and so are more vulnerable to sudden changes than other countries that can grow more of their own.

As in France in 1789, the revolutions in Tunisia and Egypt had complicated roots, articulated in one slogan used by protestors in Egypt that simply read, "Bread, Freedom, Justice." As well as being a protest about the rising price of food, both were also fueled by the nature of the autocratic regimes that had been in place for decades and were accused of corruption, fixing elections, and the suppression of free speech. High levels of unemployment, together with rapidly increasing populations that included a high proportion of young and disillusioned people, also contributed to an increasingly volatile situation.

The Arab Spring was sparked by the death of one man, Mohamed Bouazizi, a Tunisian street vendor who set fire to himself in a protest against the years of mistreatment he had endured at the hands of government officials. The fruit and vegetables he had been selling from a cart had been repeatedly confiscated and only returned after he had paid a bribe. By December 2010, the cost of living had gone up so much that Bouazizi could no longer afford to pay the bribes, so when his goods were confiscated yet again he had no way of getting them back, leaving him with no means of making a living. The dire circumstances he found himself in appear to have prompted his desperate actions and news of the circumstances of his death prompted a wave of demonstrations and riots in Tunisia against the rule of President Ben Ali. It led to Ben Ali, who had been in power since 1987, fleeing the country in the middle of January 2011 and the beginning of protests in other countries in North Africa and the Middle East.

GLUTEN

◆

By kneading bread dough, bakers create links between the proteins in wheat flour to form the composite molecule gluten. The nature of this molecule means that it is elastic, so when carbon dioxide produced by yeast fermentation is released it stretches, allowing the bread to rise. Hard wheat varieties are preferred in bread-making than softer wheats because they have a higher protein content, leading to a higher proportion of gluten in the dough when it is kneaded. The resulting bread will rise better and be lighter than bread made from soft wheat.

Pacific Salmon

Origin: The Pacific
Northwest coast

Date: From about 15,000
years ago onward

Type: Anadromous fish

+ *CULTURAL*
+ *SOCIAL*
+ *COMMERCIAL*
+ POLITICAL
+ MILITARY

Before the arrival of Europeans, the abundance of food in the coastal regions of the Pacific Northwest of North America supported a unique and extraordinary culture. The five species of Pacific salmon that returned from the ocean to spawn in the rivers of the region every year were one of the mainstays of this culture, arriving at predictable times of the year and often in huge numbers, allowing these hunter-gatherers to live sedentary lives.

SALMON NATIONS

The opening chapter of this book described how people may have first migrated to the North American continent by following herds of large mammals across the Bering land bridge. An alternative explanation suggests that people could have followed a coastal route, traveling in canoes and living off the produce of the sea as they moved from what is now Siberia to Alaska. The rising sea levels as the ice melted at the end of the last glacial period covered any traces of this migration that may have remained, meaning that, if people followed this route, any settlements they may have established on the coast would now be underwater. But, even though we cannot be certain of how they got there, by 15,000 BP people were living in North America and must surely have occupied the northwest coastal region because of its relatively mild climate and the availability of large quantities of food.

The retreating ice sheets left a green strip of land between the mountains in the interior and the ocean that provided an ideal environment for human habitation, the warming climatic conditions making the rivers of the region perfect salmon spawning grounds. Forests also began to spread northward, cloaking the interior with red cedar, western hemlock, Douglas fir, and a variety of other species and providing these First Nations with a huge resource of wood. The availability of such an abundance of food and resources led to the development of a highly complex hunter-gatherer society and an elaborate material culture in which everyday items, such as baskets

Only a fool starves in the land of the Tlingit.

Saying of the Tlingit people

and storage boxes, were converted into beautiful works of art, decorated with highly stylized and symbolic designs. The people who lived in this region when Europeans began to arrive in the 18th and 19th centuries may well have been the descendants of those original settlers and, even though the culture no doubt evolved over time, we can get a glimpse of how those first people lived from the aspects of that culture that persisted into modern times. We can also learn from those people who still live there today; for instance, the Tlingit of the coast of British Columbia, the Haida from Haida Gwaii, or the Queen Charlotte Islands as they are also known, and the Kwakwaka'wakw on Vancouver Island.

The people of these First Nations lived in large houses made from planks of red cedar, often with beautifully carved totem poles erected in front of them. Villages were situated along the coast and seagoing canoes were used for fishing and to mount raids against other tribes. Salmon runs in the late summer and autumn, comprising adults returning to rivers to spawn after spending most of their lives in the ocean, provided a huge resource of food. As well as hunting them with spears and traps, the people erected large fish weirs either spanning a river completely or stretched across a channel where the salmon were known to swim. Large quantities of fish could be caught in this way and, while some would have been cooked and eaten right away, impaled on sticks and roasted over an open fire, the majority would have been either air-dried on racks or smoked in wooden smoke houses specially built for the purpose. The huge glut of fish available during a run, which was over in a matter of days, could provide enough food to last through the leaner winter months ahead. The importance of the fish to the people of the Pacific Northwest coast has been compared to the role played by the buffalo in the cultures of the tribes of the Great Plains and has led to them being described as the "salmon nations."

SALMON RUNS

◆

Pacific salmon are anadromous, migrating from the ocean to freshwater rivers and streams to spawn, often finding their way back to the same river, even the same spot on that river, where they were born. This migration is known as the salmon run and can involve many thousands of fish at the same time, providing such predators as bears and bald eagles with a bonanza of food. It has been estimated, for instance, that, in a good year, half a million chum salmon can reach their spawning ground on the Chilkat River in Alaska, arriving in late October or November and sometimes attracting more than 3,000 bald eagles.

Contact with Europeans, beginning with Russian fur trappers in the 18th century, exposed the people of the First Nations to diseases to which they had no natural immunity. Smallpox in particular had a devastating impact, in some cases causing the deaths of over 90 percent of the population in the area of an outbreak. It was a devastating blow to the culture, causing villages to be abandoned and accumulated knowledge that had been passed down through the generations to be lost.

Violent confrontations between settlers and the First Nations did not occur as often in the Pacific Northwest as in other parts of North America; instead, trading relationships developed that in some cases led to the accumulation of great wealth among tribal chiefs. Sea otter fur was highly sought after because of the demand for it in China, where it could sell for huge sums. Over the course of the 19th century and 20th centuries, a serious decline in sea otter numbers occurred as they were hunted to the point of extinction before conservation measures were put in place. The salmon also went into decline as commercial fishing expanded in the 20th century and, even though the link between the fish and the people remained, few of the First Nations relied on the runs for food any more.

JOHN WEST
The Scottish-born John West (1823–88) started the first salmon cannery on the Oregon side of the Columbia River.

CANNERY ROW

The coastal tribes of the Pacific Northwest had long traded dried salmon to those in the interior. The potential to exploit the vast and apparently limitless supply of the fish was recognized in the mid 19th century after the technology required to preserve food in tin cans had been developed. Canneries began to open on the coast and along rivers all the way from California to British Columbia and on to Alaska. One of the main locations for the canning industry became the Columbia River in northern Oregon, where, in 1868, the Scottish-born John West founded the Westport Cannery. The industry boomed in the region and, by the 1880s, 37 canneries were operating along the river, many employing Chinese workers in the factories and operating their own fleets of fishing boats.

Pelling Stanley and Company of Liverpool were among West's British customers, and after he died in 1888 the company bought the right to use his name on their products. John West salmon became popular in Britain, mostly because it was much cheaper than the fresh fish, which remained expensive until farmed salmon began to appear regularly in supermarkets. The John West brand also began to be exported around the British Empire, which, at the time, spanned the globe, and it remains well known today even if the company has changed hands on a number of occasions and has since branched out into other fish.

SALMON FISHING
A 1914 photograph showing fishermen on the Columbia River in Oregon catching salmon in a seine net.

The boom in the cannery industry on the Columbia River continued until fish stocks became so reduced that it was no longer viable. A combination of overfishing, industrial pollution, the construction of dams that prevented salmon spawning, and the diversion of river water for irrigation came together to put an end to the industry. The last cannery on the river closed in 1980, by which time the center of the industry had long since moved to Alaska, which now accounts for 80 percent of the entire business. Conservation measures and the development of hatchery programs have gone some way to reversing the decline, particularly in Alaska, where strict regulations are now in force to ensure that salmon fishing is conducted on a more sustainable basis than it was in the past.

If I had the choice between smoked salmon and tinned salmon, I'd have it tinned.

Harold Wilson, the Labour prime minister of Britain between 1968 and 1976

CHINOOK SALMON
The chinook, or king salmon, is the largest of the five species of salmon found along the Pacific Northwest coast.

Lamb

Origin: The Fertile Crescent

Date: c.11,000 BP

Type: Livestock

+ CULTURAL
+ **SOCIAL**
+ **COMMERCIAL**
+ POLITICAL
+ MILITARY

In the world today there are more than a billion sheep, spread out across six continents and stretching from the hills of Scotland to the South Island of New Zealand. Sheep have become so widespread because of their adaptability, being capable of fitting in to a variety of farming systems and thriving in different climates and environments. Sheep-farming allows for the use of land that is of little use to other forms of agriculture. As well as meat, sheep can be farmed for wool and milk, but, in the end, its popularity rests on the fact that lots of people like to eat lamb.

SHEEP AND MEN

Sheep have had a very long association with humans, going back to our hunter-gatherer ancestors, who, no doubt, appreciated a leg of lamb as much as the rest of us. But the turning point in the relationship came about 11,000 years ago, when sheep were first domesticated in the same region of Western Asia, the Fertile Crescent, as were wheat and barley. Archaeological research suggests that the wild ancestor of the sheep was most likely the Asiatic mouflon, which still inhabits the region today, and that it was domesticated in the hills of the border region between what is today southeastern Turkey and northern Syria.

The exact way in which this domestication occurred is not known, but, as it is thought to have happened not long after people began to grow their own crops in this region, adopting a more sedentary lifestyle than had previously been the case, it is possible that the two events were connected. The population growth that most likely accompanied the cultivation of cereals would have caused an increase in hunting pressure on mouflon and a corresponding drop in their numbers. The resulting scarcity of meat could have caused people to adopt a different way of providing such an important food, perhaps initially bringing the lambs of a ewe they had killed back to their homes and raising them and then going on to breed their own sheep rather than relying on a wild source.

The first domestic sheep, like their mouflon ancestors, had hairy hides rather than woolly fleeces. By about 6000 BCE, sheep with wool were being kept in the Zagros Mountains of Iran, which forms the eastern part of the Fertile Crescent, but, as far as we know from the available archaeological evidence, it would take another 2,000 years before the wool was being used to weave textiles. The production of sheep wool as well as meat explains why it has

been farmed much more widely than goats. Sheep also do better on grassland because they are grazers, while goats prefer to browse on the leaves of trees and shrubs; this means that sheep are easy to manage in a mixed farming system in which crops and grass are alternated on the same area of land.

THE QASHQAI

Sheep have played an important role in the histories of numerous peoples around

The meadows are covered with flocks and the valleys are mantled with grain; they shout for joy and sing.

Psalms 65:13

the world and in none more so than the Qashqai of southwestern Iran, who, until recently, lived a semi-nomadic lifestyle that revolved around the movements of their sheep. The Qashqai are of Turkic descent and migrated to Iran from the plains of Central Asia about a thousand years ago to settle in the flat land to the south of the city of Shiraz. They established a farming system that involved keeping sheep and growing crops in the lowlands during the winter months and then moving their flocks in the spring to exploit the first flush of new grazing as it became available in the Zagros Mountains, making the journey of 300 miles (483 km) over the course of a month. In the early fall, with

MILKING SHEEP
A Qashqai woman milking a sheep. In the summer, the Qashqai live on the flat land to the south of Shiraz.

the grazing in the mountains exhausted and the weather deteriorating, they returned to the south, planting their crops as soon as they arrived and introducing their rams to the ewes so that lambs would be born in February and be old enough to begin the journey to the mountains toward the end of March.

The Qashqai were largely self-sufficient, living on the crops they grew in the winter and on the meat from their sheep, together with

yogurt made from sheep's milk. They also made rugs and carpets, using home-spun wool colored with natural dyes and woven in characteristic geometric patterns. The rugs were then sold to dealers in the main bazaar of Shiraz and were widely regarded as being some of the highest quality and most beautiful available. Since the 1960s, the Qashqai have adopted a more settled lifestyle and those who still travel between their traditional winter and summer grounds now usually transport their sheep by road rather than making the journey on foot. They may no longer be as dependent on the sheep as they were, but they remain a distinct ethnic group in Iran today and, while they have adapted to the times, many still keep sheep and weave carpets, maintaining the traditions on which their culture has always been based.

THE CLEARANCES

The Highland Clearances occurred in the north and west of Scotland during the 18th and 19th centuries, when people were forced off the land to make way for commercial sheep-farming. The clearances remain an emotive subject in Scotland and are often described as being a consequence of the greed and inhumanity of the landowners, who were only interested in making a profit and showed more concern for sheep than people. There is more than an element of truth in this explanation, but to gain a wider understanding of how the clearances came about it is necessary to consider the historical background, including the Jacobite Risings and the changes to British society brought about by both the Agricultural and Industrial Revolutions.

TEXEL LAMBS
Modern breeds like these Texels, originally from the Netherlands, are very different from their wild ancestors.

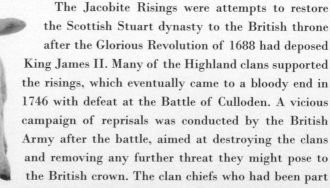

The Jacobite Risings were attempts to restore the Scottish Stuart dynasty to the British throne after the Glorious Revolution of 1688 had deposed King James II. Many of the Highland clans supported the risings, which eventually came to a bloody end in 1746 with defeat at the Battle of Culloden. A vicious campaign of reprisals was conducted by the British Army after the battle, aimed at destroying the clans and removing any further threat they might pose to the British crown. The clan chiefs who had been part

of the rebellion were either executed or stripped of their lands, while those who had stayed loyal to Britain were rewarded with the land taken from the rebels. Many were also awarded titles and incorporated into the British aristocracy.

At about the same time, the Agricultural Revolution was transforming large parts of rural Britain. The Enclosure Acts formalized the ownership of land, giving the title to individuals of what had been common land or communal open fields, depriving many people of the traditional rights they had previously held. In the Scottish Highlands, the newly created aristocracy obtained the title to much of the land and, in an attempt to make money from it, began the clearances so that they could rent farms to commercial farmers. The idea was to farm sheep for meat and wool to supply the expanding cities and towns of Lowland Scotland and the North of England, where the landless rural poor had moved in order to find work in factories and workshops.

CLEARED LAND
These ruins are all that remain on the Hebridean island of Fuaigh Mòr, cleared of people in 1841 to graze sheep.

In some parts of the Highlands, the clearances were carried out by soldiers and policemen who literally burned people out of their houses. It caused great hardship, including cases of starvation, and resulted in mass migration away from the Highlands. Some were forced to join the migration to the industrial towns of Britain, whereas others emigrated abroad in search of a better life in other parts of the British Empire or in America. Those who remained were resettled on land too poor for commercial farming, where they subsisted on small crofts and worked as fishermen, kelp harvesters, and weavers in an effort to make a living.

The sheep farms that replaced the people in the Highlands did not last very long, mainly because it proved impossible to produce meat and wool cheaply enough to compete with better quality imports from Australia and New Zealand. The Highlands changed again, becoming home to the shooting estates of the aristocracy and wealthy industrialists, while the signs of those people who had formerly lived in the region gradually eroded away; now, all that remains of their houses and townships are piles of stone. The population of the Highlands was deci-

HAGGIS

✦

In Scotland, Burns Night is held on January 25th to celebrate Scots poet Robert Burns' birthday and would hardly be complete without the haggis, made from those parts of a sheep some may think better thrown away. The heart, lungs, and various other internal organs are minced up with onions and oats and then simmered slowly in a sheep's stomach. At the Burns supper it is served with neeps and tatties (mashed turnip and potato) and accompanied with a dram of whiskey. In 1848, Thomas Burns, Robert's nephew, was one of the first settlers in Dunedin on New Zealand's South Island, where Burns Night continues to be observed among the Scottish community with traditional enthusiasm.

mated by the clearances and has never recovered. Today it is one of the least inhabited regions of Western Europe.

Many of the Highlanders who were either compelled to emigrate to North America or chose to go in an effort to escape poverty formed close-knit communities with strong connections to their homeland and have maintained their traditions and language. On the island of Cape Breton in Nova Scotia, which, of course, means New Scotland, these ties have led to it becoming a center of Scots Gaelic culture today. Over the course of the 19th century something like 50,000 Highlanders arrived on the islands, settling mostly on the northern coastline and the interior uplands, known as the Highlands, where the Gaelic language is still widely spoken and where traditional music, particularly fiddle playing, can be regularly heard.

SHEEP-FARMING IN NEW ZEALAND

Another destination for people from the Highlands, together with emigrants from other parts of the British Isles, was New Zealand, where, over the course of the 19th century, sheep-farming became the mainstay of its economy. The introduction of refrigerated steamships in the 1880s led to further growth in the production of meat because it opened up the export trade in New Zealand lamb to Britain, which was one of the reasons why commercial sheep-farming in the Scottish Highlands failed. For the next hundred years, the export of agricultural products to Britain, mostly lamb and dairy products, made up a significant part of the New Zealand economy. A serious problem emerged when Britain joined the European Union in 1973, because the preferential treatment it had previously given to imports from New Zealand could not continue as a consequence of it adopting the Common Agricultural Policy.

In 1984, the newly elected Liberal New Zealand government reacted to the economic crisis that had developed by initiating a program of reforms aimed at moving away from a reliance on agricultural exports toward a more balanced economy. Part of the restructuring involved stopping all the subsidies paid to farmers in the country to provide a guarantee for their businesses, which came as a huge shock because at that time the subsidies accounted for almost 40 percent of farm income. New Zealand farmers were forced to adapt to these new market conditions and, rather than agriculture in the country becoming bankrupt, as some people had claimed it would, farming actually became much more efficient. Farmers began to develop new markets and diversify their businesses into a variety of other commodities so that now, as well as lamb and butter, New Zealand exports kiwi fruit, wine, and a range of other products.

The number of sheep in New Zealand has declined as a result of the ending of agricultural subsidies, falling from about 70 million in the early 1980s to about 40 million today, even if that still means there are almost 10 times as many sheep in the country as there are people. Farming has gone from strength to strength in recent years and, despite the decline in actual numbers, New Zealand exports more lamb now than it did before the subsidies were stopped. No other country in the developed world has followed the model established by New Zealand, opting instead to maintain the payment of subsidies to farmers and arguing that, rather than setting an example for the future, New Zealand is a special case because more than 90 percent of its farm produce is exported.

In truth, the governments of those countries that retain agricultural subsidies lack the political will to take on powerful farming lobbies. In the European Union, the protection of national interests by those countries that benefit the most from the Common Agricultural Policy have meant that only minor reforms have been made to a subsidy system that was first developed to address the food shortages that occurred in Europe after the end of the Second World War. Although such attitudes persist, agricultural subsidy will continue to be paid even though, if the example of New Zealand is anything to go by, everybody, including farmers, would be better off in the long run if it came to an end.

I am forgetting myself into admiring a mountain which is of no use for sheep. This is wrong. A mountain here is only beautiful if it has good grass on it.

Samuel Butler, A First Year in Canterbury Settlement *(1863)*

SHEEP COUNTRY
Despite a drop in numbers in recent decades, there are still 10 times as many sheep in New Zealand as there are people.

Beef

Origin: The Fertile Crescent

Date: c. 7500 BCE

Type: Large ungulate mammal

+ **CULTURAL**
+ **SOCIAL**
+ **COMMERCIAL**
+ POLITICAL
+ MILITARY

The French have been known to refer to the English as *les rosbifs* because of their apparent predilection for roasting huge slabs of meat. It is hardly intended as a compliment, but has not overly strained the *Entente Cordiale* as the English don't consider it to be any great insult either. And, in truth, the French are not wrong: the English really do like their roast beef. By identifying the people with one of their favorite foods, the French have also provided us with an indication of the role beef, and cattle-farming, has played in England and more widely in the British Isles as a whole.

AUROCHS

The wild ancestor of cattle is the aurochs, an imposing beast considerably larger than modern domestic breeds. According to Julius Caesar, who encountered them in Germanic forests while campaigning there, they were aggressive and would attack people on sight, giving the impression that their temperaments were more like Spanish fighting bulls than dairy cows. It was one of the reasons why they were highly regarded as quarry by hunters. As well as providing a huge quantity of beef, successful hunts were also considered to confer prestige on a hunter capable of killing such a large and aggressive animal and, as far as it is possible to know now, this appears to have been the case going back far into our prehistory.

Images of aurochs feature on numerous occasions in the cave paintings of our hunter-gatherer ancestors, suggesting that these animals had a particular significance in the culture, perhaps being part of religious rituals and ceremonies as would later be the case with domestic bulls in Minoan Crete and Ancient Egypt. Whatever the truth of the matter, hunting appears to have had a dramatic impact on the numbers of aurochs and, when this was combined with habitat loss as a consequence of the adoption of farming and the spread of disease from domestic cattle, it would gradually lead to its extinction. Some animals persisted in the more isolated and remote regions of Europe until relatively recently; the last known auroch died in 1627 in a Polish forest. DNA studies of modern cattle have shown that the aurochs

was first domesticated about 10,000 years ago in the Fertile Crescent of the Middle East. We don't know exactly how this happened, but one theory put forward in recent years suggests that it was originally caught in the wild for use in religious rituals and was then held in captivity to ensure the animals were available whenever such rituals needed to be performed. Once the wild populations began to decline, making it difficult to catch enough for ritual purposes, people started to breed the captive ones and, from that point onward, integrate them into the farming system.

WILD CATTLE
A 17,000-year-old cave painting of an aurochs from the Lascaux Caves in southwestern France.

Evidence from archaeological sites in the region, such as the 12,000-year-old Göbekli Tepe in southeastern Turkey, indicate that the aurochs was certainly the object of veneration before it was domesticated. At Çatalhöyük in central Anatolia, which dates to about 9000 BP, skulls and horns of what appear to be domestic cattle were plastered, painted, and hung on the walls of houses. This has been interpreted by some archaeologists as being an indication of a cult of bull-worshipping at Çatalhöyük and other sites where similar examples of bucrania, as these installations are called, have been found. An alternative and rather more straightforward theory sees the bucrania as evidence of feasting in which the remains of the cattle have been displayed afterward as a reminder of the occasion.

And Adam gave names to all cattle, and to the fowl of the air, and to every beast of the field.
Genesis 2:20

FEASTING IN THE ORKNEYS

If we have no way of knowing what the inhabitants of Çatalhöyük had in mind when hanging bucrania on their walls, we can be more certain of what was happening in the Orkney Islands on a particular occasion roughly 4,300 years ago, when a huge feast was held that involved the slaughter of 600 cattle, enough to feed as many as 10,000 people. The debris from this feast has been found by archaeologists excavating one of the most remarkable Neolithic sites ever to be found in the British Isles, discovered in 2003 on a narrow spit of land in Orkney, the Ness of Brodgar, which separates two lochs. The site has been described as a temple complex and consists of at least 12 large buildings enclosed by a massive stone wall which was 10 feet (3 m) wide at its base and would likely have been at least as tall.

Archaeological excavations
on the Ness of Brodgar in
Orkney have uncovered 12
large buildings enclosed
within a massive wall.

When archaeologists discover anything that they can't explain, they
often describe it as having some sort of ritual purpose, but in the case
of the buildings on the Ness of Brodgar this description appears entirely
justified. The interiors of the three largest buildings in the middle of
the complex have been laid out in a similar way to that of Maes Howe,
a nearby Neolithic chambered tomb of about the same age, except that
these buildings have three entrances, including one at either end, as if
the purpose of the buildings was for people to walk through them.
Inside, there are a number of hearths, as well as numerous recesses in
the walls and alcoves separated from the main central space by stone
walls. The amount of work required to build such structures, together
with the imposing size of both the buildings themselves and the wall
surrounding them, certainly suggests that the complex was built for a
special purpose. The Neolithic houses found at Skara Brae, which date
to the same period and are not far away from the Ness of Brodgar, are

much more modest in size. The
difference between the two has led
to comparisons being drawn with
medieval cities, in which the inhabitants demonstrated their devotion
and, in some cases, their wealth by
constructing enormous cathedrals
that towered over the buildings
around them.

The first building work on the
complex began about 5,000 years

SKARA BRAE
The interior of one of the
Neolithic houses at Skara
Brae, showing what appears
to be stone storage boxes.

ago, not long after farming first arrived in the British Isles, and could represent a change in the way people viewed the world and their place in it that either accompanied the transition to agriculture or, according to some academics, caused it in the first place. Hunter-gatherers tend to venerate the environment in which they live and the animals they hunt, whereas farmers are more concerned with fertility and the changing seasons. The bull has symbolized fertility in numerous cultures around the world, whereas many of the megalithic structures in the British Isles, including Stonehenge, which is about 4,500 years old, were built in such a way as to indicate the moment when the seasons change. The winter and summer solstices can be marked at Stonehenge, for instance, because of the careful alignment of the stones, which allows people standing within the circle to see exactly when the sun rises and sets on the longest and shortest days of the year, showing the beginning and end of winter.

The people who built Stonehenge were cattle farmers and their culture had much in common with those who built the temple complex in the Orkneys. The style of pottery used by both, known as grooved ware, originated in the Orkneys, leading to speculation that this culture arose there first and then spread southward throughout the British Isles. Then, for reasons we don't understand, the temple complex at the Ness of Brodgar was not only suddenly abandoned but the only building still standing at the time, the one where the feasting took place, was intentionally demolished and covered over, a job that would have entailed almost as much work as constructing the building in the first place. In doing so, the people not only preserved the site for the archaeologists of today, but also that last huge feast, perhaps held to mark the last moments of the building.

Chemical analysis of the cattle bones found at the site shows that farming on the Orkneys at that time was quite sophisticated. The bones have a high nitrogen content, suggesting that farmers were fertilizing

ZEBU CATTLE

✦

Zebu are the humpbacked cattle of the Indian subcontinent, the result of a separate domestication of Asian aurochs that occurred about 8,000 years ago in the early Neolithic phase of the Indus Valley civilization in what is now Pakistan. They are more tolerant of hot and dry conditions than European breeds and are now found in tropical and arid countries around the world. The huge Brahma bulls often seen in rodeos were bred from zebus imported into America from India in the late 19th century and have since become an important commercial breed.

KOBE BEEF

✦

Kobe beef is some of the most expensive meat in the world and considered a delicacy in Japan. It comes exclusively from Hyōgo Prefecture of Honshu and is raised according to strict standards to ensure the quality of the meat. Only the Tajima strain of wagyu cattle is used and these are fed on grain and brought on slowly to produce the characteristic rich marbling of fat through the meat and tender flavor. It is sold under a trademark in Japan, legal protection not recognized in other countries so that, since very little Kobe beef is exported, most of what is sold under that name abroad is not the real thing.

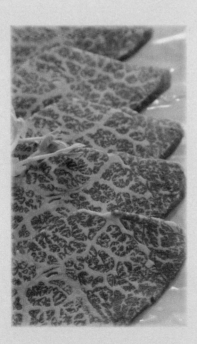

their fields to increase the growth of grass, most likely spreading manure from the cattle and quite possibly using seaweed collected from the shore as well, a practice that continued on the islands into the 20th century. The reason these people abandoned and demolished their temple building, which, in one form or another, had been in use for almost a thousand years, is not known. Perhaps there had been some form of radical shift in their religious beliefs so that it was no longer necessary, or maybe they were in the process of moving away from the islands themselves, taking as many of their cattle with them as they could and eating the rest in one last immense party before leaving for good.

CATTLE CULTURE

Clues to the place cattle held in the culture of the British Isles beyond what can be uncovered through archaeological excavation can be found in the stories that were passed from one generation to the next in the oral culture of Ireland. These Celtic myths, as they are sometimes called, appear to have their origin in the Iron Age, which lasted from the 6th century BCE to the 1st century CE, and were written down by monks in the Christian abbeys of Ireland, preserving them for us to read today. The longest story to have survived is usually known as *The Táin*, short for the full Irish title of *Táin Bó Cúailnge*, which has been translated into English as *The Cattle Raid of Cooley*.

The Táin forms part of the Ulster Cycle of stories and, in common with a number of others, features the exploits of the Irish hero and renowned warrior Cúchulainn. In *The Táin*, Cúchulainn defends Ulster from an attack by neighboring Connacht, whose warriors are intent on driving off the great brown bull, Donn Cúailnge, because it is wanted by their queen Medb. Her lower-ranked consort, Ailill, owns a white-horned bull called Finn-bennach, the only other bull in all of Ireland held in as high esteem as Donn Cúailnge. Medb wants the Ulster bull because she can't bear the thought of Ailill being richer than she is.

The story unfolds in a series of intense battles in which Cúchulainn kills hundreds of the warriors from Connacht but fails to stop them running off with Donn Cúailnge. It climaxes in a single combat between Cúchulainn and his childhood friend Ferdiad that lasts for four days and only comes to an end when Cúchulainn uses a magical weapon, the *gae bolga*, against Ferdiad that penetrates his body and splinters into numerous barbs, finally killing him. It ends with a battle between the two armies and then a bull fight that is almost as epic as the one between Cúchulainn and Ferdiad and in which Donn Cúailnge gores the white-horned bull to death and then returns to Ulster with its entrails hanging from his horns.

The Táin is vivid and blood-thirsty, comparable in many ways to the story of Achilles recounted in *The Iliad*, and, while involving elements of fantasy, can also give us some insights into Iron Age society, particularly the importance people attached to their cattle. In the story, wealth can be measured not only by how many cattle a person owns, but by the quality of the animals; the possession of a great bull confers prestige on the owner that is coveted by others. Of course, as *The Táin* and the other stories of Celtic mythology come from an oral tradition, before the introduction of writing, it is impossible to say for certain that the values expressed in any of them are an accurate reflection of the period when they were first told or that they remained unchanged over the centuries before being written down. Nevertheless, it would not be unreasonable to conclude that Iron Age Ireland, in common with the rest of the British Isles at that time, was a cattle culture.

IRISH HERO
An illustration from 1911 of Cúchulainn, the great hero from the stories of the Ulster Cycle of Irish mythology.

Give them great meals of beef and iron and steel, they will eat like wolves and fight like devils.
William Shakespeare, Henry V

From Herefordshire to the World

Cattle-farming, then, has had a long history in the British Isles and, if we can jump forward a few thousand years, one which led to the British passion for eating beef. As we have already seen in the chapter on lamb, great changes were occurring in British agriculture in the late 18th century, not all of which were carried out with the same degree of inhumanity as the Highland Clearances (see page 28). In the rural county of Herefordshire, for instance, a number of cattle farmers were in the process of improving their herds in an effort to produce the best beef animals they could breed. By the end of the century, they had bred the Hereford, with its distinctive red-brown back and white face which, at least in my opinion (and bearing in mind that I grew up on a farm in Herefordshire, so might be a little biased), today produces some of the best beef to be found anywhere in the world.

By the early 19th century, the Hereford had been stabilized as a breed and, in about 1817, the first ones were exported to America. It took several decades for the breed to become established, but once it became more widely known, it began to replace the cattle previously ranched, such as the shorthorn and the Texas longhorn, in all but the most arid areas. Its success in America was replicated in other parts of the world, in South America and Australia in particular, so that the Hereford became the most widely distributed of all breeds of cattle and remains an important part of these farming systems today.

By the 1970s, the Hereford had declined in Britain because of the introduction of breeds from continental Europe, including the Charolais,

THE HEREFORD
A young Hereford bull, with the red-brown back and white face characteristic of the breed.

Limousin, and Simmental, which were bigger and, crucially for the changing beef market at the time, produced less fatty meat. The Hereford was bred to have a relatively high fat content in its meat, the marbling that gives it such good flavor, whereas continental breeds, originally draft animals, were bigger and more muscular and without as much fat. The lower fat content was a desirable quality in a market where people were becoming more health conscious, but the meat could become too dry when it was cooked. This problem was overcome by feeding the cattle grain, which increased the fat content and also meant that the animals grew more quickly than Herefords and so could be sold for slaughter at a younger age.

In more recent years, the Hereford has made something of a comeback. This has been in part because of breeding programs to increase the size of the breed, but also because of a rising appreciation among British consumers of the better quality of beef obtained from Herefords and other British beef breeds like the Aberdeen Angus compared to their continental cousins. Beef from Herefords and Angus cattle can be more expensive because they grow more slowly, a consequence of them eating more grass and less grain, but this also contributes to the better flavor of the meat.

The resurgence of the Hereford and the Angus in recent years suggests that the British have not lost their taste for beef, which has even managed to survive the health scares caused by the bovine spongiform encephalopathy (BSE, also known as mad cow disease) crisis of the 1980s and 1990s and the potential for the disease to be passed on to humans. Other health concerns have been raised about beef, mostly over eating too much of it. There are also a number of environmental issues concerning cattle-farming in general, such as the destruction of natural habitat to provide grazing land and the large amounts of greenhouse gases that are produced by cattle as a consequence of their digestion of grass. Nevertheless, the roast beef of old England remains a signature dish of the country, particularly when served with Yorkshire pudding and horseradish sauce, and, despite the concerns, it looks set to continue to do so for some time to come.

SUNDAY ROAST
The traditional British dinner of roast beef and Yorkshire pudding, together with roast potatoes, vegetables, and gravy.

When the mighty roast beef was the Englishman's food,
It ennobled our brains and enriched our blood.
Our soldiers were brave and our courtiers were good.
Oh, the roast beef of old England,
And English roast beef.

From the song "The Roast Beef of Old England"
by Henry Fielding

Dates

Origin: The Middle East and North Africa

Date: c.7000 BP

Type: Fruit of the date palm

+ **CULTURAL**
+ SOCIAL
+ **COMMERCIAL**
+ POLITICAL
+ MILITARY

The date palm is widely distributed across the desert regions of North Africa and the Middle East, one of the few cultivated plants capable of growing in such hot and dry conditions. It is reputed to have 800 different uses altogether, but perhaps the most important of all of these is the food it produces. The date has been a staple in the diet of people in the region for thousands of years, a valuable source of carbohydrates and essential vitamins in a part of the world where few other comparable foods are to be found.

FOOD OF THE DESERT

Dates provided people with food for thousands of years before the palm trees were deliberately cultivated, which, as far as we can tell, began 7,000 years ago in what is now Iraq or Iran and possibly farther east in the Indus Valley of Pakistan as well. Once the method of cultivating date palms had been discovered, the trees appear to have spread quickly across arid regions, mainly because the fruits can be stored for long periods once they have been dried so that they can be used as provisions during long journeys across the desert. Trade routes developed across both the Arabian and Saharan deserts, particularly after the domestic camel began to be used to carry goods around 3,000 years ago, when caravans carrying merchandise began to cross immense distances of desert by traveling from one oasis to another.

Arab traders transporting such trade goods as gold, incense, and ivory, not to mention slaves, were often guided across the inhospitable deserts by the people of the nomadic tribes of the region, the Bedouin of Arabia and the Berbers of North Africa, and while en route were sustained by a diet of camel's milk and dates. In 1352, the great traveler and writer Ibn Battuta (1304–69), who journeyed throughout the Islamic world, joined a caravan to cross the Sahara Desert from north to south and left us with an account of his experiences in which he assessed the prosperity of the towns and oases he visited by the quality of the dates he found.

DATE PALM
Large bunches of dates growing in the crown of the female date palm. A mature palm can produce over 100 pounds (45 kg) of fruit.

Ibn Battuta set out on his journey from the Moroccan city of Sijilmasa on the northwest edge of the desert, which was then a major trading post on the western branch of the trans-Saharan trade route, before later declining in importance when first Portuguese and then British sailors made such overland trade routes redundant over the course of the 16th and 17th centuries. After 25 days in the desert, he arrived at Taghaza, now in northern Mali, where he observed that everybody was engaged in the salt trade and that even the houses were made of it.

From Taghaza, Ibn Battuta continued southward to the Malian kingdom, crossing the most arid part of the desert. The leaders of the caravan sent scouts ahead to the oasis town of Oualata, on the southern edge of the desert, to arrange for water to be sent back to them, a common practice during such long and arduous journeys. It took almost six weeks to reach the oasis, completing the caravan journey of almost a thousand miles. Ibn Battuta had little to say about the 50 days he spent in the town, other than to comment on how hot it was and that it, "boasts only a few small date-palms," but that there was plenty of mutton to eat.

Oualata was the northernmost outpost of the Mali Empire, which existed from the 13th century until about 1600, and from the oasis Ibn Battuta traveled on to Niani, the capital city of the empire, where he was underwhelmed by the hospitality he received from the Malian king during the course of his eight-month stay. He then returned to Morocco, traveling through Timbuktu which, at that time, had yet to attain the wealth it would later accrue as a result of its Saharan trade links. He then accompanied another caravan moving northward across the desert, transporting 600 female slaves from West Africa to the slave markets in Marrakesh and Tangier, before finally arriving at home from what would prove to be the last of his great journeys.

> **I reached the city of Sijilmasa, a very beautiful place. It has abundant dates of good quality.**
> *Ibn Battuta*

TAGINE

✦

The tagine is a North African stew of meat and fruit originally cooked over open fires by the nomadic Berbers of Morocco. It is named after the distinctive earthenware pot it is cooked in, a large dish covered with a cone-shaped lid that allows steam to circulate without being lost so the tagine does not require very much water to cook. One of the best recipes for tagines is a combination of lamb and dates, often complemented in Morocco by the addition of preserved lemons, which bring an acidity to the dish to enhance its rich flavors.

Beer

It was my Uncle George who discovered that alcohol was a food well in advance of medical thought.

P. G. Wodehouse, The Inimitable Jeeves

Origin: Sumer

Date: By 2000 BCE and most likely much older

Type: Malted grains and water

+ *CULTURAL*
+ *SOCIAL*
+ *COMMERCIAL*
+ POLITICAL
+ MILITARY

Beer, it could be argued, is in reality very wet bread. The two are made from much the same basic ingredients and both involve a yeast fermentation, even if the purpose of that fermentation is different; to make bread rise and, in beer, to convert sugar into alcohol. In numerous cultures around the world, beer has been an important constituent of people's diet, providing a clean and safe drinking supply before effective sanitation systems were developed, lubricating social gatherings, and, on occasion, giving a reason, or an excuse, to get together. It was also involved in the birth of civilization, at least in its literal meaning of "living in cities," which is as good a place as any to begin a discussion of the place of beer in our history.

BEER AND CIVILIZATION

The first cities began to develop from about 5500 BCE in Sumer, the southern region of Mesopotamia, the land between the Tigris and Euphrates rivers in what is now Iraq. The surpluses of grain provided by the cultivation of the fertile soils along the banks of these two rivers was enhanced by the development of irrigation systems, allowing for a large number of people to live together in communal settlements. We don't know exactly why people came together in this way at this particular moment in history despite having equally productive farming systems; perhaps it was done in order to protect themselves from outside threats to their security. Whatever the reason, as more people began to live in cities there was also a growth in the specialization of trades, including bakers and brewers, together with the development of a civil administration to manage the affairs of these cities, which included, of course, the collection of taxes.

As cities grew in size, the administrators developed a system of accounting to keep track of the various agricultural and trade goods produced. The system involved impressing symbols onto clay, recording both the collection of taxes and pay-

ments to people for work they had done, which was often in the form of bread and beer. This was the beginnings of writing, a further sign of what we would now think of as civilization, and the symbol used to indicate beer was a large jar of the type used to store it after it had been brewed. Numerous pictures from both Mesopotamia and Ancient Egypt have been found depicting people seated around one of these large jars drinking beer through long straws, showing that beer drinking was as much a social activity then as it is now.

> **Beer ... Now there's a temporary solution.**
> *Homer Simpson*

Once writing became established, Sumerian scribes began to record a wide range of other events beyond simple record keeping, including a recipe for making beer dating from 1800 BCE in the form of a song to Ninkasi, the Sumerian goddess of beer. The "Hymn to Ninkasi," as it is known, describes how the goddess added a type of barley bread called *bappir*, which was flavored with honey and dates, to a vat containing malted barley and water and then, after the beer had brewed, how it should be filtered out into the storage jars. The song goes on to praise the goddess for providing beer, giving the singers a "blissful meal" and a "happy liver."

The beer-drinking culture of the Sumerians spread through the rest of Mesopotamia and is thought to have been picked up by the Egyptians, becoming a central part of their culture as well. The workers who built the Great Pyramid of Giza, for instance, were paid in bread and beer, the two staples of the Egyptian diet, each person receiving three loaves of bread and two jars of beer containing about 4 pints (2 l). It is thought that these workers were agricultural laborers who worked on monumental building projects during the summer months while the annual flooding of the River Nile had inundated their fields. For the rest of the year, they cultivated wheat and barley on the fertile soils left behind by the flood and paid taxes to the pharaoh in the form of a percentage of their crops, which was then given back to them as bread and beer when they worked on building his pyramid.

EGYPTIAN BEER
This wooden model depicting beer being brewed was found in an Egyptian tomb and dates to c. 2000 BCE.

The first known written laws come
from Ancient Mesopotamia and
these can be regarded as a further
sign of the development of civilization. The Babylonian king Hammurabi (died c.1750 BCE) appears to
have been something of an autocrat,
establishing laws for almost everything, including the brewing and sale
of beer. The Code of Hammurabi
was carved into a stone column, or
stele, which is now in the Louvre in
Paris, and amongst the numerous
laws it sets out are strict price con-
trols for brewers and innkeepers, suggesting that the king considered
keeping an eye on what they were charging for their beer an important
part of his role as monarch. Under the code, beer was categorized into
20 different types, eight of which were made purely from barley. There
were also wheat beers, beers made from a mixture of grains, black
beers, and beers brewed specially for export to Egypt. It amounted to
state-imposed control over all aspects of the business, perhaps in part
to facilitate the collection of taxes but also to prevent overpricing or
fraud. It appears that some Babylonian innkeepers had been trying to
sell inferior beer at inflated prices and Hammurabi was attempting to
put a stop to such shrewd practices.

Hammurabi may have been the first to adopt laws governing beer
production and sale, but he was by no means the last. One of the most
famous is the Reinheitsgebot of 1516, often called in English the Bavarian Beer Purity Law, which set out regu-
lations to ensure that Bavarian beer was
only made from malted barley, hops,
and water. The original law also regu-
lated the prices that could be charged
for beer in Bavaria, as the Code of Hammurabi had done, together with setting
out the penalties for breaking the law.
The purpose was to ensure that wheat
and rye were used to make bread rather
than beer, but it came to be seen as a
sign of the quality of Bavarian beer and

the law was adopted across other German states as well. At the time the law was passed, the role yeast played in brewing had not been discovered. During the 19th century there was an amendment to include it on the list of permitted ingredients. Even though the Reinheitsgebot is still adhered to by many breweries across Germany, it is not actually still legally enforced, having been lifted in 1988 because it infringed European law.

By far the most common type of beer bought around the world today is lager, named after the German word *lagern*, which means "to store." This style of beer evolved from the Bavarian practice of storing beer in caves during the summer to keep it cool, where a fermentation from the bottom of the barrels occurred at low temperatures to produce a particularly clear beer when compared to the top-fermented beers made at higher temperatures. In 1842 the Bavarian brewer Josef Groll took this bottom-fermented beer-making process to the Bohemian town of Pilsen, now in the Czech Republic, where he developed the style of pale lager known as Pilsner using Saaz hops, a locally grown variety of so-called noble hops that are not as bitter as those used in other styles of beer. The resulting golden-colored beer was not only popular because of its clean taste, but also kept better than the dark top-fermented beer previously produced in the city and, as word got around about its quality, the technique for brewing it began to spread as well.

PILSNER URQUELL

✦

The brewery in Pilsen, or Plzeň as it is written in Czech, where pale lager was first made in 1842, is still going, making the same type of bottom-fermented lager today even if it uses modern equipment and is now owned by the huge brewing conglomerate SABMiller. In 1898, the beer was named Pilsner Urquell, which means "the original pilsner," to distinguish it from the numerous imitations of the style that had appeared by then. It is still sold under the same name today. It has a much fuller flavor than the mass-produced versions of pilsner lager brewed in other parts of the world, which can often taste quite bland in comparison.

The development of refrigeration toward the end of the 19th century allowed cold bottom-fermented beer to be brewed anywhere, beginning the transformation of lager from a popular style of beer in central Europe to it becoming by far the best-selling beer in the world, as it is today. These days, Pilsner-style lager is brewed in numerous places, even if many of the brewers making these beers are not always as keen to maintain the standards of purity set out in the Reinheitsgebot as they have been in Germany and the Czech Republic.

For a quart of ale is a meal for a king.
William Shakespeare, The Winter's Tale

Soybean

Origin: China

Date: From at least 5000 BCE

Type: Protein- and oil-rich legume

+ **CULTURAL**
+ SOCIAL
+ **COMMERCIAL**
+ POLITICAL
+ MILITARY

SHENNONG
A typical image of the Divine Farmer, painted in Japan during the 19th century.

The soybean has some extraordinary qualities. It consists of 20 percent oil and 40 percent protein, more of each than is found in any other plant, and it contains all of the essential amino acids necessary for a healthy diet. It has a very long history of cultivation in China and, considering its properties, it is perhaps surprising that it was not more widely cultivated outside Southeast Asia until relatively recently, even if it has now gone on to be grown extensively in many parts of the world.

THE DIVINE FARMER

The soybean was first domesticated in central China in the valley of the Yellow River, the so-called cradle of Chinese civilization, by 5000 BCE and quite possibly very much earlier. As more archaeological research is carried out in the region, it is becoming increasingly apparent that farming began in China almost as early as it did in the Fertile Crescent, based on the cultivation of rice together with a number of other staple crops. Early Chinese farming did not include very many animals so the high protein content of soybean meant that it was a vital component of the diet and its importance would be recognized in these societies.

In Chinese mythology the discovery and cultivation of the soybean is attributed to Shennong, one of the Three Divine Sovereigns of the predynastic period, usually dated to about 2800 BCE. The stories concerning Shennong, which literally means the Divine Farmer, were not actually first written down until about 2,000 years later and, even though it is thought Shennong may well have existed, the stories can only be considered legends. In the mythology, Shennong's people were said to have lived on nothing more than weeds and worms until he discovered the five sacred grains of rice, wheat, barley, millet, and beans (which are, of course, pulses rather than grains) and then invented both the methods needed to cultivate them and the implements to be used. The success of farming in the Yellow River valley allowed the people of the region, the Han Chinese, to prosper and spread to other areas, the beginning of a population explosion that would result in the Han becoming the largest ethnic group in the region, a situation that remains the same today; Han Chinese make up about 95 percent of the population of the modern country.

Stories about Shennong are still widely told in China today and festivals celebrating him are held to mark important moments in the farming calendar, particularly the sowing of seeds in the spring. Soybeans remained central to the Chinese agricultural system and have spread to those areas of Southeast Asia where the Han migrated, but despite their nutritional properties they were not cultivated in any great quantity anywhere else in the world until the 20th century. One of the reasons for this is that soybeans require a great deal of processing before they become edible. In the raw state the protein in the beans cannot be absorbed by the human digestive system. They also contain a toxin which has to be denatured by cooking.

EDAMAME
The Japanese dish is made from whole soybean pods that are picked before they have fully ripened, then boiled and served with salt.

One of the few occasions when unprocessed soybeans are cooked is in the Japanese dish edamame, in which the young green pods are boiled and served as an appetizer, but otherwise they are used to make a variety of other foodstuffs. Soy milk is used to make tofu, whereas fermented beans can be pounded into a paste from which soy sauce is made. In Japan, the paste is used to make miso, the base for numerous dishes and, when added to dashi, a clear broth, to make miso soup. The Japanese also make natto from whole beans that have undergone a bacterial fermentation. It produces a sticky white slime that forms strings when the beans are pulled apart and this, together with the pungent smell, can make it a little challenging for people who are not accustomed to it.

SOYBEANS IN AMERICA

Soybeans were introduced to America in the 18th century but did not really begin to become established as a major crop until after 1904, when an industrial process was developed to extract the oil. It began to become more common during the First World War, when the protein-rich meal left after the oil was extracted was used as a meat substitute. After the war was over, its popularity declined and the beans were considered only fit to be fed to animals. In the 1920s it was grown more as a cover crop than a commercial one, farmers making use of its nitrogen-fixing properties and then ploughing the whole plant back in to the soil rather than harvesting it. These properties would prove useful in the aftermath of the Dust Bowl in the Midwest in the 1930s, when large areas of open prairie were ploughed up and planted with wheat and corn only for enormous quantities of topsoil to be blown away in great dust storms after a prolonged drought.

The Dust Bowl came on top of the Great Depression, sparked by the stock market crash of 1929, which, together with the overproduction of wheat and other grains as a consequence of the huge areas being planted, caused a crash in the agricultural market. As part of the New Deal, President Franklin D. Roosevelt introduced a range of agricultural policies, beginning in 1933, which set out to address the problems in production as well as in the market itself. One of these policies was to place controls on the number of acres of wheat and corn that individual farmers could grow in an attempt to reduce the overproduction and rebalance the market.

Corn is an efficient way to get energy calories off the land and soybeans are an efficient way of getting protein off the land, so we've designed a food system that produces a lot of cheap corn and soybeans resulting in a lot of cheap fast food.

Michael Pollan, The Omnivore's Dilemma

No controls were put in place on the amount of soybean planted, so those farmers who had reached their wheat and corn limit switched to it. Soybean is relatively drought resistant and deep rooting, so growing it rather than leaving the ground bare was a way for the farmers to stabilize the soil, preventing it from being blown away, and with the added bonus of increasing its nitrogen content at the same time.

DUST BOWL
Drought and high winds caused topsoil to be blown away, shown here in a 1936 photograph of a farm in South Dakota.

More soybean was planted during the Second World War, to be used again as a meat substitute, but it would not become common in American agriculture until the 1970s, when it began to be used much more widely in the food-processing industry and in the intensive production of livestock. From then on, its cultivation really took off so that now it is the second most widely grown crop in America after corn. Soybean oil has been put to an enormous range of uses: it is the most common cooking oil in America, marketed as vegetable oil; it is found in a wide range of processed foods, such as margarine and various sauces and salad dressings; and it has been used to make biodiesel and for numerous industrial applications, in, for instance, the manufacture of paint and printing ink. The protein-rich meal left after the oil has been extracted is almost all used as livestock feed, a small amount being ground into soy flour and made into, amongst other things, the textured vegetable protein found in a huge range of processed foods and used to replace meat protein in such foods as prepared meals for vegetarians.

Almost all of the soybeans grown in America are now of genetically modified varieties, first developed in the 1990s as a means of making the bean plants resistant to particular brands of herbicides, which could then be used to kill weeds

TOFU

✦

Tofu is made by adding a coagulant such as gypsum (calcium sulfate) to hot soy milk so that the proteins solidify as bean curd. This is then strained to remove excess water and pressed into small blocks in much the same way as cheese is produced from milk. The resulting tofu can be hard or soft, depending on the amount of coagulant used, and has a rather bland taste; this can be enhanced by using it in recipes with other, more fully flavored ingredients because it will then absorb those flavors.

without damaging the crop. Although many of the environmental and health concerns raised over the years about genetically modified foods have yet to prove as disastrous as some people had predicted, there are nevertheless a whole range of potential problems, from the spread of transgenic genes into the wider environment to the dominance of a small number of extremely large and powerful multinational companies in the agricultural market, whose primary interests are in their profit margins rather than in maintaining a sustainable farming system or in producing safe food. The soybean, along with corn, has radically changed the face of American farming, but it remains too early to tell if this has been a change for the better or worse.

Corn

Origin: Southern Mexico

Date: By at least 5000 BCE

Type: Staple food of the region

+ **CULTURAL**
+ **SOCIAL**
+ **COMMERCIAL**
+ **POLITICAL**
+ MILITARY

Corn, or maize as it is sometimes called, has been a staple food in Central America, where it was first domesticated, for thousands of years and remains an important foodstuff in Mexico today. Cornmeal, the flour obtained by grinding dried corn, is used to make tortillas and a wide range of other foods. It was also an important food source for the first European settlers in North America and in the subsequent opening up of the continent. Corn is now the most widely grown crop in America, even if almost the entire crop goes into the processing industry rather than being eaten in its natural state.

CORN AND CIVILIZATION

The cultivation of corn was the foundation stone on which the great empires of Central and South America were built, including the Aztecs of Mexico and the Inca of Peru. It has not been firmly established exactly how it was first domesticated and an academic debate continues over whether the corn we know today was developed by the selective breeding of teosinte or if it actually descends from a different and now extinct wild ancestor that at some stage cross-bred with teosinte. The wild plant is certainly very different from corn, producing small hard kernels in spikes rather than large ears of corn, but it is certainly possible that naturally occurring mutations and selective breeding by early farmers could have resulted in the productive plant we know today. But, however it came about, by about 5000 BCE, and quite possibly considerably before then, a version of corn with relatively large ears was being grown in the Oaxaca Valley of southern Mexico.

From the Oaxaca Valley, corn is thought to have spread throughout Mexico and both farther north into what is now southern USA and to the south into South

MEXICAN CORN
Detail from a mural painted by Diego Rivera (1886–1957) showing Aztec men and women cultivating and processing corn.

America, even if there are some indications that a separate domestication may also have taken place in the coastal region of Peru. Agricultural systems grew up in a number of places based on the cultivation of corn and other domesticated plants, including various species of beans and squashes, and these regions experienced a considerable rise in population that led to the development of complex and stratified societies. One of the first of these were the Olmecs, who, from about 1500 BCE, began to live in cities and build step pyramids on the coastal lowlands of the Tabasco region of southeastern Mexico.

The Olmecs have been described as the "mother culture" of Mesoamerica, as the region is sometimes known, because many of the characteristics of their culture would later appear in those of the Toltecs, Aztecs, and Maya. As well as city-living and step pyramids, the Olmecs developed the first writing system to be used in the region, drew charts of the stars, and may have developed the first calendar. It has also been suggested that their religion involved ritual blood-letting and human sacrifice, as later ones in Mesoamerica certainly did, but this has yet to be confirmed by any definite evidence.

In about 400 BCE, the Olmec civilization underwent a sudden and catastrophic decline in which its cities were abandoned and population numbers crashed. The reason why this happened is not fully understood, but it would appear likely that, whatever was behind the crash, it caused a reduction in the amount of corn that could be grown, leading to food shortages and, most likely, clashes between people over the dwindling food reserves that ultimately caused the culture to fall apart. All that remains of the Olmecs today are the artifacts held in museums and the ruins of their cities in the rainforests of southern Mexico — a demonstration of the importance of a staple food such as corn, which can cause the destruction of a civilization as well as allowing it to flourish in the first place.

THE THREE SISTERS

✦

The agricultural systems used by pre-Columbian farmers in Central and South America were often based on the cultivation of corn, beans, and squash, known as the Three Sisters (as featured on the reverse of the US dollar coin pictured below), which were usually grown together on the same patch of ground. It is an example of companion planting, in which each constituent benefits the overall system: the tall stalks of the corn provide support for the climbing beans, which improve the soil thanks to the nitrogen-fixing bacteria in nodules on their roots, while the low-growing squash covers the ground, inhibiting the growth of weeds and preventing the soil from drying out.

INDUSTRIAL CORN

Since the early 1970s a transformation has occurred in American agriculture based on a vast increase in the cultivation of corn, almost all of which has been used either to feed livestock and poultry, in the food-processing industry, or for nonfood industrial purposes. The current farming system for growing corn in America could be compared to the farming practiced by the Olmecs because it involves the cultivation of corn along with beans, in this case soybeans, and the absence of livestock, even if, beyond these two similarities, the systems could hardly be further apart. The large-scale cultivation of corn in America today relies heavily on the widespread application of fertilizers and the use of herbicides and pesticides, while the livestock that were formerly part of the farming landscape across the country are now mostly intensively reared in feedlots or sheds.

> **While the surgeon general is raising alarms over the epidemic of obesity, the president is signing farm bills designed to keep the river of cheap corn flowing, guaranteeing that the cheapest calories in the supermarket will continue to be the unhealthiest.**
>
> *Michael Pollan*, The Omnivore's Dilemma

Over the same period as this agricultural transformation has occurred, there has also been a rapid rise in the occurrence of obesity, diabetes, and heart disease among American people and, at least according to some commentators, a link exists between these two phenomena in the current use of high-fructose corn syrup (HFCS) in a vast range of foods and drinks. In the 1970s, the US government introduced tariffs on imported sugar, artificially maintaining its price in America above world trade levels, while continuing to support those farmers who were growing corn with subsidy payments, leading to a vast increase in the amount grown. As a consequence, most of the big food and drink manufacturers switched from using cane sugar as a sweetener to HFCS, while, at the same time, the availability of so much cheap corn meant that it was an inexpensive way to fatten beef cattle intensively in feedlots while the grassland they had previously occupied was ploughed up to grow even more corn.

SYRUP BARRELS
New York dock workers loading barrels of corn syrup onto a barge on the Hudson River in a photograph taken in about 1912.

It is difficult to establish the exact cause of a rise in obesity because social factors play a part as well as dietary ones, such as a tendency toward leading a sedentary lifestyle and not getting enough exercise, but since it is clear that people in America, and in many other parts of the developed world, are eating more carbohydrates now than they were in the past, it is apparent that this must have played some part in the problem. Much of the increase of carbohydrate in the diet is due to people eating more processed foods than they used to and, in particular, consuming more soft drinks, which often contain large amounts of HFCS.

As well as the potential health problems associated with eating too much carbohydrate, the agricultural system that produces the cheap corn has an inherent instability at its center because it relies on the continuing support of the US government. Should the government's farm policy change by either ending the import tariff on sugar or reducing the subsidy paid to farmers, the current methods of corn production could become economically unviable, forcing farmers to change the way they farm. The food-processing and farm lobbies in America have a great deal of influence in shaping government policy at present, so it is unlikely that any major changes will occur in the foreseeable future, but, at the same time, should it happen then it will be American farmers who will suffer the most. The food and drink manufacturers will be able to switch to buying sugar from other sources, but farmers who have invested heavily in cultivating corn will have a much harder time adapting.

In his book *The Omnivore's Dilemma*, Michael Pollan has pointed out the absurdity of the situation the US government has created by supporting an industrial food system that is causing wide-ranging health problems in America. Too many vested interests are involved in keeping the system as it is for any meaningful change to come from the level of the government, so finding a solution will most likely have to rest with American consumers, who have the ability to decide for themselves what food they buy. Should a large-scale shift toward a healthier diet begin to occur, then food manufacturers will either have to respond or see their businesses decline as others who are producing what people want to buy take over.

PROCESSED CORN
Most of the corn grown in America today is used in the food-processing industry or fed to livestock.

HIGH-FRUCTOSE CORN SYRUP

✦

The industrial process to make high-fructose corn syrup (HFCS) was developed in the late 1960s in Japan and involves using enzymes to convert some of the glucose in regular corn syrup into fructose, which is much sweeter to the taste. Medical research has suggested, though not confirmed, that the nature of the metabolic pathway of fructose in humans leads to greater gains in weight than for comparable amounts of other sugars, which implies that the current widespread use of HFCS in America is particularly damaging to public health.

Noodles

Origin: China

Date: c. 2000 BCE

Type: Thin strands of flour and water

✦ **CULTURAL**

✦ **SOCIAL**

✦ **COMMERCIAL**

✦ POLITICAL

✦ MILITARY

Noodles may be simple, made from a dough of flour and water, formed into strands and cooked, but it is not a straightforward matter to define exactly what constitutes a noodle because of the great variety of forms that exist around the world. Most are made from either wheat or rice flour, but all sorts of other flours have also been used, and there are numerous ways of making the resulting dough into noodles. So, rather than get bogged down in the question of how to define a noodle, here we consider the impact strands of flour and water have had on history without worrying too much about what they are called.

ANCIENT NOODLES

In 2002, archaeologists found an upturned bowl on the floor of a house they were excavating at the Bronze Age site of Lajia, which dates to about 2000 BCE, on the banks of the Yellow River in central China. The site had been buried beneath 10 feet (3 m) of river sediment, the bottom layer of which appeared to have been deposited by a huge flood caused by an earthquake and had led to the abandonment of the site. When the bowl was lifted, it was found to be filled with sediment and, at the bottom, the well-preserved remains of long thin strands of what looked very much like noodles. The airless conditions caused by the sediment had prevented the noodles from decaying, which, when they were analyzed, proved to be the same age as the overall site and had been made from the flour of two types of millet, apparently mixed together to give the noodles both strength and elasticity so that they could be stretched out.

The 4,000-year-old noodles from Lajia resembled lamian noodles found in China today, which are made by hand using a method of twisting and folding the dough, in this case normally made from wheat flour, and then using the weight of the dough itself to stretch the noodles out. It is impossible to say for certain if these ancient noodles were made in the same way, even if the similarities would suggest that they were, but their discovery certainly appears to have settled a long-standing debate concerning the origin of this type of food. In the past, arguments have been put forward stating that noodles were first made in Italy and then spread eastward, going in the reverse direction of the old trade network known as the Silk Road, or that Arab traders who were transporting silk and other goods across parts of the route between China and Europe were the first to make them before passing them on to the Chinese and Italians along with the goods they were trading. The early date of the Lajia noodles points firmly toward a Chinese origin, even if there is no reason why the Italians or Arabs could not have independently come up with the same method of preparing their food.

PASTA

The Italians may not have been the first to eat a form of noodles, which we all now know as pasta, but it nevertheless has a very long history in the country. The Roman poet Horace wrote about a dish he called lasagna in the 1st century BCE and, although what he describes bears little resemblance to the layered pasta dish of today, it was based on flat sheets of a wheat dough. The first known reference to strands of pasta that can be compared to spaghetti comes from Sicily in the 12th century, which, before being conquered by the Normans in 1071, had been an Arab emirate for over two hundred years. We can only speculate now on whether the Arab influence on Sicily

PASTA-MAKING
An illustration from a 14th-century book in Latin showing two Italian women rolling dough and drying pasta strands.

extended to the introduction of pasta, but from that island it appears to have then spread throughout the Italian peninsula. In its dried form, it would prove a significant food for the powerful city states of Venice and Genoa, both of which rose to prominence in the medieval period because of the wealth they accrued from their extensive commercial links across the Mediterranean and beyond and because they possessed powerful navies.

The introduction of pasta into Italy used to be credited to the most famous of all Venetian merchants, Marco Polo, who journeyed along the Silk Road to China in the late 13th century and left an account of his travels that includes a reference to noodles. But, by the time of his journey, pasta was already a staple food in Italy and, as it turns out, research has shown that the story of its association with Marco Polo was probably a promotional gimmick put out by the National Association of Macaroni Manufacturers of America, no doubt

SPAGHETTI
Pasta may have first been
made in Sicily before
spreading throughout
the rest of Italy.

attempting to drum up some trade with a romantic story about their products. The introduction of tomatoes into Italy after the European discovery of the Americas by Christopher Columbus (originally from Genoa) provided the final ingredient for the sort of sauces, or ragus as they are known, that are now recognized all over the world as being typically Italian.

In the 19th century the introduction of an industrial process to make pasta led to it becoming the national food of Italy and to it being exported to numerous other countries. Mass emigration to America, particularly from the poorer southern parts of the country, led to the development of large Italian American communities in many cities, together with restaurants that served pasta and pizza. This exposure to Italian food combined with the convenience and long shelf life of pasta have no doubt also contributed to its popularity in America and many other countries, enhanced further by a rising appreciation of the Italian lifestyle and the food that goes with it. The references to Italian food in Hollywood gangster films, which would not be complete without a scene of Mafia hoods eating in a restaurant or cooking while they planned their next hit, could well have served as advertisements for pasta, much as other aspects of American culture have popularized hamburgers and hot dogs around the world.

One example of a cultural reference to the Italian lifestyle and, in particular, to the perception of Italians eating at large and boisterous family meals can be found in the writing of the Japanese novelist Haruki Murakami. A recurring motif in his novels is a scene in which

In 1971 I cooked spaghetti to live, and lived to cook spaghetti.

Haruki Murakami, The Year of Spaghetti

the main character cooks spaghetti on his own, signifying his disloca-
tion from wider society. Murakami is using the perception of the Italian
meal as a social event to highlight the loneliness of his character, who
has no family or friends to share his spaghetti with. The effect would
not work so well if Murakami's character had been cooking udon,
Japanese wheat noodles that are very similar to spaghetti, because they
do not have the same association with a social
event, often being eaten by Japanese people
when they are on their own. The character
cooking spaghetti suggests that, even though he
is Japanese, he feels like a foreigner in his own
country, separate from the mainstream of society, while, at the same time, also suggesting
that he is both modern and worldly, preferring
to eat Italian food at home rather than a more
traditional style of Japanese food.

Beyond the literary aspects of Murakami's
use of spaghetti to create an effect in his novels,
it also demonstrates how certain foods can circulate around the world. From their beginnings
in Southeast Asia, noodles traveled westward,
possibly with Arab merchants who had trade
links with China, into Europe and then on to
America. The Italian style of eating noodles
with a sauce rather than in a soup or broth
has then traveled back eastward to Japan and
to other countries in the region, completing a
circular journey during which the noodles,
under the name of pasta, have acquired different cultural symbols without actually changing
all that much.

NOODLES IN AMERICA

Noodles did not only arrive in America with the
pasta brought by Italian immigrants. They also
came from the other direction in their original
form with those Chinese people who crossed the
Pacific Ocean in the early 19th century.
A particularly large burst of immigration
coincided with the Californian Gold Rush of
1848 and the numbers of people leaving China

YAKISOBA PAN

◆

As an example of a cross-cultural
food, it is hard to beat the Japanese
sandwich yakisoba pan, which literally
means "fried noodles in bread." It
involves putting chow mein, originally
a Chinese noodle dish, in a hot dog
bun and adding yakisoba sauce, a
Japanese version of Worcestershire
sauce. To mix things up even further,
Japanese pickled ginger and French
mayonnaise are often added as a
garnish, resulting in what might give
the impression of being a culinary
double-carbohydrate mess, but in
reality is, apparently, delicious.

swelled further after the outbreak of the Taiping Rebellion in 1850, a bloody civil war that lasted for 15 years and is thought to have resulted in the deaths of 20 million people. As well as working in the Californian goldfields, many thousands of Chinese laborers were employed building the First Transcontinental Railroad, constructed between 1863 and 1869 and beginning in San Francisco, the port where most Chinese immigrants arrived in America.

The Chinese, like the Italians, brought their food with them to America, some opening restaurants to cater to their fellow countrymen and then branching out to provide Chinese food for Americans of all ethnicities. Chop suey, a dish now found in Chinese restaurants around the world, was thought to have originated in America when, so the story goes, hungry gold miners demanded that a Chinese cook feed them even though he had run out of ingredients. Rather than risk angering his customers, who, according to most versions of the story, were not entirely sober, the cook put together whatever he could find, threw in some noodles and, in the process, invented a new dish. Recent research has suggested that this story is just another case of the sort of mythology that develops around popular food. A similar dish made from leftovers and bulked up with some noodles existed in Guangdong Province in southern China, where many of the immigrants into America had come from, so, if the story has any credibility at all, which is doubtful, then the Chinese cook was simply making a dish he knew but would not normally serve to customers.

Large Chinese communities grew up in the port cities of America where immigrants arrived, particularly in New York and San Francisco, which still have the two largest Chinatowns in the country. A similar pattern emerged in Britain on a much smaller scale, where Chinese communities developed in London and Liverpool. It wasn't until after the Second World War that more Chinese immigration occurred, mostly from the British colony of Hong Kong, as well as from other parts of the British Empire and Commonwealth such as Malaysia and Singapore, where there are large Chinese communities. Many of the first generation of immigrants worked in the catering trade and, from the 1960s, Chinese restaurants and takeouts began to spread out from the cities so that now Chinese food is available in almost every town in the country.

CHINATOWN
East Broadway in Manhattan, New York City, forms part of one of the oldest and largest Chinese enclaves outside China.

Noodles, then, have crossed cultural boundaries on numerous occasions in history, becoming one of the most widely consumed foods across the world in the process. The development of instant noodles by the Japanese company Nissin Foods in 1958 only served to enhance their appeal, even if, let's be honest, cooking noodles from scratch is not an incredibly labor-intensive process. Instant noodles are made by precooking the noodles and then flash frying them to dry them out so that they only need to be rehydrated in hot water to be ready to eat. For those of us too lazy even to think of anything to go with our instant noodles, Nissin Foods came up with the Cup Noodle next, a plastic pot of noodles with the flavorings already added, only requiring hot water to make a convenience food. In Britain, the much maligned Pot Noodle is a similar product and has become the butt of numerous jokes about lazy students who can hardly be bothered to get off the sofa to boil a kettle never mind cook something to eat. The nutritional benefits to be gained from instant noodles in whatever form they are sold may be a little dubious, but they nevertheless demonstrate the potential for noodles to be reinvented to fit in with different cultures and lifestyles, a quality that has seen them transported from the banks of the Yellow River 4,000 years ago to the supermarket shelves of today.

MI KROP

✦

Like many dishes in Thailand, mi krop is based on a Chinese recipe, in this case chow mein, but then given a twist to make it uniquely Thai. Fine rice vermicelli are deep fried until they are golden brown and crisp (*mi krop* means "crisp noodles") and then pork, chicken, or prawns are added to the noodles after being stir-fried with Thai fish sauce, garlic, lime juice, palm sugar, and vinegar. Diced and fried tofu is also often added and the dish is then garnished with bean sprouts, coriander, and chili. The lime juice and vinegar complement the sweetness of the palm sugar, giving the finished dish a lightness and freshness typical of Thai cuisine.

I've been to a parallel universe, I've seen time running backwards, I've played pool with planets, and I've given birth to twins, but I never thought in my entire life I'd taste an edible Pot Noodle.

Spoken by the character Dave Lister in the BBC sci-fi series Red Dwarf

CONVENIENCE FOOD
A bowl of Myojo Singapore Curry Noodles, made by Nissin Foods. Just add hot water, wait three minutes, and enjoy.

Olive Oil

Origin: The eastern Mediterranean

Date: c.12th century BCE onward

Type: Cooking and salad oil

- ✦ **CULTURAL**
- ✦ SOCIAL
- ✦ **COMMERCIAL**
- ✦ POLITICAL
- ✦ MILITARY

Today, more than 90 percent of the world's olive oil is pressed from olives grown around the Mediterranean Sea, principally in Spain, Italy, and Greece. Its association with the region has a very long history going back at least 7,000 years and, in all likelihood, considerably further. In antiquity, the oil was used as a fuel for lamps and as a lotion to be rubbed into the skin as well as for cooking. It was also an important commodity for trade, carried around the region and beyond by, amongst others, the Phoenicians, the great merchant seamen of antiquity who contributed a great deal to what we now think of as Western civilization but whose achievements have often been overshadowed by the Greeks and Romans.

PHOENICIAN TRADE NETWORKS

In the early 12th century BCE, the great empires of the eastern Mediterranean region that had flourished up until that time, including the Egyptians and Hittites, suffered a sudden decline. This is usually attributed to waves of invasions and attacks by the Sea Peoples, but, in truth, we are not entirely sure who these people were, or if they were actually responsible for the collapse rather than simply exploiting weaknesses that existed after it had occurred. But, whatever the cause, over a period of less than 50 years, most of the cities in the coastal region between Egypt and Greece were destroyed, plunging the region into what is sometimes described as a Dark Age from which it did not begin to emerge until the rise of the Assyrian Empire in the 10th century BCE and then the classical Greek civilization from about the 8th century BCE.

The Phoenicians stepped into the power vacuum created in the Mediterranean by the collapse to develop extensive trading networks. They were not a single unified entity, but a collection of city states much like those that would later make up Ancient Greece, based at Tyre, Sidon, Byblos, and a number of smaller cities on the coast of Canaan, now Lebanon. Characteristically coned-shaped Phoenician amphorae, used for transporting wine as well as olive oil, have been found all over the Mediterranean region, showing the extent of the trade networks, which spread out to the Atlantic coasts of North Africa, Spain, and France and on to Britain.

The economic revival that accompanied the development of trade would lead to an economic recovery across the regions disrupted by the 12th-century collapse, creating the conditions in which Greece could begin to flourish and, ultimately, develop into what we now regard as the first modern civilization. As well as trading with other states, the Phoenician merchants spread technological innovation, particularly in ship design, and introduced the concept of the phonetic alphabet, which used symbols to convey sounds rather than to depict individual words. The Greek alphabet developed from the Phoenician one with the addition of vowels and the Romans then adapted it to form the letters still widely used today.

AMPHORAE
Phoenician merchants transported olive oil around the Mediterranean region in amphorae like these.

The Greeks and Romans continued to have extensive dealings with the Phoenicians throughout much of the classical period and were particularly keen to obtain a dye found in murex sea snails known as Tyrian purple, which was incredibly expensive and used to color the robes of high-ranking people. The name we know the Phoenicians by now actually comes from the Greek word for the dye and continued in use even after the majority of the Phoenician people had left their original homeland on the coast of Canaan after 539 BCE, when it was conquered by the Persians. The majority of the Phoenician population moved to the colonies they had previously established along the North African coast, principally to Carthage, in modern-day Tunisia, where they continued to trade around the Mediterranean and to establish an empire that would go on to challenge the Roman Empire in the Punic Wars before being destroyed by Rome in 146 BCE.

A vivid example of the extent of the olive oil trade in the Mediterranean region can be seen in Rome today. Monte Testaccio is an artificial hill on the eastern bank of the River Tiber made from the broken terracotta shards of millions of amphorae that had been used to bring olive oil into the city.

For the Lord your God is bringing you into a good land, a land of brooks of water, of fountains and springs, flowing forth in valleys and hills; a land of wheat and barley, of vines and fig trees and pomegranates, a land of olive oil and honey.

Deuteronomy 8:7–8

These large amphorae, each containing about 20 gallons (76 l) of oil, were used to transport it from Spain to the city, where it was stored in large tanks in the Horrea Galbae, the warehouses used by the Roman state to store food. The amphorae were then smashed and thrown on to what amounted to a garbage pile nearby, accumulating in a mountain as over 100,000 amphorae were arriving in the city each year. The dumping occurred between the 1st century BCE and the 2nd century CE, long after others had taken over the trade networks set up by the Phoenicians and after the destruction of their Carthaginian Empire, but it can nevertheless be seen as a sign of the commercial business they had originally established and which provided the economic model for those engaged in trade in the region after them.

OLIVE PRESSES IN EKRON

The Phoenicians were merchants, the archetypal middlemen who facilitated the trade in olive oil, but they were not farmers. They were happy to leave the cultivation of olives and the pressing of the oil to others, which included the various peoples who lived in the interior of Canaan, which, after the invasion of the Israelites in about 1000 BCE, would become known as Israel and Judah. Evidence of the extent of olive oil production in this area has been uncovered in an archaeological excavation carried out at Tel Miqne in Israel, about halfway between Jerusalem and the Mediterranean Sea. An inscription found at the site has identified it as Ekron, mentioned in the Bible as being one of the five cities of the Philistines, an ethnic group thought to have originally come to the region from the Aegean Islands who gained a reputation for uncivilized behavior, most likely a consequence of being in a state of almost constant war with Israel.

The excavation discovered more than a hundred olive presses dating to the 7th century BCE, at which time the region was a vassal state of the Assyrian Empire, making Ekron the largest known center of olive

EKRON PRESSES
These olive presses have been reconstructed from original parts found during archaeological excavations of Ekron.

oil production to be found from the ancient world, capable, it has been estimated, of producing 1,120 tons (1,000 tonnes) of oil a year. Presumably some of this would have been used in the city and its surroundings, but it is also likely to have provided the Phoenicians with some of the oil they would trade across the Mediterranean region.

Another source indicating the importance of olive growing in this area comes from the Assyrians, who left records stating that the tribute paid to them by King Manasseh of Judah, who ruled from 686 BCE to 642 BCE, was entirely made up of olive oil. Manasseh was the son of Hezekiah, who, according to both the Assyrian records and the Bible, had led a rebellion against the Assyrian king Sennacherib, so it is possible that the olive presses of Ekron were geared up to produce such large quantities of oil in order to appease the Assyrian rulers of Judah rather than for trading purposes. A period of calm followed the conciliatory approach adopted by Manasseh, which, according to the Bible, lasted for 55 years, before the return of unrest. This was one of the causes of the invasion of Judah by the Babylonian king Nebuchadnezzar and the subsequent Siege of Jerusalem in 597 BCE, which would result in the destruction of the Temple of Solomon and the exile of the Jews of Judah to Babylon. We can only speculate now how different history would have been if, rather than rising against Nebuchadnezzar, they had continued to appease him with olive oil instead.

EXTRA VIRGIN OLIVE OIL

✦

The Madrid-based International Olive Oil Council states that, for an olive oil to be described as "virgin," it must be extracted using only mechanical means at a temperature below 86°F (27°C) and without being treated with any chemical solvents, which are routinely used to extract any remaining oil left in the pulp to produce pomace oil. To be described as "extra virgin," the oil must have a low acidity and pass a taste test carried out by a panel of experts. The labels on expensive bottles of extra virgin olive oil often include the phrase "first cold pressed," which is not strictly necessary because all olive oil described as extra virgin should come from the first, and usually only, cold pressing.

Spartan Black Broth

Origin: Ancient Greece

Date: 5th century BCE

Type: Blood soup

Ｔhe Ancient Greek city-state of Sparta was famous for the fighting capacities of its army and is remembered today for the heroic last stand of the 300 at the Battle of Thermopylae in 480 BCE, fought against an invading Persian army. The military prowess of the Spartans was based on the harsh training regime it imposed on its soldiers, designed to instill discipline and loyalty, which began at an early age and extended to every aspect of their lives, including their food.

+ CULTURAL

+ SOCIAL

+ COMMERCIAL

+ POLITICAL

+ MILITARY

SPARTAN LIVING

On tasting black broth, a traveler from the city of Sybaris, whose inhabitants were famed for enjoying the good life, is said to have remarked, "Now I know why the Spartans are not afraid to die." The broth was the staple food eaten by Spartan soldiers, made from pig's blood and vinegar, which was used to stop the blood from clotting. Unfortunately, no recipe for the broth has survived, but presumably it was not unlike the blood soups made in a number of European countries today in which cuts of meat are slowly simmered for a few hours and the resulting broth thickened by the addition of a mixture of blood and vinegar to produce a rich and nutritious meal more like a stew than a soup.

Spartan society was strictly organized along militaristic lines and was divided into three main classes: at the top were the citizens, followed by a class of workers and traders called the *perioikoi*, who were free but did not have the rights of citizens, and at the bottom were the *helots*, slaves with no rights at all. At birth, the boys of Spartan citizens were inspected by a council of elders and those not thought healthy enough to grow into soldiers were thrown over a cliff. At the age of seven, the surviving boys were separated from their families and entered the *agoge*, the harsh training regime designed to make soldiers of them that lasted until they were 20, when, if they were considered to have passed the training, they were elected to a *syssitia*, a small group of soldiers who lived and ate together in what could be described as an army mess. Those that were not thought ready had until the age

BLOOD SOUP
No recipe for Spartan black broth has survived, but it may have been similar to Schwarzenauer, a blood soup from northern Germany.

**Go tell the Spartans, stranger passing by,
that here, obedient to their laws, we lie.**

Epitaph on the memorial to the 300 at Thermopylae

DAVID'S LEONIDAS
Leonidas at Thermopylae
(1814) by the French artist
Jacques-Louis David, painted
in the neoclassical style.

of 30 to be elected to a *syssitia* and, if they
failed, were then forced to return to Spartan
society to become *perioikoi*. Once a soldier
joined a particular mess, he would eat with
his colleagues every day, the main part of
every meal being black broth, one part of an overall military system
aimed at creating a body of men who would fight and die for each other
as well as for the glory of Sparta.

The invasion of Greece by a huge Persian army, estimated to be
150,000 strong, provided the Spartans with an opportunity to demonstrate to the rest of Greece why their soldiers had gained such a fear-
some reputation. A small force of Spartans, made up of 300 men led by
King Leonidas, met about 7,000 other Greek soldiers at Thermopylae,
a narrow pass between the shoreline of the Aegean Sea and steep-sided
mountains through which the Persian army would have to travel in
order to enter Greece.

Before the battle began, the Persian king Xerxes
demanded that the Greeks throw down their weapons, to
which Leonidas is famously reported to have replied,
"Come and get them." The fighting lasted for three days,
during which the Greeks inflicted terrible casualties on
the Persians, until a traitor informed Xerxes of a
path through the mountains that he could use to
attack the Greeks from the rear. When he became
aware of the Persian plans, Leonidas dismissed
the bulk of the Greek army, remaining at
Thermopylae himself with his 300 Spartans
and about 700 others to fight a rear-guard
action. In the event, the Spartans were overwhelmed
quickly, almost all of them being killed and, in truth, the
battle only delayed the Persian advance for a matter of
days. The decisive encounter of the war came at Salamis a
month later, when the Greek navy led by the Athenians
defeated the Persians, but nevertheless the courage shown
by the Spartans at Thermopylae is still regarded as being
one of the greatest acts of courage in military history.

SPARTAN WARRIOR
A modern bronze
statue of Leonidas
based on an ancient
statue of an unknown
Spartan warrior
found by
archaeologists.

Garum

Garum is made from fish intestines and other parts of the fish that are otherwise thrown out.

Pliny the Elder, Natural History

Origin: The Roman Empire

Date: c. 4th century BCE to 5th century CE

Type: Fermented fish sauce

+ **CULTURAL**
+ SOCIAL
+ **COMMERCIAL**
+ POLITICAL
+ MILITARY

FISH SAUCE
Garum was probably similar to the fermented fish sauces made in Southeast Asia today.

The popularity of some foods within a particular culture can sometimes mystify outsiders, who may fail to understand what the fuss is about or, in some cases, be astonished at what other people are prepared to eat. In the case of the Roman Empire, the food nobody else could understand was a fish sauce called garum, widely used across all levels of society, from emperors to slaves, as an ingredient in numerous recipes and as a table condiment.

A ROMAN OBSESSION

From the descriptions left by a number of Roman writers, including Pliny the Elder and Seneca, garum was made from the parts that remained after fish had been salted and barreled. The heads, guts, and everything else left over were all salted and put either in tanks or jars, depending on the size of the operation, then left in the sun to ferment naturally over the course of several months. According to Pliny, almost any small fish could be used and, once the garum had been made, it was then skimmed off as a thin liquid, leaving a thick sludge called *allec* which was also used in cooking.

At the height of the empire, garum was being made in industrial quantities. The smell coming from the open tanks was apparently truly revolting and garum factories, common in coastal areas across the empire, were almost always situated outside and, presumably, downwind of towns. In some cases the location of garum-making was stipulated in local laws, ensuring that the smell did not ruin the atmosphere of Roman towns. The resulting sauce could not have tasted as disgusting as it sounds from the way it was made, perhaps being something like the fish sauces of many Southeast Asian cuisines today and being used in a similar way to how soy sauce is used in Chinese cooking. In common with these modern sauces, garum was probably rich in glutamate, giving it a complex taste somewhere between being savory and salty without quite being either and, as it is not easy to describe, for which the Japanese word umami has been adopted in English.

The Romans appear to have inherited their taste for garum from the Greeks, in common with many other aspects of their culture, and it has been suggested that their fondness for the sauce, and its value as a tradable commodity, acted as an inducement for them to expand the territory under their control in coastal regions around the Mediterranean. No evidence exists to support such a suggestion, but, once colonies had been established, the production of garum did provide new territories with a potentially lucrative commodity that could be traded all

the way across the Roman Empire. So, if the fish sauce had nothing to do with the expansion of the Roman Empire, it played an important role in the economies of its coastal colonies, allowing them to be self-supporting and giving them at least a degree of autonomy within the empire, even if they ultimately remained under Roman control.

The Romans recognized different grades of garum and, according to Pliny, the best, known as *garum sociorum*, came from the southern part of the province of Hispania, now Spain, and in particular from the city of Cartagena. Significant Roman ruins remain in the city today, particularly the amphitheater in the center, but no sign of a garum factory has been found, which would most likely have been outside the city walls and may have since been built over. The remains of the garum tanks from the Roman towns of Baelo Claudia and Carteia, both near Gibraltar on the southern tip of Spain, have survived and can still be seen today. Amphorae that contained garum have been found in Pompeii and in a number of shipwrecks that date from the Roman period.

The sauce was still being made in the Eastern Roman Empire, or the Byzantine Empire as it is known, in the medieval period, disappearing after the Ottoman conquest of Constantinople in 1453, but it does not appear to have survived for long after the fall of the Roman Empire in the West. Perhaps the barbarian invaders who are sometimes said to have been responsible for the collapse were no more attracted to the idea of a sauce made from fish guts than we are today.

LEA & PERRINS WORCESTERSHIRE SAUCE

✦

According to one version of the story, Worcestershire sauce was first made in the 1840s after Mr. Lea and Mr. Perrins, dispensing chemists from Worcester, were asked to make a strongly flavored curry sauce from a recipe brought back from India. The result, made from anchovies, tamarind, vinegar, and a whole variety of other spices and flavorings, proved to be far too strong, but, after being left in a basement for a few years, it fermented on its own and, in the process, improved in flavor. Worcestershire sauce probably doesn't taste much like garum did, but it does show that making a sauce out of fermented fish is not necessarily quite such a mad idea as it might first appear to be.

Kimchi

Origin: Korea

Date: 1st century CE onward

Type: Fermented vegetables

+ **CULTURAL**
+ **SOCIAL**
+ COMMERCIAL
+ POLITICAL
+ MILITARY

The Miracle on the Han River, as the period of extraordinary economic growth experienced by South Korea since the 1960s is sometimes called, has transformed the country from being one of the poorest in Southeast Asia into one of the most highly developed in the world. The social changes that have accompanied this transformation could have resulted in the separation of the Korean people of today from their past, but, to an extent at least, this has not happened and kimchi, the national food, has played a part in the continuity between the traditional and modern worlds. It is a side dish of fermented vegetables, served at almost every meal, and most commonly made from Chinese napa cabbage, often prepared with salted fish and chili pepper, but it can also be made from a wide variety of other vegetables.

> All Koreans are thus part of one large kimjang community, which transcends regional and socio-economic boundaries within Korean society.
>
> *From the South Korean government's UNESCO application*

KIMJANG

A survey carried out by the government of South Korea in 2013 found that 95 percent of its citizens eat kimchi of one sort or another at least once a day. The survey formed part of its application to UNESCO (United Nations Educational, Scientific and Cultural Organization) to have kimjang, the traditional preparation of kimchi, recognized as part of its Intangible Cultural Heritage program in which important aspects of different cultures from around the world are given a UNESCO designation in much the same way as are World Heritage sites like the Pyramids of Giza or the Taj Mahal.

In the past, the hard winters experienced on the Korean peninsula made food preservation a necessity and the fermentation of vegetables has a long history, going back at least to the Three Kingdoms period of Korean history that began in the 1st century CE. Over the centuries, some of the ingredients used may have changed as recipes have adapted to different conditions — chili, for example, coming into wide use after it was introduced in the early 17th century — but the traditional way of making kimchi has remained much the same. In late November or early December, Korean families get together, sometimes with friends and neighbors as well, in what has become a festival of kimchi-making.

In more recent times, the development of refrigeration and the availability of imported fresh food throughout the year has meant that it is no longer as important to make kimchi, but many people have kept up the tradition because it brings the family together at a particular time of year, not unlike the Western festivals of Thanksgiving and Christmas.

Baechoo kimchi, made principally from napa cabbage, is made by salting whole cabbages in brine overnight and then, after washing off the excess salt, stuffing them with a mixture of other ingredients, including the chili powder that gives the kimchi an extra spicy kick. In the traditional method, the stuffed cabbages are then packed into large earthenware jars called *onggi* that are buried up to the necks outside. As well as ensuring the smell when the jars are opened, which can be quite powerful, does not permeate the house, the cooler temperatures outside lead to a slow fermentation, producing a better quality of kimchi, without it freezing completely, which would otherwise stop the fermentation occurring. These days, special kimchi fridges are available for people who don't have a garden, allowing them to keep their kimchi separate from other foods so the smell does not contaminate everything else. It also means that people who don't have much space can still make their own, as more than half the families in South Korea still do, keeping up the tradition even if they live in a tiny apartment in Seoul.

Kimchi is now widely available in many parts of the world, particularly where there is a Korean community, and for Koreans at home and abroad it is both a reminder of the traditions of the past and a demonstration that it is perfectly possible to keep such practices going today. Some of the ways of making kimchi may have been adapted to the world in which we now live, but the associations kimjang has with the family and with getting together in a communal activity means that, even though commercially-made kimchi is available to buy, the version made at home is always going to taste much better.

TRADITIONAL KIMCHI
A kimchi storage hut and *onggi* at the Korean Folk Village living museum in Yongin near Seoul.

GOCHUJANG

✦

Gochujang is another Korean fermented food, a paste made from red chili powder, rice, soybeans, and salt that used to be made in the same sort of earthenware *onggi* as kimchi but is now more often bought ready-made. It is both a table condiment and an ingredient, used in the marinade for bulgogi, a popular dish of grilled beef, and often added to bibimbap, rice mixed with vegetables. The paste contains a serious amount of chili powder, but the fermentation process mellows the flavor so that it remains spicy but doesn't blow your head off.

Chocolate

What you see before you, my friend, is the result of a lifetime of chocolate.

Katharine Hepburn

Origin: Mesoamerica

Date: From at least the 4th century CE

Type: Processed seeds of the cacao tree

+ **CULTURAL**
+ SOCIAL
+ **COMMERCIAL**
+ **POLITICAL**
+ MILITARY

There are some people in the world who claim not to like chocolate, but they appear to make up a very small minority of humanity. Most of the rest of us love the stuff and don't believe that anybody could really not like it. The size of the global business, reported to be worth over $50 billion a year and climbing, suggests that, since it emerged from its homeland in Central America 500 years ago, it has captured our hearts and minds in a way few other foods can match.

MAYA GOLD

In 1994 the British company Green & Black's began to make a chocolate bar from cocoa they had bought from the Toledo region of southern Belize called Maya Gold, named after the people who produced the cocoa. The company described it as being, "rich, dark chocolate with a twist of orange, nutmeg, cinnamon, and just a hint of vanilla" — and it tastes as good as it sounds. It was also the first product of any description to achieve a Fairtrade certification in Britain, awarded because Green & Black's adopted ethical trading practices, buying directly from the Toledo Cacao Growers' Association, a cooperative of small farmers, and paying them a fair price.

The Maya have had a long history with chocolate, going back in their recorded history to the beginning of what is called the Classical Mayan period in about 400 CE and most probably for at least a thousand years before that. Chocolate is produced from the seeds, the cocoa beans, found in the large pod-like fruit of the cacao tree (*Theobroma cacao*) native to Central America. It appears to have been domesticated by the Olmecs, who preceded the Maya, living to the north of the Mayan territory on the Yucatán Peninsula. The Olmecs may have been the ones who passed chocolate on to the Maya, as they are thought to have done with many other aspects of their culture, such as the characteristic step pyramids of Mayan cities. Wherever it came from, the Maya certainly grew plantations of cacao trees for the cocoa beans to make chocolate and they either consumed it as a bitter-flavored drink, sometimes spiced with chili or vanilla, or as a porridge after it had been thickened by the addition of corn.

The importance attached to chocolate by the Maya can clearly be seen on artifacts recovered by archaeologists that date to the classical period. Some vases found in Mayan graves were decorated with illustrations of cacao tree cultivation and of people making chocolate and drinking it, whereas others show scenes of chocolate being used in religious rituals and royal ceremonies. References to chocolate have also been found in the Mayan books that survive; the vast majority were either destroyed by the Spanish after the conquest of Mexico or deteriorated naturally because the type of paper used, made from bark, decomposed quickly in the tropical conditions.

MAYAN CHOCOLATE
A Mayan dish showing a woman using a grinding stone, or metate, to prepare chocolate.

The Maya developed extensive trading networks across Central America and appear to have used cocoa beans as a form of currency in the place of gold. The beans are lightweight, durable, and were considered to be highly valuable by the Maya and by the other civilizations of Central and South America, making them an almost perfect commodity for exchange. By the 9th century CE, the classic Maya civilization was in decline and the cities on the Yucatán were abandoned. The exact reason for this collapse and the accompanying dramatic drop in the population is not known for certain, but may have been a consequence of a long period of drought that had a devastating impact on the Mayan agricultural system.

During his third voyage to the New World in 1502, Christopher Columbus encountered a large Mayan trading canoe carrying a cargo of cocoa beans, making him the first European to see the raw material from which chocolate is made even if it is not clear that he was aware the beans were used to make a drink. By that time, the Aztec Empire had come to dominate much of the region from its capital city of Tenochtitlan, now the site of Mexico City, and the Aztecs had adopted many of the Mayan practices, including drinking chocolate. The cacao trees could not be grown in the more arid conditions of central Mexico, so the Aztecs obtained cocoa beans either by trade with the Maya or by demanding the beans in taxes. When the conquistador Hernán Cortés arrived

MOLE SAUCE

✦

Mexican restaurants around the world often serve chicken mole, which almost always means that the meat comes in a chocolate sauce. It may not sound all that appetizing, but, when made well, the chocolate should not overwhelm the dish, instead giving it a thick and smooth texture with only a hint of sweetness and complementing the flavors of tomato and chili pepper, two of the other main ingredients. In Mexico, moles come in a number of distinct varieties in which chili is the common ingredient and the one containing chocolate is called mole poblano, suggesting that it originated in the southern state of Pueblo.

in Tenochtitlan, he found that the Aztec king Montezuma drank numerous cups of the chocolate drink, up to 60 a day according to an account written by one of his companions, and, although they were not at first impressed with the drink, after the subsequent conquest it would eventually be taken back to Spain.

THE SCRAMBLE FOR CHOCOLATE

The Spanish introduced chocolate to Europe, initially into the royal court of Spain and from there it spread to Italy and France, helped by the increasing availability of sugar to sweeten its bitter taste. But it still had to be imported from the tropical regions of the New World, so remained expensive and was not widely drunk outside of high society. By the early 17th century, chocolate had begun to appear in the Spanish Netherlands, territory in the southern region of the Low Countries under the rule of the Habsburg monarchy of Spain that included modern-day Belgium, now noted for the high quality of the chocolates made there. Over the course of the next few centuries, it would become known as "the Battlefield of Europe" because of the wars fought between the major powers of the day on its territory, a situation that would repeat itself in the 20th century during both the First and Second World Wars. At the end of the War of the Spanish Succession, fought between 1701 and 1714 over the issue of whether a Habsburg or Bourbon monarch should succeed the infirm Charles II of Spain, the Spanish Netherlands came under control of the Austrian Habsburg Empire.

Belgium did not actually become independent until 1830, a situation recognized by the great powers of Europe in 1839, and this coincided with a dramatic increase in the sales of chocolate as a consequence of the industrialization of the processes involved in making it. In 1828 the Dutch chocolate maker Coenraad van Houten developed a hydraulic press that could extract cocoa butter from beans to leave cocoa powder, establishing the processing method known in the business as "dutching" that has since been refined, but nevertheless remains the principal step in chocolate-making today. As well as making drinking chocolate, the dutching process also made it possible for solid bars to be made by reconstituting the required amounts of the butter and powder together, which, once van Houten's patent on the dutching process had run out in 1838, opened up the way for other chocolate makers to begin producing bars.

DRINKING CHOCOLATE
The Chocolate Girl (c.1743) by Jean-Étienne Liotard, showing a maid serving a mug of drinking chocolate and a glass of water.

The British chocolate manufacturer J. S. Fry & Sons, located in Bristol, is usually credited with being the first company to establish the method of bringing cocoa butter and powder together into a form that could be molded into a bar, which went on sale in 1847, and this was followed two years later by the first bar made by the Cadbury brothers in Birmingham. The manufacture of chocolate bars in factories was one part of a great social shift that had been happening since the late 18th century, brought on by the Industrial Revolution, during which cities across Europe expanded rapidly and what we would now describe as a consumer society developed in which people bought branded products.

The rapid increase in sales of chocolate brought about by the availability of relatively inexpensive bars and other chocolate products led to a shortage in supply of cocoa that was exacerbated by the regular occurrence of plant diseases in the plantations that had been established in Central and South America. The biology of the tree meant that it could only be grown in the tropics and, by the time the shortage of cocoa was becoming apparent, the only parts of the tropical world that had not already been colonized by one European power or another were in Central and West Africa.

The British and French had been involved in West Africa for a long period by this time as a consequence of the transatlantic slave trade and, after it was abolished, began to look for other ways of exploiting these territories. Britain actively began to colonize the Gold Coast, now Ghana, and Nigeria, while the French secured Sierra Leone and the Ivory Coast, and both began to exploit the natural resources of the region, which included diamonds and gold.

FIVE BOYS
An advertising image from about 1910 for Fry's Five Boys milk chocolate, made in Bristol and sold from 1902 to 1976.

PERCENTAGE COCOA

✦

Many chocolate makers now include a figure on the label of their chocolate bars giving the percentage of cocoa they contain. Green & Black's Maya Gold, for instance, contains 55 percent cocoa, whereas its two dark chocolate bars have 70 percent and 85 percent and its milk chocolate bar 35 percent.

This figure refers to all the cocoa products obtained from the processing of the beans, combining the amount of cocoa butter and cocoa powder used to make the bar. The remaining percentage points are mostly made up of sugar together with any additional flavorings.

They also established plantations producing palm oil for use in making soap, cotton, rubber, and cocoa beans.

In the 1870s, Belgium became involved in the Scramble for Africa, as it was known, in which European powers competed with each other to take control of those few parts of the continent that were not already colonized. After the British had shown little interest in the Congo region, the explorer Henry Morton Stanley, who had traveled through it as part of his trans-Africa expedition from 1874 to 1877, approached King Leopold II of Belgium in an attempt to gain support for a further expedition to the region. Leopold was much more receptive than the British had been, jumping at the chance to establish a colony for himself in Africa, but needed to gain the approval of the great powers in Europe in order to achieve this.

STANLEY'S CONGO
An illustration from *The Congo and the Founding of its Free State* (1885) by Henry Morton Stanley, whose expeditions led to the Congo becoming a Belgian colony.

While Stanley returned to the Congo, Leopold and the Belgian government began a campaign to win support for their colonial policy, stressing that its main purpose was "a civilizing mission" rather than purely an attempt to exploit the natural resources of the region. At a conference held in Berlin in 1884, Belgium's claim to a large part of the Congo region was recognized, enabling Leopold to set up what was, in effect, a private empire headed by himself known as the Congo Free State. Any pretence that Belgium annexed the region for the benefit of the indigenous people was quickly dropped and, instead, one of the most brutal colonial regimes of the period was put in place aimed solely at extracting as much of its natural resources as possible. Once the enormous scale of the misrule, which included mass murder and the widespread use of forced labor, became known in Europe, it caused a scandal that would eventually force Leopold to give up his personal rule over the Congo Free State, even if it remained a Belgian colony.

Leopold's initial intention may have been to develop the Congo region with plantations of cocoa to supply Belgium's chocolate makers, but these were quickly abandoned, most likely because that would have involved large investments before any return would have been available. In contrast, both the British and French began to plant large areas of cocoa trees in their West African colonies, in the process cashing in on the rising demand for chocolate across Europe and around the world. Needless to say, this was motivated by the potential to profit from the plantations rather than any philanthropic desires, but the contrasting histories of the former colonies of Ghana, the Ivory Coast, and what is now the Democratic Republic of Congo after each gained independence in 1960 illustrates how the exploitative imperial policies adopted by Belgium went on to have a greater detrimental impact in the postcolonial period than those followed by Britain and France.

The Ivory Coast and Ghana are now the world's first and second largest producers of cocoa, a commodity that has increased in value in recent years and for which demand is still rising. Since it gained independence, the Democratic Republic of Congo has experienced almost constant turmoil, including the despotic and corrupt rule of Joseph Mobutu and devastating civil wars in which it has been estimated that five million people have been killed and from which the country is only slowly beginning to emerge now. Despite a wealth of natural resources and an abundance of agricultural land, the country remains one of the poorest in Africa and, as a consequence of the violence and political instability, has only a minor industry in cocoa production. The potential to develop this industry at a time when demand for chocolate is rising is one of the few indications of a brighter future for the country, should it ever be able to put the horrors of its colonial and postcolonial past behind it.

CONGO BARS

✦

In 2013, the Seattle-based ethical chocolate maker Theo, working in partnership with the Eastern Congo Initiative, a charity set up by Ben Affleck, bought 381 tons (340 tonnes) of cocoa beans from farmers in the Democratic Republic of Congo. The company launched two bars, Congo Vanilla Nib and Congo Pili Pili Chili, made from these beans, together with vanilla and chili also sourced from the Democratic Republic of Congo. The bars are priced at $5, of which $2 goes to the Eastern Congo Initiative.

IVORIAN COCOA
An Ivory Coast farmer picking cocoa pods. The Ivory Coast is the largest producer of cocoa in the world.

Paella

Paella has as many recipes as there are villages, and nearly as many as there are cooks.

Llorenç Millo, a chef from Valencia

Origin: Spain

Date: 8th century

Type: Mixed rice dish

+ **CULTURAL**
+ SOCIAL
+ COMMERCIAL
+ POLITICAL
+ MILITARY

Paella is now widely thought of as being typically Spanish and is named after the wide flat-bottomed pan in which it is cooked. It comes from the countryside around Valencia and is primarily a rice dish made with either meat or seafood that, at least in the form it is most commonly made now, dates back to the 18th century. But its roots can be traced much further back to the conquest of the Iberian Peninsula by the Moors in the 8th century that created the Islamic state of al-Andalus.

LA ALBUFERA

One of the primary reasons Valencia is the home of paella is because it is at the heart of one of the largest rice-growing regions of Spain. Much of the rice is grown in paddy fields around La Albufera, a freshwater lagoon to the south of the city that is separated from the Gulf of Valencia by a narrow spit of land. Up until the 17th century, it contained salt water, but gradually became less brackish becauseof the diversion of freshwater into it from canals, allowing rice-growing in irrigated paddy fields. By the 19th century, laborers in these paddy fields and the orange groves that surround them had begun to make paella using local ingredients, including water voles caught in the paddy fields as well as chicken, rabbits, and whatever else was available or, alternatively, from any fish or seafood they had. These two paellas, meat and seafood, are now regarded as being the authentic Valencian ones, whereas others, of which there are hundreds, are modern interpretations of the classic dish.

Large flat-bottomed pans were used to cook paella over wood fires to prepare a midday meal, the wood smoke adding to the flavor of the dish, and the varieties of short-grain rice being grown, including bomba and calasparra, were of a type that absorbed the flavors in the pan. It was traditionally eaten with wooden spoons straight from the pan, workers sitting around it sharing their meal in a way that is reminiscent of Arab eating habits and may well be another sign of the influence of the Moors. A distinguishing feature of a traditionally cooked paella, separating it from the otherwise similar rice dishes made in other parts of the world, such as risotto in Italy and the pilafs widely made across Central Asia and the Indian subcontinent, is that a paella is not supposed to be stirred while the rice is cooking so that a crisp layer of toasted rice, known as the *socarrat*, forms at the bottom of the pan.

SEAFOOD PAELLA
The traditional method of making paella, cooked outdoors over a wood fire, here with mussels, prawns, and octopus.

At its heart, then, paella is a simple country dish originally made to feed people who had been working hard and required a hearty meal at lunchtime. Over the course of the 19th century, the city of Valencia grew into the major port it is today, attracting the workers from the fields to become city dwellers and, in the process, bringing their food with them. The first recorded use of the name paella comes from a Valencian newspaper dating to 1840, even if it was most probably known by that name for some time before then, and it became a standard item on the menus of restaurants in the city in the later part of the 19th century. It was also regularly cooked by the middle classes on trips into the countryside in which the tradition of the dish being cooked by men was preserved, much as in other countries where men often take charge of the barbecue when cooking outdoors.

SPANISH RICE
Varieties suitable for making paella such as bomba are grown in the rice fields of La Albufera.

ARROZ

The Spanish word for rice, *arroz*, comes from the Arabic word usually transliterated as *orez*, giving us a clear signal of the origin of rice growing in Spain. The initial encroachment of the Moors into the Iberian Peninsula was made in 711 by a small force led by Tariq ibn Ziyad near Gibraltar. Over the course of the next 60 years, almost all of the territory of what is now Spain and Portugal, and what was at the time part of the Kingdom of the Visigoths, was conquered, becoming al-Andalus, part of the Umayyad Caliphate, the empire centered on Damascus that had continued the period of the expansion of Islam that began in the previous century during the lifetime of the prophet Muhammad.

Many of the invading Islamic forces came from North Africa and were ethnically Berber as well as Arab. They brought with them the techniques of dry-land agriculture that included the use of irrigation and they put their knowledge to use in the more arid regions of southern Spain. Where there was sufficient water, they also introduced paddy field rice growing. Rice had spread to the Arab world from the East, most likely by a process of diffusion from the rice-growing region of the Indus Valley and then into Iran. Before the rise of the Islamic Caliphates, rice was being grown at oases on the Arabian Peninsula and in the Nile valley and it is possible that dishes not unlike paella would have been prepared in these places.

In 750, the Umayyad dynasty lost the Caliphate in Damascus to the rival Abbasids and the Umayyads were forced to leave the Arabian Peninsula, instead establishing a separate emirate in al-Andalus with its capital at Córdoba. Over the course of the next two hundred years, al-Andalus developed into one of the most advanced and cultured cities in Europe, noted for what was, at least by the standards of the day, the toleration of people of other faiths besides Islam. One of the greatest examples of Moorish architecture is the Great Mosque of

ARROZ NEGRO

✦

The Valencian dish *arroz negro*, or black rice, is made in the same way as paella. Some squid is fried in oil for a few moments and then removed from the pan and a *sofrito*, made by frying onions, garlic, bell peppers, and tomatoes, is prepared. Spanish short-grained rice is added and fried briefly, before stock, into which paprika and the blue-black ink from the squid has been stirred, is poured in and the pan left to simmer for about 40 minutes until almost all the liquid has been absorbed by the rice. The cooked squid is then placed on top of the rice to reheat for a minute or two and the almost jet-black dish is ready to serve.

Córdoba, built over the course of two centuries and finally completed in 987. Its remarkable interior, composed of 856 stone columns with characteristic double arches, can still be seen today, even if the mosque was converted into the Cathedral of Córdoba after 1236, when the city was taken by the Christian monarch King Ferdinand II of Castile as part of the Reconquista of Spain.

The Moors were finally expelled from Spain altogether in 1492, in the same year that Columbus departed on his voyage to the New World, leaving after almost 800 years of rule. The period left a legacy that can still be seen today, particularly in the south of the country. As well as such architectural masterpieces as the Mosque-Cathedral in Córdoba and the Alhambra palace in Granada, the Moors were in part responsible for introducing a culture of science and learning that would have an influence on the emergence of medieval Christian Europe from the so-called Dark Ages. And even though paella is a relatively recent addition to Spanish cuisine, and, these days, world cuisine, and is particularly associated with Valencia, it is also a reminder of the influence of the Moors more than 500 years after the last of their rulers was forced out of Spain.

TARIQ IBN ZIYAD
A military leader of the Moors who led the first incursion and subsequent conquest of Spain.

Spice

Origin: Across the East Indies

Date: From the 8th century

Type: Pepper, nutmeg, cloves, cinnamon, and many others

+ CULTURAL
+ SOCIAL
+ **COMMERCIAL**
+ **POLITICAL**
+ **MILITARY**

From the medieval period onward, spices were extremely valuable commodities, traded across the extent of the known world. Pepper, cloves, nutmeg, cinnamon, and a huge variety of other spices were almost perfect commercial goods; they were very expensive, lightweight, and came from places only known to a few people, giving them a monopoly on the business. The trade had huge consequences for history, influencing the development of the Republic of Venice, the opening up of sea routes around the world by Portuguese and Spanish traders, and the rise to prominence in the 17th century of Dutch and British commercial ventures in the East Indies.

THE WEALTH OF VENICE

The market for spices from the East existed around the Mediterranean from ancient times, going back to the Egyptians, and continued through the classical period. One of the ways in which spices arrived in the region was along the Silk Road, an overland network of commercial travel from China and Central Asia, which, after the collapse of the western Roman Empire in the 5th century CE, arrived at Constantinople, the capital of the Byzantine Empire. An alternative to the Silk Road involved a combination of sea and land transport, bringing spices across the Indian Ocean and through the Red Sea to the Byzantine city of Alexandria on the Mediterranean coast of Egypt. This Spice Route, as it is sometimes called, was controlled by Arab traders who kept the

eastern sources of the spices they were trading secret; it would become increasingly important because of frequent interruptions to trade along the Silk Road caused by instability in Central Asia.

By the 8th century CE, Venice began to develop as a trading city because of its location at the head of the Adriatic Sea, making it a gateway for goods to be transported into central and northern Europe. By that time it had become an independent city-state, but it had previously been part of the Byzantine Empire and had retained its commercial links with Constantinople and Alexandria, becoming over the preceding centuries very wealthy through the trade in spices, together with other goods transported from the East. In the early medieval period, the huge demand for spices in Europe saw them become very expensive and because their exact origins remained unknown and the trade controlled by Arab merchants, Europeans could not circumvent them by buying spices directly from their sources. It would be centuries before it was known in Europe that pepper came from the Malabar Coast of southwestern India, cinnamon from Sri Lanka, cloves from the Maluku Islands of Indonesia, and nutmeg from the tiny Banda Islands to the south of the Malukus, which together were known in Europe as the Spice Islands.

From about 1200 onward, Venice enjoyed an almost complete monopoly on the European spice trade that lasted for the next three centuries, even if it began to drop with the decline of the Byzantine Empire and the eventual fall of Constantinople in 1453 to the Ottomans. Many of the most beautiful buildings that line the Grand Canal today were built during this golden age, including the Doge's Palace and the marble-fronted Ca' d'Oro, both constructed in the characteristic Venetian Gothic style of the period. Over the course of the 16th and 17th centuries, trade routes to the East switched to the seaways that had been opened up around the African continent, allowing spices to be traded directly into northern Europe without going through Venice. As the city went into decline, fewer grand buildings were constructed to replace the old ones, leaving the city with the faded elegance and romantic charm that many of us find so attractive today.

TELLICHERRY PEPPER

✦

Pepper is now grown across the tropical regions of the world, from Vietnam to Brazil, but remains an important crop on the Malabar Coast of Kerala in the southwest of India. One of the best available to buy in the West is Tellicherry pepper, an anglicized version of Thalassery, a commercial town in the north of the region that has had a long history in the spice trade. Tellicherry pepper is rich and pungent, grown in the hills of the Western Ghats, and, in its highest grade, known as Tellicherry Garbled Special Extra Bold, it is considered by many to be the finest in the world.

CINNAMON STICKS
True cinnamon is the inner bark of a number of related Sri Lankan trees. It has been traded for thousands of years.

THE AGE OF DISCOVERY

By the 15th century the Silk Road across Asia had declined as a consequence of the fragmentation of the Mongol Empire established by Genghis Khan two centuries previously and, toward the end of the century, as the Ottoman Empire began to displace the Byzantines, the Spice Route also became more difficult and expensive. In an effort to end the monopoly of Venice on the highly lucrative spice trade and to break the monopoly by Arab merchants and the Ottomans, the rising maritime powers of Spain and Portugal began to look for ways of opening up direct trade links with the East themselves.

> **But in truth, should I meet with gold or spices in great quantity, I shall remain till I collect as much as possible, and for this purpose I am proceeding solely in quest of them.**
>
> *From a journal entry in 1492 by Christopher Columbus*

The most famous voyage of this new Age of Discovery was the one undertaken by Christopher Columbus in 1492, in which his intention was to find a route to the East Indies by heading west from Spain. Columbus was unsuccessful in his initial aims, having miscalculated the distances involved in sailing around most of the world, but inadvertently discovered the New World when he made landfall on an island in what is now the Bahamas rather than, as he thought, arriving in the Indies. Others were embarking on what were, at the time, more sensible ventures, exploring the coast of Africa looking for a way to sail around the continent in the hope of then continuing on eastward. In 1497, the Portuguese mariner Vasco da Gama led an expedition of four ships around the Cape of Good Hope on the southern tip of the African continent then traveled up the eastern coast to Mombasa (he was the first European known to have visited the city), before crossing the Indian Ocean in May 1498 to Calicut on the Malabar Coast of India,

CITY OF SPICES
A 1572 panorama of Calicut, which developed into a major trading center for spices from the East.

CALECHVT CELEBERRI MVM INDIÆ EMPORIVM.

now known as Kozhikode. In doing so, he had arrived in the main spice-producing region of the subcontinent, where most of the pepper sold in Europe originated; it was also a major trading post for those spices that came from farther east.

On the journey home, da Gama lost two of his ships and at least half of his men, but nevertheless arrived in Lisbon with a cargo of spices, principally pepper and cinnamon, which has been estimated as being worth 60 times the cost of the expedition. It also opened up the way for further trading missions to Calicut and the establishment of what would become the Portuguese Empire, making Portugal the first European country to begin settling overseas colonies. It was the beginning of a relatively short golden age for Portugal in which Lisbon became the main mercantile port for trade with Africa, the East, and South America, Brazil having been claimed for Portugal by Pedro Álvares Cabral in 1500. His ships had sailed westward into the Atlantic after either being blown off course during a storm or on a secret mission to look for a route to the East to take advantage of the spice trade.

The Portuguese established a colony in the southern Indian province of Goa early in the 16th century in order to further exploit the spice trade and from there began to send out expeditions to find the location of the Spice Islands. They annexed the city of Malacca on the Malay Peninsula in 1511 and, after learning of the location of the Spice Islands, moved on to take the islands two years later. Ferdinand Magellan was one of the Portuguese sailors involved in the search, but then, after falling out of favor with the Portuguese authorities, in 1519 he led a Spanish expedition to find a way to the islands by sailing around the South American continent. On November 1st, 1519, the expedition entered what would become known as the Straits of Magellan, between the South American mainland and Tierra del Fuego, and went on to make the first European passage from the Atlantic Ocean to the Pacific. Magellan died in the Philippines the following year, but his expedition returned to Spain in 1522, completing the first circumnavigation of the globe. The expedition had passed through the Spice Islands, and Spain would later claim a share of sovereignty over them as a result, but it was hardly a viable commercial route for the import of spices to Europe, which would remain under the control of the Portuguese until the beginning of the 17th century.

SPICE TRADER
An illustration from 1453 of a dealer weighing out spices in the German city of Nuremburg.

THE SPICE WARS

The wealth to be gained from the spice trade had not gone unnoticed by the emerging European powers of England and, in particular, the Dutch Republic. In 1592, English ships of the Royal Navy captured the Portuguese ship *Madre de Deus* off the Azores as it was returning to Lisbon from the East Indies loaded with 1,008 tons (900 tonnes) of cargo, including 476 tons (425 tonnes) of pepper as well as chests full of gold, silver, and jewels. It was one of the largest prizes ever taken, estimated at a value of half a million pounds at the time, and made the English very aware of the riches to be gained from trade with the East. In 1600, the East India Company was set up in London in order to exploit this potential and, two years later, the Dutch Republic followed suit, establishing the Dutch East India Company, or, in Dutch, the Ver-eenigde Oost-Indische Compagnie (VOC). Both companies had been granted charters by their respective governments allowing them to take and defend overseas colonies, raising armies and building fortresses if necessary; so, even though both nominally remained commercial companies, they had the power to act as if they were nation states.

The Dutch were already involved in the spice trade by this time and for much of the 17th century were more prominent than the English, taking on the Portuguese in a series of military encounters in various parts of their empire sometimes known as the Spice Wars. Over the course of almost 60 years, from 1602 to 1661, the VOC established itself in the Far East, breaking the monopoly on the spice trade held by the Portuguese and creating what was, in effect, a Dutch overseas empire centered on Batavia, the capital of what became the Dutch

DUTCH MALACCA
An 18th-century illustration of the trading port on the Malay Peninsula ruled by the Dutch from 1661 to 1824.

East Indies, now Jakarta in Indonesia. They also took over Malacca on the Malay Peninsula, giving them control of the Straits of Malacca, which separate the peninsula from the island of Sumatra; one of the most important stretches of water on the passage from the East Indies to Europe.

The conflict was finally settled by a treaty signed by the Dutch and Portuguese at Utrecht in 1661 in which the Dutch kept all the territory they had gained in the East Indies but agreed to give up New Holland, the colony they had established in northern Brazil. Despite several attempts, the Dutch had failed to capture Macau, the Portuguese trading post on the Pearl River delta in southern China, from where they controlled the trade with China and Japan for much of the 17th century. By the beginning of the following century, the British, as they had become after the Act of Union between England and Scotland in 1707, became more active in the region, and, as they were not prepared to allow the Portuguese a monopoly of trade with China through Macau, set up their own station on the other side of the delta that would later become known as Hong Kong. The two colonies remained in British and Portuguese hands until the late 1990s, Hong Kong finally being returned to the Chinese in 1997 and Macau following two years later.

The British became more firmly established on the Indian subcontinent over the course of the 18th century as the East India Company founded an increasing number of trading posts, including on the Malabar Coast to exploit the spice trade. The company also began to make inroads in the Malay Peninsula and, in 1819, Sir Stamford Raffles founded Singapore as a free port on its tip, from where it was in prime position to control commercial shipping through the Straits of Malacca, which, by that time, had become part of the main seaway between India and China. By the 19th century, spices were being grown in numerous different locations around the world, reducing their value as trade goods, but by that time the commercial and financial networks set up initially on the back of the spice trade were dealing with a vast array of other commodities.

THE BANDA ISLANDS

◆

Up until nutmeg trees began to be grown in tropical countries in the 19th century, the only source of nutmeg and mace, both obtained from the fruit of the tree, were the tiny Banda Islands, volcanic outcrops between Sulawesi and New Guinea. In the 17th century, the Dutch were so keen to monopolize the nutmeg trade that, as part of the settlement of the Second Anglo-Dutch War in 1667, they were prepared to concede their colony on Manhattan Island to the English in order to gain full control of the Bandas. Once they had taken possession of the Dutch colony, the British changed its name from New Amsterdam to New York.

NUTMEGS
The reddish-brown outer seed covering, or aril, is used to make mace, while the seed within provides nutmeg.

Salted Herring

Origin: Baltic Sea, North Sea, North Atlantic

Date: 12th century

Type: Preserved fish

The extraordinary abundance of herring in the North and Baltic Seas in the early medieval period led to it becoming the most important commercial fish in Europe at that time. The salted fish became a staple in the diet of people across large parts of northern Europe and it was one of the first commodities traded by what would develop into the Hansa, or Hanseatic League as it is often called in English, a cross-border mercantile association of towns and cities that, in some respects, can be seen as a forerunner of the modern European Union.

+ **CULTURAL**
+ **SOCIAL**
+ **COMMERCIAL**
+ POLITICAL
+ MILITARY

THE HERRING AND THE HANSA

The reason vast shoals of herring teem in these northern seas compared to those farther south is simply because cold water has the capacity to hold more dissolved oxygen than warm water does, so it can support larger quantities of the microscopic plankton and other main invertebrates that the herring feed on. The Danish chronicler Saxo Grammaticus (c.1180–1220), for instance, wrote of herring shoals in the Danish Sound, the narrow stretch of water separating Copenhagen from Malmö, so dense that boats struggled to sail through them and claimed that the fish could be picked from the water by hand. It sounds, it must be admitted, like a fisherman's tale, but even if Saxo was exaggerating slightly, a further indication of the vast scale of the herring fishery is contained in records from the northern French town of Arras dating back to the 15th century. By comparing the number of barrels of the salted fish bought by merchants in the town to its population, it

has been calculated that, on average, every person in Arras consumed more than 200 salted herring a year, so most people must have eaten the preserved fish nearly every day.

The fish eaten in Arras were most likely Atlantic herring (*Clupea harengus*) from the North Sea and North Atlantic that had been landed at Boulogne, one of the many fishing ports in Europe and the British Isles that grew wealthy because of the herring trade. Marine biologists now recognize the

smaller herring of the Baltic Sea as a subspecies (*Clupea harengus membras*) of the Atlantic herring and it has a slightly lower oil content, even if, at 10 percent of body weight, it remains packed with the sort of healthy oils nutritionists are always reminding us to eat more often. It also accounts for the method of preservation used from the medieval period and into modern times, in which the cleaned herring were packed in barrels with brine within 24 hours of being caught, before the oil could become rancid and spoil the fish. Cod, the other major commercial fish of the period, has a lower oil content and can be dry salted and then air-dried because it does not spoil so quickly.

The Baltic herring spends much of the year feeding in deep water and comes into shallower coastal waters to spawn at a number of different times of the year. The spawning grounds on the tip of the Falsterbo Peninsula, at the south-

The herring, who finds in the shinning waves
Board, lodging and washing free,
Though small is, of all kind Neptune's gifts,
The sweetest by far to me.
Alexander of Neckham (1157–1217),
  De laudibus divinae sapientiae

ernmost tip of Sweden, are active in the spring and, during the 12th century, the Scania Market began to operate in August and September principally to sell barrels of salted herring, the fish having been caught in the sea immediately adjacent to where it was sold and then salted as soon as it was landed on shore. Merchants came from all over northern Europe to buy the fish, including from Lübeck, a city near the Baltic coast of what was then the Holy Roman Empire and is now Germany. The limiting factor on the amount of salted herring that could be sold was not the fish themselves, but the availability of salt and, as a consequence, a two-way trade developed in which Lübeck merchants supplied the Scania fishermen who ran the market with salt from the Lüneburg salt springs in northern Germany, about 50 miles (80 km) inland from Lübeck, and then bought large quantities of the resulting salted herring, much of which they then sold on to merchants from towns farther inland.

HANSEATIC LÜBECK

The trade in salted herring boomed because of the difficulty of transporting fresh fish any distance away from coastal regions before it went off and also because of the Christian practices of abstaining from eating meat during the 40 days of Lent and of eating fish on Friday. It was cheap and plentiful, becoming a staple food in the diets of many people throughout the year and leading to it being regarded as the food of the poor. But despite the low price, the sheer scale of the trade meant that the Lübeck merchants at the center of it began to grow wealthy. They formed trade guilds within the city and developed commercial links with numerous other towns and cities along the Baltic coast and extending westward along the shore of the North Sea and eastward into what is now Russia.

Lübeck was in a position to control the trade exchange between east and west, in which the raw materials from the eastern Baltic and Russia, including timber and resin, together with other commodities like wheat, amber, and furs, were sent to the cities of Western Europe, while manufactured goods, particularly cloth, went in the other direction. By the middle of the 13th century, Lübeck had formed trade associations with other cities to protect the monopolies they had established

and to prevent the trade networks being attacked by thieves and pirates. Trade agreements between cities also allowed merchants to establish offices and warehouses in each other's ports, so that business could be conducted without interference, and these mutually beneficial arrangements formed the basis of the Hanseatic League. Once the association had been formed, it was governed by a council, the Hansetag, which met in Lübeck, but it was for the most part an informal system and the council only came together infrequently to discuss matters relating to trade between the members of the league, who were otherwise free to conduct their affairs as they saw fit.

By the start of the 15th century the Hanseatic League was at its height, extending westward as far as Bruges and with offices in a number of English cities, including London, and stretching as far east as Novgorod, a city to the south of modern St. Petersburg. An indication of the wealth accumulated by Hansa merchants can be seen in Lübeck today, where many examples of churches, guild halls, and merchants' houses built in the distinctive style of the Brick Gothic remain, even if many others were destroyed during the Second World War. Brick was used as the principal building material because no suitable stone was available in the region, whereas there was a plentiful supply of clay for brick-making. Further examples of Brick Gothic buildings can be seen across much of northern Germany, many showing the high-stepped gables characteristic of the architectural style, whereas Lüneburg provides us with a fascinating reminder of a Hansa town. Few new buildings were constructed in the center of the town after 1560 because its fortunes went into a serious decline, preserving its medieval street plan as well as many of the houses built by the people who were involved in the salt business. By the middle of the 16th century, the Scania Market had ceased trading as a consequence of a major drop in the herring stocks in the Baltic Sea around the Falsterbo Peninsula, depriving Lüneburg of one of its major customers, and, at the same time, it faced increased competition to the south from salt produced on the Atlantic coasts of France and Portugal.

By that time the Hanseatic League as a whole was beginning to contract. The rising powers of Sweden and Denmark, together with the emerging Dutch Republic, were challenging the Hansa monopoly on trade through the Baltic region, while the focus of European commerce was becoming more international as trade routes to the Far East and across the Atlantic eclipsed those controlled from Lübeck. With the decline in the Baltic herring, even the trade on which it had first built its wealth began to shift to fishing ports on the North Sea and North Atlantic coasts, where the Atlantic herring remained abundant. The

SURSTRÖMMING

✦

Fermented herring is considered a delicacy by some in northern Sweden, where it is called *surströmming*. The herrings are first brined and then canned, where, in the absence of air, a natural fermentation takes place to preserve the fish. It is traditionally eaten outdoors because the smell is said to be unbearable if a can is opened in the house. The German food writer Wolfgang Fassbender has suggested that the hardest part of eating *surströmming* is overcoming the urge to throw up because of the horrendous stench before getting the chance to discover what it actually tastes like.

salted herring trade may have been overshadowed by other more lucrative commodities after the Hanseatic League had become established,
but the fortunes of the fishery and the trade association in the Baltic
region continued to mirror each other, rising together and then declining at the same time as well.

The league persisted in a much reduced form for another 200 years,
finally involving only Lübeck, Hamburg, and Bremen out of almost
200 towns and cities that had been members at its height, until it was
finally dissolved in the 1750s. Some cities continued to include the word
Hansestadt, or Hansa Town, in their names long after it had ceased to
have any real meaning. In 1980 a new version of the Hanseatic League
was established, based in Lübeck again and open to all those towns that
had participated in the original alliance. In 2007, Lüneburg was admitted as a member, changing its name to Hansestadt Lüneburg in recognition of its past and joining what has become a loose association of
about 180 towns and cities extending across much the same region as it
had almost 500 years earlier, including the modern city of Novgorod
and King's Lynn, where the only remaining original Hanseatic building
in Britain is to be found.

The trade links of the past are nothing more than a distant memory
now and the new Hansa describes its purpose as not being in commerce,
but in promoting cultural exchange and tourism. It is, for instance, now
possible to follow the original path of the old salt road from Lüneburg
to Lübeck, on which the salt to preserve herring was hauled by horse

and cart on the first part of its journey to Scania Market. The road was superseded by a canal in 1398, making it one of the oldest man-made waterways in Europe, enabling the salt to be transported in much greater quantity. The canal gradually fell into disuse with the decline in the herring trade, but the salt works in Lüneburg persisted right up until 1980, before finally being shut down and converted into the German Salt Museum.

HERRING TODAY

Herring is still popular in countries around the Baltic, even if it is more usually eaten either fresh or pickled these days rather than salted. In Britain, the herring fishery remained important right up to the 1970s, when decades of overfishing in the North Sea and North Atlantic resulted in a crash in its numbers. The extraordinary fecundity of the herring, in which the female can lay 40,000 eggs in one spawning, allowed the species to recover quickly, but, just as populations were increasing in the 1990s, it was subjected to industrial-scale fishing for fishmeal to be fed to livestock, a practice that risked the fish being eradicated as a commercial species. In an effort to prevent further overfishing, the European Union introduced much stricter regulations, resulting in a steady recovery in herring populations so that the Atlantic herring fishery is now regarded as being sustainable.

In Britain, herring appears to have retained its reputation for being the food of the poor and, after its decline in the 1970s, the market for it never fully recovered even after it had become widely available again. In these health-conscious days, it is hard to imagine a return to eating salted herring or the fish ever again having the sort of influence on history as it did during the period when the Hanseatic League was still functioning. Nevertheless, the silver of the sea, as it used to be known, is now sustainably fished and is rich in all the right sort of oils, so it must surely be due to make a comeback someday soon.

OMEGA-3 FATTY ACIDS

◆

Herring contain one of the highest levels of long-chain omega-3 fatty acids of any fish. The health benefits to humans of these fatty acids, known as EPA and DHA, were first described in the Inuit people of Greenland, who eat lots of fish and exhibit almost no incidence of heart disease. Medical research has shown that taking dietary supplements containing EPA and DHA does not reproduce the same effect, leading to the conclusion that a complicated metabolic pathway is involved in reducing the likelihood of heart trouble. One less scientific conclusion that can be drawn from this is to eat more herring because it's good for you.

PICKLED HERRING
Salted herring are no longer common in Europe, but pickled herring such as these rollmops remain widely available.

Frankfurter

**Laws are like sausages. It is better
not to see them being made.**

Otto von Bismarck

Origin: Frankfurt am Main

Date: From the 12th century

Type: Finely ground smoked
pork sausage

+ **CULTURAL**
+ **SOCIAL**
+ COMMERCIAL
+ POLITICAL
+ MILITARY

For such a straightforward foodstuff, usually made to use up cheap cuts of meat, the range of sausages available around the world is truly astonishing. In Germany alone there are said to be over a thousand different types, including the frankfurter, a long thin sausage made from finely ground pork and then smoked and scalded. It is probably the best-known German sausage outside of the country, largely because of its associations with American food and, in particular, with the worldwide phenomenon of the hot dog.

ON THE MAIN

By the 12th century, the city of Frankfurt am Main had grown into a commercial center largely because of its central position on the River Main, one of the major tributaries of the Rhine, which linked it to other cities across central Europe. Fairs were held regularly in the city and, in 1152, the Holy Roman Emperor Frederick I, better known now as Frederick Barbarossa, became the first of many Holy Roman Emperors to be elected by a council of prince-electors in the city, going on to be crowned in the city of Aachen a few days later. No direct evidence exists to show that any particular sausages were made or consumed at either the fairs or the elections of emperors at this time, but it was considered traditional by the 16th century and it is not unreasonable to suppose that this tradition began with the first emperor to be elected in Frankfurt.

The Holy Roman Empire was the successor state to the Carolingian Empire established by Charlemagne across central Europe in the late 8th century, but by the 12th century had declined as a consequence of internal divisions and the rising powers of the popes of Rome, who had challenged the authority of the emperors across much of the region. Frederick Barbarossa, which literally means "Red Beard," set out to restore the empire to its former glory, initiating successful military campaigns against the states of northern Italy that had become independent and, in the process, re-establishing the power of the Holy Roman Emperors at the expense of the popes. Over the course of the next few centuries, Frankfurt grew rich, trading with the Italian city-states and with the rising commercial cities in the Low Countries.

Frankfurt was granted the status of an Imperial Free City in 1372 within the Holy Roman Empire, allowing the city council to elect their own leaders and largely to govern themselves while remaining under the overall rule of the emperor. The city flourished, becoming in 1564 the place where emperors held their coronations as well as elections. At the first of these coronations, in which the Holy Roman Emperor Maximilian II was crowned, a special sausage was made to celebrate the event, which may have been actually called a frankfurter.

The truth is that we don't know exactly when and where a long thin sausage made like they were in Frankfurt actually became known as a frankfurter. By the early 19th century, similar sausages were being made by a butcher in Vienna who, it has been suggested, had learned the method while working in Frankfurt and then adapted it by using a mix of pork and beef, but it is impossible to say for sure if these Vienna sausages, or wieners as they would become known in America, were the ones later called frankfurters or if the name was first applied to the ones actually made in Frankfurt itself. What we can say is that, over the course of the 19th century, around eight million Germans emigrated to America, taking with them, amongst other things, the sort of food they were used to eating at home, including their sausages which, with a few tweaks and additions, would become one of the archetypal American foods.

BARBAROSSA
An illustration of the red-bearded Frederick Barbarossa, flanked by his sons, from the 12th-century *Chronicle of the Guelphs.*

FRANKFURT AM MAIN
A watercolor from 1889 showing Frankfurt in the 17th century, when it was an Imperial Free City of the Holy Roman Empire.

CONEY ISLAND AND THE BALL PARK

In Frankfurt the sausages that would come to bear the city's name were eaten at public events and fairs and this association, knowingly or otherwise, would continue in America, where frankfurters were slapped in a bread bun and called hot dogs. As well as being a convenient lunch-time meal bought from one of the lunch carts that plied their trades in American cities in the 19th century, hot dogs were eaten on days out and at baseball games because they were cheap and could easily be eaten while on the move or while watching the game. Besides tasting great, particularly with the addition of a little mustard, relish, or sauerkraut, hot dogs were the food of the masses, eaten and enjoyed by everybody up to and including the president, particularly if he was keen to demonstrate to the electorate that, despite the high office he held, he was really just a regular American guy.

A hot dog at the ball park is better than a steak at the Ritz.

Humphrey Bogart

The origin of the hot dog in America is now shrouded in so many legends that it is impossible to know where it was first made or who made it, but then again, let's be honest, it doesn't take a genius to make a sausage sandwich. In one of the numerous versions of the story concerning how it came about its name, the hot dog is said to have first been called the dachshund sandwich, presumably because both are long and thin and come from Germany, and the name was shortened when a newspaper man on a tight deadline didn't know how to spell dachshund (I looked it up).

One of the earliest successful hot dog operations was started in 1870 by Charles Feltman, a German immigrant who had arrived in New York as a 15-year-old in 1856 and had begun his catering career with a food cart. Coney Island was already a popular resort with New Yorkers by that time, being immediately to the south of Brooklyn and yet different enough so that going there felt like a proper day out from the city.

LUNCH CARTS
Vendors selling hot frankfurters for 3¢ each or two for 5¢ on Broad Street, New York, in about 1906.

The opening of the Brooklyn Bridge in 1883 and the extension of the railway system in the early 20th century made getting to the island even easier, but it was the opening of a subway station in 1915 that really caused the resort of take off.

NATHAN'S FAMOUS
Still a Coney Island institution, Nathan's Famous now has more than 300 outlets around America.

In 1916 Nathan Handwerker, one of Feltman's employees, decided to go it alone, opening Nathan's Famous near the subway station. The hot dogs were half the price they were at Feltmans, 5¢ instead of 10¢, and it took some time for people to overcome initial suspicions about the content of such cheap sausages. According to one story, Handwerker offered free hot dogs to doctors from a nearby hospital as long as they were wearing their white coats, and the sight of a queue of doctors at Nathan's Famous apparently convinced those people who had been reluctant to trust the food that it was safe. Whether that story has any truth to it or not, Nathan's became a Coney Island institution and it remains in the same place today, on the corner of Surf and Stillwell. And, despite the gradual decline of the resort from its heyday in the 1920s and 1930s, a trip to Coney Island today would somehow not be complete without a hot dog or two from Nathan's.

The same could be said for a trip to the ball park because baseball and hot dogs have been associated with each other right from the beginning of the Major League in 1893, so much so that it is now hard to imagine how it would be possible to have a more American experience. Both developed out of the great melting pot of cultures thrown together in the 19th century as people came to the Land of the Free in search of a better life, in the process creating a vibrant and dynamic culture that would go on to change the world.

CHICAGO-STYLE

✦

In the Windy City, hot dogs are served "dragged through the garden," or, in other words, with everything on: mustard, relish, pickles, tomatoes, peppers. Everything, that is, except ketchup. Chicagoans are of the opinion that ketchup has no place on a dog and no amount of persuasion could convince them otherwise. An alterative to the Chicago-style dog is the Maxwell Street Polish, made from a Polish sausage with onions and mustard, first served at Jim's Original stand, which, before the district was redeveloped, was in the market on the corner of Maxwell and Halstead and is now on East 95th Street.

Peking Duck

A man who stands on a hill with his mouth open will wait a long time for a roast duck to drop into it.

Confucius (c.551–478 BCE)

Origin: Beijing

Date: From the 14th century

Type: Roast duck

✦ **CULTURAL**

✦ SOCIAL

✦ COMMERCIAL

✦ **POLITICAL**

✦ MILITARY

The dish known in the West as Peking duck and as Beijing *kaoya* in China has become one of the best-known examples of Chinese cuisine, now served in restaurants in numerous countries around the world and thought of as a national dish at home. It was first made in the way it is today in the mid 19th century in Beijing, either in the imperial kitchens of the Forbidden City, the huge palace complex of the Qing dynasty emperors, or in one of the numerous restaurants of the city, but its origins can be traced back much further in Chinese history, at least as far as the Mongol Yuan Dynasty in the early 14th century.

BEIJING ROAST DUCK

The characteristic feature of Peking duck is that the skin is crispy while the meat remains moist. This is achieved by, first, pumping air into the duck through the neck cavity to separate the skin from the fat and then coating it in maltose syrup. It is then hung up in an oven and cooked at quite a high temperature so that the fat drips off it while the skin becomes crisp and takes on a deep brown color. It is served in restaurants in Beijing in three courses, beginning with the crispy skin, then the carved meat, usually eaten rolled up in a fine pancake with thinly sliced cucumber and green onions or Chinese chives and with a sweet soybean sauce, and finally a broth made from what remains of the duck after the meat has been carved.

The earliest written record we have of roast duck in China cooked in a way that resembles modern Peking duck comes from the book *Yin-shan Zhengyao*, or *Principles of Food and Drink*, compiled in 1330 by Hu Sihui, a court dietician in the imperial household of the Yuan Dynasty emperors. He was responsible for ensuring that the emperor and his family ate a healthy diet and his book was as much about the medical properties of food as the culinary aspects. The traditional diet of the Yuan Dynasty, established by Kublai Khan, the grandson of Genghis Khan, reflected their heritage as nomads on the Mongolian steppes, but Hu Sihui, who was of Mongol descent himself, wrote about the cuisines of the different ethnicities of China and those from further afield, including those

of the Turkic tribes of Central Asia and the Persians. He placed great emphasis on moderation and the consumption of a variety of fresh fruit and vegetables, promoting the sort of balanced diet nutritionists would approve of today.

After the Yuan Dynasty collapsed in 1368, Hu Sihui's writings would prove influential with the Ming Dynasty, who initially ruled from Nanjing and then in 1421 moved back to Beijing. When the imperial court returned to Beijing, which literally means "the northern capital," it brought with it influences of southern Chinese cuisine, together with the variety of duck that would become the breed now used to make Peking duck and that is generally known in the West by that same name. Restaurants specializing in roast duck began to open in Beijing during this period, some of which lasted through the succeeding Qing Dynasty, the last of the imperial Chinese dynasties, and the revolutionary period of the first half of the 20th century. A few of these restaurants are still serving duck in the People's Republic of China today, demonstrating that good food remains good food whatever political system is being followed.

The spread of Chinese cuisine around the world has meant that it is possible to eat Peking duck, or, at least, a version of it, all over the place these days, including at the Chinese restaurant five minutes' walk from where I live. The version sold in Britain is called crispy aromatic duck and is usually cooked for longer than Peking duck would be in Beijing so that the meat is drier and less fatty and the skin and meat are usually served together rather than separately. It is often served with hoisin sauce, which is similar to sweet soybean sauce but for some reason is almost always called plum sauce, despite not having any of the fruit in it.

QUANJUDE

✦

The Quanjude restaurant was first established in Beijing in 1864 and its chefs are credited with introducing the now widely imitated method of roasting ducks by hanging them from racks in an oven. The modern restaurant is enormous, in a year serving two million ducks to its five million customers, and has been visited by numerous world leaders on state visits to China. It famously hosted a Chinese government dinner given in 1971 for the US National Security Advisor Henry Kissinger, who apparently enjoyed the duck, and the discussions held at the dinner table are said to have paved the way for the groundbreaking visit of President Richard Nixon to China in the following year.

Roast duck is prepared by revolving a young duckling on a spit in an oven. The chefs of Inspector Feng's family excel in preparing this dish.

Yuan Mei, Recipes from the Suiyuan Garden *(1716–97)*

Cassoulet

Origin: Languedoc

Date: 1355

Type: Meat and bean stew

✦ **CULTURAL**

✦ **SOCIAL**

✦ COMMERCIAL

✦ POLITICAL

✦ MILITARY

Cassoulet is a hearty meat and bean stew from Languedoc in southern France, known in the Occitan language of the region as *caçolet* and named after the cassole, the large earthenware pot with sloping sides it is cooked in. It is associated with both Toulouse and Carcassonne, but in reality it is from the countryside, originally cooked as a midday meal for people who worked on the land and were in need of something more substantial than a sandwich for lunch.

CASTELNAUDARY

The citizens of the small town of Castelnaudary are of the opinion that cassoulet does not come from either Toulouse or Carcassonne. According to them, cassoulet comes from their town and, at least if the town council website is to believed, they consider it to be the "*Capitale Mondiale du Cassoulet*," the Cassoulet Capital of the World. The town is roughly halfway between Toulouse and Carcassonne and stands on the Canal du Midi, which dates back to the late 17th century and forms one part of an inland waterway across France that links the Mediterranean Sea with the Atlantic Ocean.

For several hundred years, the town was a major port on the canal, possessing one of the largest basins for overnight stopovers for barges, most of which would have been carrying wheat and wine, the two principal commodities of trade. Commercial barges carried freight on the

GRAND BASIN
A view of Castelnaudary across the Grand Basin of the Canal du Midi.

canal right up to the 1970s, but by that time the volume had decreased to such an extent as to be insignificant because of the construction of the railways in the 19th century and then in the 20th century a switch to road transport. These days, the canal is mostly used by pleasure craft and the rise in tourism in the second half of the 20th century is most probably what lies behind the attempts by the citizens of Castelnaudary to identify the town with cassoulet. At about the same time as a tourist boom was beginning in the 1960s, the dish was discovered by chefs and food writers, who transformed it from the rustic stew of the *paysans*, the people of the French countryside, into a restaurant dish now found in varying degrees of authenticity on menus all over the world.

One of the first books, and still probably the best, to be published outside France that described the sort of French cooking that was a part of everyday life, as opposed to the haute cuisine of high-end French restaurants, was *French Provincial Cooking*, by Elizabeth David, first published in 1960 in Britain. For people living in a country where the food rationing introduced during the Second World War had only come to an end in 1954, it offered a glimpse of a different way of life in which such simple pleasures as eating and drinking well were celebrated. As Britain recovered after years of postwar austerity and people began to be able to afford to go on holidays abroad, one of the principal destinations was France, not only because it was just on the other side of the English Channel and the weather was better there than in Britain, but also because of a perception of a way of life in France which, if it had ever existed in Britain in the first place, had largely been lost.

British tourists were among the first to discover the delights of a boating holiday in the Canal du Midi, beginning in Toulouse and going down to the South of France. Castelnaudary provided a perfect stopover on the way, where the original cassoulet, as promoted by the town council, could be sampled in one of the town's restaurants together with a couple of glasses of the local *vin rouge*. After a leisurely lunch, a genuine cassole made in the nearby village of Issel could be purchased

CASSOULET IN CASTELNAUDARY

✦

The four main ingredients of Castelnaudary cassoulet are pork, haricot beans, duck confit, and Toulouse sausages, which are cooked with onions, garlic, and a bouquet garni of herbs. The beans are soaked overnight and then placed in a cassole with all the ingredients except the confit, which only needs to be heated through, and the sausage, which is fried separately first. Water is then added to cover the pork and beans and the cassole goes in the oven for several hours. The crust that forms on the surface of the cassoulet as it cooks is folded in on several occasions and then the confit and sausage go in for the final half hour of cooking. The crust that forms during this last phase is left on the cassoulet and it is now ready to serve.

as a memento of the trip and then, despite best intentions, probably left in a cupboard at home and forgotten. In the meantime, the people of Castelnaudary had established a new way of making a living after the decline of commercial traffic on the canal and if that involved inventing the Festival of the Cassoulet, held in the town since 1999, in order to promote themselves, then what is the harm in that?

THE BLACK PRINCE

Cassoulet was, according to one story at least, first made in Casteln-audary in 1355 during the Hundred Years War, a series of conflicts between the kings of England and France over possession of large swathes of French territory claimed by successive Norman and Plan-tagenet English kings. In October of that year, when the town was being besieged by the forces of Edward of Woodstock, the son of the English king Edward III and better known today as the Black Prince, its people are said to have brought their remaining food supplies together and cooked everything communally in one large cauldron,

THE BLACK PRINCE
A 15th-century illustration of Edward, the Black Prince, shown holding the Royal Standard of England.

ending up with a stew containing pork, duck, and whatever else they had. The resulting cassoulet may have fortified them to continue the fight against the Black Prince, but unfortunately it did not lead tovic-tory; the town fell at the end of October and the prince's army ran-sacked it, killing many of its inhab-itants and burning down the castle and many of the houses.

Historians of the period have pointed out that during the Great Raid, as the Black Prince's cam-paigns in Aquitaine and Languedoc are known, his forces only remained at Castelnaudary for a total of two days, overcoming the modest defenses of the town easily before moving on in search of plunder elsewhere. It would hardly have left the people of the town time to organize a defense, let alone invent a new dish. And, as even the Castelnaudary Town Council are prepared to acknowledge today, haricot beans, the ingredient that gives cassou-let its particular character, originally came from the New World, dis-covered by Columbus in 1492, so were not likely to have been integral to a stew being made more than a hundred years beforehand.

In Britain, the Hundred Years War is remembered now for Henry V's victory at the Battle of Agincourt in 1415 (or at least in Shakespeare's version of it), while the French think of Joan of Arc, who revived French fortunes in the war during 1429, and their eventual victory in 1453, which brought to an end the possession of land in France by English kings. In both Britain and France today, people have exercised the power of selective memory to concentrate on those parts of the Hundred Years War they are interested in, like the English victory at Agincourt or the eventual French victory in the war as a whole, without worrying too much about the overall picture or about questioning the historical accuracy of the stories that have grown up surrounding the events.

In Castelnaudary, much the same has happened with cassoulet. In truth, there is no more reason to suppose that the town has any greater claim on the dish than anywhere else in the region and it is probably the case that not too many of its citizens are really overly concerned about cassoulet's association with the Hundred Years War or the Black Prince. Its importance to them is in how it has revived the fortunes of the town in more recent times; at the Hôtel de France in the town, for instance, they operate their own canning factory so, as well as selling Castelnaudary cassoulet in the restaurant, their

The wise will heed M. Colombie's advice about eating the cassoulet at midday on a day when no great exertion is called for afterwards.

Elizabeth David, French Provincial Cooking

customers can take a can of it home with them or, failing that, order it online. In this sense, cassoulet, together with the idea of French cuisine and the lifestyle that goes with it, has been used to mold the history of the town, boosting its economy and providing its people with jobs and livelihoods. And as well as this, when it is made properly, like it is in Castelnaudary, cassoulet tastes pretty good.

Turnips

I was raised almost entirely on turnips and potatoes, but I think that the turnips had more to do with the effect than the potatoes.

Marlene Dietrich

Origin: Northern Europe

Date: From the 14th century

Type: Root vegetable

✦ CULTURAL

✦ *SOCIAL*

✦ COMMERCIAL

✦ POLITICAL

✦ MILITARY

The turnip may be the butt of jokes in most of the countries where it is grown, many suggesting that it is only eaten by peasants or alluding to the effects it can have on the digestive system, but in France it is held in higher regard and is one of the key ingredients of navarin of lamb, one of the classic dishes of French cuisine. The turnip has also played a significant role in history as a part of a new system of farming first developed in the 14th century in the Low Countries that would lead to enormous social changes across Europe and pave the way for the Industrial Revolution of the 19th century.

THE ROTATING TURNIP

By the 14th century the mercantile cities of the Low Countries, including Bruges and Antwerp in modern-day Belgium, were expanding as a consequence of the wealth generated through the wool trade and their commercial links with the northern cities of the Hanseatic League (see page 88). As well as a growth in population, people from many other parts of Europe were coming to the region, providing its farmers with both an opportunity and a problem. Their markets were expanding, but the amount of land suitable for agriculture was limited, preventing them from taking full advantage, while the sale of such foodstuffs as salted herring imported from the Baltic region plugged the gap.

The solution to this problem was to introduce a particular type of crop rotation that allowed farmers to double the productivity of their land, an innovation for which they have rarely received any recognition but one that would form the basis of agriculture for more than 500 years and remain important in many farming systems today. At the heart of this new way of farming was the turnip, not specifically grown as a food crop even if it provided a cheap source of sustenance during the winter months, but as fodder for animals and, in particular, for sheep. Up until then, arable farming had required long periods of fallow in which a third of the land was left unproductive at any one time to allow it to recover after crops had been grown. As well as restoring the

fertility of the soil, the fallow period also inter-rupted the life cycles of the various pests and diseases of arable crops that would otherwise build up over time and could dramatically reduce the quantity of grain harvested.

The advance developed by farmers in the Low Countries was to integrate livestock and arable farming, breaking up the cultivation of cereal crops by growing fodder crops, which are subject to a different range of pests and diseases, and including a grass and clover phase into the rotation for livestock to graze. The benefits of this grazing phase were threefold; as well as pro-viding pasture and winter fodder for livestock, the grass and clover phase further reduced the build-up of pests and diseases as well as actively improving the fertility of the soil. This is a con-sequence of the cycling of manure from cattle and sheep, both directly while they graze and through the spreading of the muck and straw that has accumulated in the sheds they are kept in over winter, and because growing the legumi-nous clover results in an increasing amount of nitrogen in the soil. Like all legumes, clover forms a symbiotic relationship with soil-borne bacteria in which the clover forms nodules in its roots to house the bacteria and also provides the microorganisms with food in the form of root sap, while the bacteria fixes atmospheric nitro-gen in close proximity to the roots of the plant, thereby nourishing it.

The success of farming in Flanders and in the neighboring regions of Holland contributed to the increasing prosperity of the Low Countries, which by the 16th century had become the lead-ing trading nations in the world. Over the course of the century, Antwerp developed into one of the largest and wealthi-est cities in Europe, whereas the Dutch could afford to begin the hugely expensive process of large-scale land reclamation that would transform the country in succeeding years. It would, of course, be ridiculous to claim that the wealth of Antwerp or the extraordinary

NAVARIN OF LAMB

✦

In France, turnips, or *navets*, as they are known, are harvested when they are young and still relatively sweet so that, in a navarin of lamb, they don't have that bitter aftertaste associated with the fully grown vegetable. The dish is made using a cheaper cut of lamb that is cooked slowly over the course of several hours together with the turnips, other root vegetables, onions, garlic, and herbs. The result is similar to such dishes as Irish stew or Lancashire hotpot, with the exception that no potatoes are used in the navarin, but plum tomatoes are often added to enhance the broth.

flowering of culture during the Dutch Golden Age of the 17th century were entirely based on the farmers of the region growing the most humble of root vegetables, but it would not be unreasonable to suggest that the turnip played a modest role in creating the economic conditions that allowed these phenomena to arise.

TURNIP TOWNSHEND

The farming innovations developed in Flanders did not result in an immediate flood of imitators in other parts of Europe. It was not taken up in the arable regions in the east of England until the 17th century and then only sporadically. One of the reasons for this was that much of the arable land was farmed in an open field system, in which local people held commoners' rights to cultivate strips of land and to graze animals during the fallow periods. A change to a system based on a continuous rotation without the fallow did not begin to occur until the enclosure of these open fields began, a legal process in which the ownership of the land was formalized, which usually meant that local people lost their rights and the title of the land was obtained by the aristocracy and other large landowners.

VISCOUNT TOWNSHEND
Townshend introduced crop rotations using turnips onto his estate at Raynham in Norfolk.

The enclosure of the countryside and the introduction of new farming methods such as crop rotation, when taken together with the development of new machinery and the improvements made in the breeding of livestock, are what constitute the British Agricultural Revolution, which used to be described as if it was entirely the work of a few enlightened men. One of these was Charles Townshend (1674–1738), later the 2nd Viscount Townshend, a senior politician and diplomat who owned a large estate in Norfolk and is often credited with introducing the four-course, or Norfolk, rotation into Britain.

Townshend had been a diplomat in the Dutch Republic from 1709 to 1711 and had seen for himself how productive the farming system developed in the Low Countries could be, so he had introduced a version of it onto his estate. In Flanders, farmers were using a rotation involving up to seven phases, but in Britain this was generally simplified to four, beginning with winter wheat, sown in the fall and then harvested in the following summer. Immediately after the wheat harvest, turnips were then put in, a fast-growing crop that could tolerate the relatively cold conditions of the fall to produce a fodder crop for the winter. Next spring, barley was planted and, once that was harvested, the final phase of the rotation was to sow a mixture of grass and clover seed that could then be used for grazing and to make hay until the ground was ploughed up to begin the rotation again with another wheat crop.

THE TURNIP
An illustration from the *Vienna Dioscurides*, a 6th-century illuminated manuscript.

The extent to which Townshend was actually responsible for introducing this system to Britain is open to question because records exist of farmers growing turnips in rotation with cereal crops decades before he did. Nevertheless, whatever role he played in the beginning, he was certainly a great advocate of the use of improved farming methods, a fact noted by the poet Alexander Pope, who wrote that all he ever talked about was turnips, earning himself the nickname of Turnip Townshend. But, as dull a conversationalist as he may have been, farming productivity more than doubled as a result of the widespread adoption of the four-course rotation, or farming systems similar to it, at a time when the British population was rapidly expanding.

These days the turnip is not as widely grown as it used to be, even in those mixed-farming systems that still make use of crop rotation. Other crops have taken its place, and its reputation as being the foodstuff of people who could not afford to eat anything else has limited its appeal as many Western countries have become more affluent. It is hard to imagine the turnip making any sort of comeback, but the part it played in enabling the adoption of more productive agricultural systems and the social changes that followed means that the most maligned of vegetables can legitimately be said to have changed the course of history.

Baldrick, I've always been meaning to ask: Do you have any ambitions in life apart from the acquisition of turnips?
Edmund Blackadder from the BBC TV series Blackadder the Third

ORGANIC ROTATIONS

✦

Organic farming began to develop in the 1920s and 1930s as a reaction against what its proponents saw as the unnatural practices of relying on synthetic chemical fertilizers and pesticides to produce food. One of the principal methods employed since it first began, to manage soil fertility and reduce the impact of pests and diseases, is crop rotation. It is a little ironic that organic farming is often labeled as being "alternative" because it actually employs methods that have been in use for hundreds of years, while it is so-called "conventional" farming that has undergone much more radical change.

Roquefort Cheese

Origin: France

Date: 1411

Type: Blue cheese

+ **CULTURAL**
+ **SOCIAL**
+ **COMMERCIAL**
+ POLITICAL
+ MILITARY

If the French can be said to be obsessive about food, then that obsession reaches a peak over their cheeses. Whereas the rest of us have to make do with only a couple of types, and some people are apparently prepared to eat cheese that comes out of a can, the French can choose between a huge variety, many preserving a regional character that has disappeared from many other types of food in this globalized world. Opinions differ about which French cheese is the best of all, but the one that would surely make it onto the top 10 list of any serious cheese-lover must surely be Roquefort, a crumbly and moist white cheese from the South of France, made from sheep's milk and cut through by veins of blue-green mold.

THE CAVES OF COMBALOU

According to European Union law, the only cheese that can legally be labeled as Roquefort comes from the place that provided it with a name, the village of Roquefort-sur-Soulzon on the limestone plateau of the Larzac in southern France. The geography of this region has had an influence on the nature of Roquefort cheese. Water tends to percolate through limestone rather than flow over it, so there are few rivers and streams on the Larzac and this lack of water, together with the rocky ground and thin soil, make it only suited to sheep-farming. The farmers of the region keep Lacaune sheep, bred to be milked, and the cheese made from the milk of these ewes is then aged for at least three months in the caves of Combalou, a limestone escarpment that rises above the village of Roquefort.

The caves were originally carved out of the limestone by the action of water running through the rock, which also has fissures running through it, known as *fleurines*, which were the result of volcanic activity in the region during the Jurassic period some 150 million years ago. These *fleurines* have the effect of creating a microclimate

Roquefort should be eaten on one's knees.

Grimod de la Reynière
(1758–1838)

in the Roquefort caves that is maintained at a constant temperature and humidity all year round, making them cool and slightly damp, the perfect environment for maturing the cheese. The climate in the caves also encourages the growth of the sort of mold in its soil used in the making of the cheese, the fungus *Penicillium roqueforti*, which is also used to make other blue cheeses like Stilton and Gorgonzola and is in the same genus as the fungi used to make antibiotics. At one time, the mold used to inoculate the cheese

ROQUEFORT
A view looking down on Roquefort-sur-Soulzon from the limestone escarpment of Combalou.

was cultivated in the caves by the cheese makers, who left bread on the soil that would then be colonized, but these days, in one of the few concessions to modernity, it is cultured in laboratories from mold obtained in the caves because it allows the cheese makers to use a purer and more consistent strain.

PROTECTING ROQUEFORT

Cheese has been made on the Larzac going back at least to the Roman period 2,000 years ago and no doubt for a considerable period beforehand. It is said to have been the favorite cheese of Charlemagne, the king of the Frankish Empire in the 8th century, even if this story is based on an account written by a monk in the abbey of St. Gall in Switzerland that does not actually mention the particular cheese by

MATURING CHEESE
Roquefort cheese is left to mature for at least three months in the microclimate of the caves of Combalou.

name. If we cannot be certain that Roquefort was the cheese alluded to in such early sources, then we can have more confidence in the law signed by King Charles IV of France in 1411 that specifically names it and gives the inhabitants of Roquefort the sole right to sell the cheese they have made in the caves of Combalou under that name. The law was presumably enacted to protect both producers and consumers against people attempting to pass off lower-quality imitations as the real thing, demonstrating that Roquefort was as highly regarded then as it is now.

The law passed by Charles IV was the first to designate an individual foodstuff for protection by a specific name and it was upheld by the parliament of Toulouse on a number of occasions in succeeding centuries, pre-empting legislation in the early 20th century to establish the *Appellation d'Origine Contrôlée* (AOC), or protected designation of origin. This was first introduced in 1919 in an effort to regularize the wine trade by specifying the boundaries of each region and was based on the idea of *terroir*, the concept that the wine made in a particular place is influenced by the geography, soils, and climate where the vines grow as well as by the type of grape being used and the methods of production employed. The nature of cheese-making in Roquefort has obvious parallels with wine because of the nature of the limestone landscape in the Larzac region and, in 1925, the AOC was extended to include it, the first foodstuff to be given a designation.

In 1935 an institute was established to oversee the AOC designations, setting out regulations that had to be followed for a product to qualify for a designation, which by then had become a symbol of quality as well as a guarantee that it was the real thing. For Roquefort cheese these regulations determined that, to bear the AOC label, it must have been made in the village from milk of ewes from the surrounding farms and that the mold used had come from the caves of Combalou, where the resulting cheese had to be kept while it matured. By giving customers the assurance that they can buy their favor-

LACAUNE SHEEP
Roquefort is predominantly made from milk from Lacaune ewes kept on the Larzac plateau and in the surrounding area.

THE CHEESE MAKERS
A group of women from
Roquefort in about 1907,
taking a break from
making cheese to pose
for a photograph.

ite cheese in confidence, the AOC has also ensured that cheese-making has continued in Roquefort and that the farmers of the Larzac have a market for their ewes' milk, preserving the traditional industries of the region and providing employment for local people where few other opportunities exist. Today, there are seven companies making Roquefort cheese in the village, the largest of which is La Société des Caves de Roquefort, or La Société as it is often called, which accounts for about 70 percent of the cheese sold around the world.

The success of the AOC has seen it enlarged and since 1992 incorporated in a number of European Union laws. These are the Protected Designation of Origin (PDO), Protected Geographical Indication, and Traditional Specialities Guaranteed schemes, all designed to ensure that particular agricultural products and foodstuffs associated with regions and made in a traditional way are protected from imitation. To take just one of numerous examples, since 2008, when a PDO designation was awarded, a Melton Mowbray pork pie must come from the town of Melton Mowbray in Leicestershire, England, and be made with the correct ingredients in the traditional way as set out in the terms of the designation. Up until that point, anybody making a pork pie could label it as a Melton Mowbray pork pie in the hope of cashing in on the reputation of the name no matter where they were based or how they made it. Products as diverse as Parma ham and marzipan from Lübeck have a similar level of protection, preserving the regional character of these foods while the rest of what we eat appears to become ever more the same.

> **How can you expect to govern a country that has 246 types of cheese?**
>
> *Charles de Gaulle*

Potato

Origin: The Andean altiplano of Peru and Bolivia

Date: From the 15th century

Type: Edible tubers of *Solanum tuberosum*

+ **CULTURAL**
+ **SOCIAL**
+ COMMERCIAL
+ **POLITICAL**
+ **MILITARY**

The potato is a remarkable plant. It can grow in a wide range of climates and altitudes, it is much more productive than any other staple crop, and its tubers are so nutritious that it is possible for people to live on them alone. It has contributed to changing the course of history in numerous ways, from the rise of the Inca Empire in its native Peru to the wars in Europe of the 17th and 18th centuries and the terrible famine that occurred in Ireland in the middle of the 19th century.

THE RISE AND FALL OF THE INCA

The wild ancestor of the modern potato does not immediately give the appearance of being a very promising food source. The tubers are small and bitter to the taste, and the entire plant, which is a member of the nightshade family, contains toxins that have to be processed out before it becomes edible. The way in which these plants were first domesticated and how the toxins were bred out of the tubers is not clearly understood, but from DNA studies carried out in recent years it appears that the domestication first occurred in the Andean altiplano in the region around Lake Titicaca. This area now straddles the border between Peru and Bolivia, and it was then the subject of a selective breeding program over the course of many generations to reduce the levels of toxins.

The homeland of the Inca people was in the Andes immediately to the northwest of the region where the potato was first domesticated and by the early 15th century they were beginning to expand out of their heartlands around the city of Cuzco. The high altitude of the area meant that corn, the staple crop of much of South America, would not grow, so the farming system of the Incas was based on potatoes and other crops that could tolerate the conditions. The high nutritional content of the potato compared to corn and other staple crops was one of the reasons why the Incas came to dominate the region; it gave them an advantage over their neighboring states because it allowed a larger population to develop and the Incas to support a larger army.

The beginning of the classic period of the Inca Empire is usually dated to 1438, when the leader Pachacuti, which literally means "earth-shaker," ascended to the throne and began the military campaigns that, over the course of the next 40 years, would see the empire expand to occupy all the territory in the Andes and along the western coast of South America from central Chile to Columbia. The Incas ruled over numerous different cultures, imposing taxes on them and using their people to carry out public works, including building an extensive road network that was used to administer the empire and to transport agricultural goods. They also began to construct monumental buildings, some of which can still be seen today in Cuzco and in the mountaintop site of Machu Picchu, both of which show the remarkable stoneworking skill achieved by Inca craftsmen.

The Inca Empire rose relatively quickly, but did not last very long before suffering a spectacular fall. The Spanish conquistador Francisco Pizarro landed in Ecuador in 1532 with a force of only 168 men and 27 horses, having previously led small expeditions to the region, with the specific intention of colonizing the territory for the Spanish crown. Despite their small number, they enjoyed a huge advantage over the Incas in terms of military technology and also began to make alliances among those peoples within the empire who were dissatisfied with their subordinate positions to the Inca rulers. The empire was already unstable, having gone through a period of civil war in which the Inca ruler Atahualpa had defeated his brother to become emperor. The effects of this divisive war had been compounded by the spread of infectious diseases, including smallpox, which had inadvertently been introduced to the continent by the Spanish.

In July 1532, Atahualpa invited Pizarro to meet with him, but, after demanding that the Inca submit to

THE EARTH-SHAKER
A 17th-century Spanish portrait of Pachacuti Inca, who is said to have first established the Inca Empire.

MACHU PICCHU
The mountaintop site is thought to have been originally built for Pachacuti.

POTATO PLANT
Plate labeled "*Papas Peruanorum*" from *Hortus Eystettensis* (1613) by Basilius Besler of Nuremburg. Now known as *Solanum tuberosum*, or, more commonly, the potato.

Spanish rule and convert to Christianity, Pizarro took him prisoner and, in the following year and despite the payment of a huge ransom in gold and silver, had him executed. The Inca Empire struggled on for some time afterward, but the infectious diseases decimated the population and an increasing number of Spanish colonists arrived, lured by stories of the fabulous wealth of the Incas. The Spanish took over the Inca gold and silver mines in the Andes, using forced labor from among the indigenous people and feeding them on potatoes grown in the high mountains.

Other than as a means of providing food for laborers in the mines, the agriculture system of the Incas, which was adapted to the Andean region, was largely ignored by the Spanish. Instead, they brought their own animals and crops with them as they colonized South America. Potatoes were taken back to Spain at some point around 1570, possibly having been first cultivated in the Canary Islands. From Spain they gradually spread around Europe, but were not widely cultivated for human consumption, despite their nutritional benefits; rather, they were grown either as animal feed or to be used for medicinal purposes.

POTATO WARS

One exception to the general lack of interest in the potato across Europe was in providing a cheap source of food for armies and, over the course of the 17th and 18th centuries, potato cultivation spread around the continent in the wake of numerous periods of warfare and unrest. The Thirty Years War was fought almost continuously from 1618 to 1648 between Protestant and Catholic states and is considered by historians to have been the last major conflict on the European continent to occur before the widespread adoption of potato cultivation. As more and more states were drawn into the conflict and it eventually became a confrontation between the Bourbon and Habsburg dynasties rather than a purely religious war, whole regions of central Europe were devastated as invading armies from both sides either requisitioned whatever crops they found to feed themselves or destroyed them in the fields to prevent them falling into the hands of the enemy.

Famine and disease followed close behind the Thirty Years War, together with an almost complete breakdown in law and order. It can hardly be said that the wars that came after it were any less destructive in terms of the actual fighting, but the impact on the general population was not as great because of potato cultivation, which was often adopted as a direct response to the prospect of conflict. One war followed another: the War of the Grand Alliance (1688–97), the War of the Spanish Succession (1701–14), the War of the Austrian Succession (1740–48), and the Seven Years War (1756–63), to name only the major conflicts. As well as providing food for civilians, the potato also kept the armies supplied, so they were less likely to forage for food in the countryside around where they were deployed.

The War of the Bavarian Succession, fought in 1778 by an alliance of German states led by Prussia against Austria, is known as the Kartoffelkrieg, the Potato War, in Germany, even if it is said to have acquired the name as a consequence of both armies spending more time eating potatoes than fighting each other, rather than any suggestion the conflict had anything directly to do with the potato. An alternative theory states that the name came from the habit of the soldiers from both armies of throwing potatoes at each other rather than engaging in armed conflict. Whatever the case, little actual fighting occurred and the dispute that started the war between Frederick the Great of Prussia and Joseph II of Austria, who both wanted to expand their territory into Bavaria, was in the end settled by negotiation. The only significance of this minor war today is that it marked the beginning of antagonism between Austria and the emerging power of Prussia, which would become more evident in the following century and in 1871 would result in the unification of Germany under Prussian domination and to the exclusion of Austria.

As more people began to grow potatoes across Europe as a consequence of the long periods of

CHUÑO

✦

The Incas and other ethnic groups from the high Andes preserved potatoes by a process of freeze-drying, producing what is known in the Quechuan languages of the region as *chuño*. Two types are still made today; for black *chuño* the potatoes are exposed to freezing temperatures at night and left out in sunlight during the day, which causes them to turn black, and, during the day, they are trampled underfoot to remove the water from them. White *chuño*, known as *tunta* in Bolivia, involves a similar process but the potatoes are also washed to remove the blackened parts and then often ground into flour.

POTATO PICKERS
An oil painting from 1875 by the German Impressionist painter Max Liebermann showing potato pickers hard at work.

war, the potential benefits became obvious, particularly as the continent was in the middle of what is sometimes described as the Little Ice Age, a cold period that lasted roughly from the 1650s to the 1850s in the northern hemisphere. In London, the River Thames regularly froze over in the winter; across Europe, serious food shortages occurred until the potato, which is more frost tolerant than most cereal crops, began to be more widely grown. The adoption of the potato as a staple food in Europe has also been cited as one of the reasons for the population growth across the continent in the 18th and 19th centuries, particularly when taken together with the advances made in agricultural technologies such as the crop rotations discussed in the previous chapter. In Britain, the potato fed the rising numbers of factory workers who moved to cities during the Industrial Revolution. In Ireland, it allowed for an enormous increase in population but with very little industrialization, a situation that, when the potato crop failed, would result in tragedy.

THE GREAT HUNGER

The famine in Ireland that began in 1845 and is known in the Irish language as *an Gorta Mór*, the Great Hunger, fundamentally changed Irish history and remains a controversial subject today. At the extremes of the debate, the famine has been described as an unavoidable tragedy caused by the destruction of the Irish potato crop by a sudden infestation of late blight, a disease of potatoes that had spread from continental Europe, or, alternatively, as an attempt by the British government to use the crisis as a means of destroying the Catholic culture of the west of Ireland in what amounts to a case of genocide.

The truth of the matter probably lies somewhere between these two extremes, but what cannot be disputed is the terrible scale of the catastrophe that unfolded, in which at least a million people died either from starvation or from the epidemics of diseases, particularly typhus, that spread through populations of people already weakened by living in desperate circumstances. A further million people emigrated as a consequence of the famine, many going to the industrial cities of England, such as Manchester, Liverpool, and Birmingham, where large Irish communities formed, whereas others traveled farther, to Australia,

New Zealand, and, in particular, to America, sailing across the Atlantic in what became known as "coffin ships" to escape the famine and, in doing so, changing the histories of the places where they went. By the 1880s, a quarter of the population of New York and Boston were either Irish or of Irish descent and there are now almost 10 times as many Irish Americans as there are people living in Ireland.

There is such a tendency to exaggeration and inaccuracy in Irish reports that delay in acting on them is always desirable.
British Prime Minister Sir Robert Peel, speaking in October 1845

The potato arrived in Ireland quite early compared to many other parts of Europe and its nutritional qualities as well as its capacity to grow in conditions that did not suit cereal crops ensured that it became widely grown, particularly among the people of the west coast, most of whom were poor and had access to only small plots of land. The population soared as more and more potatoes were grown, from about a million in 1600 to four million by 1800 and then, in 1845, on to 8.5 million. The traditional method of inheritance, which involved dividing plots between children, meant that the amount of land available for each family gradually became less and less, while much of the land was actually owned by absentee landlords, who often lived in England and employed agents to manage their affairs. Poor people usually paid the rent on their cottages and plots of land by laboring rather than in wages, so they were forced to live a subsistence lifestyle on what they could grow themselves on what had become increasingly small holdings.

The size of the holdings meant that people became dependent on the potato, the only crop that was productive enough to support a family living on such small plots of land and, by the 1840s, most people were growing a single variety of potato, the Irish lumper, which grew well in the wet conditions of the west of Ireland but had a very low resistance to disease. The nature of potato growing, in which succeeding crops are grown on from seed potatoes of the previous crop, also meant that there was little genetic diversity in the potatoes grown across much of Ireland, so that, once a disease began, it could potentially infect the entire crop across a wide area.

THE GREAT FAMINE
A drawing from the *Illustrated London News* in 1849 attempting to convey the desperate search for food by starving people in Ireland.

Late blight is still the most serious disease of potatoes. It is thought to have spread to continental Europe from North America, possibly being carried in seed potatoes imported from America to Belgium, and, once it had arrived, it began to spread through crops in northern Europe in the early summer of 1845, before spreading to England in August and then first being reported in Ireland in September. The blight, *Phytophthora infestans*, is an oomycete, a fungus-like microorganism that produces spores that spread in the wind. When these infect a potato plant, they cause it to wilt and die rapidly and its tubers to rot in the ground.

The blight of the potato crop so much complained of in Belgium and several of the English counties has affected the crop and that to a considerable extent in our immediate locality and the surround districts.

From a report in the Cork Examiner *in September 1845*

Today blight is controlled by preventative means because, once a crop has become infected, there is no way of stopping the infection from killing the plant and by the time it has become visible in one plant the chances are it will have already spread to the rest of the crop. So when the weather is conducive to blight, which favors warm and wet conditions, potato crops are sprayed with a fungicide that is designed to remain on the surface of the plants to stop the blight spores from becoming established.

In Europe in 1845, no means were available to prevent the blight, leading to major crop losses and serious food shortages, but most people managed to get by on other crops or could afford to buy food. In the west of Ireland the situation was different; poor people were reliant on potatoes to feed themselves and any pigs they kept. In 1845, about a third of the entire potato crop was lost and in the following year the devastation became much worse when three-quarters of the crop succumbed to the disease.

Late Blight
Blight infection begins with blotches on the leaves and quickly spreads through the plant so that the potatoes rot in the ground.

More than three million people in Ireland were entirely dependent on the potato and the failure of the crop left them destitute, a situation made even worse when landlords began to repossess properties when rents were not paid. The British government's response to the disaster as it unfolded was, at best, too slow and inadequate, prompting the Irish nationalist John Mitchell to write after the famine was over, "The Almighty, indeed, sent the potato blight, but the English created the Famine." Perhaps the most damning aspect of the apparent lack of concern for the desperate situation faced by many people was that, throughout the course of the famine, which lasted until 1851, Ireland was exporting cereals, livestock, and other agricultural products to England, a trade that was not stopped because, as the starving people of the west coast were too poor to buy food, there was no market for it in Ireland. For the most part, the relief measures that were instituted by the government were only provided to those who were absolutely destitute, putting them into workhouses or laboring on pointless public works. It had the effect of forcing people out of their houses and off their land in order to obtain what little relief was available, which served to exacerbate the crisis even further rather than solve it.

Modern accusations of genocide against the British government of the day are impossible to prove because there is no clear evidence of murderous intent at the start of the famine. But the callous disregard for the lives of what were, after all, British people, the whole of Ireland being part of Britain at that time, have cast a long shadow over relations between Britain and Ireland and fueled the republican movement both in Ireland and among the huge Irish diaspora in America and around the rest of the world.

COLCANNON

◆

The Irish dish of colcannon is made by mashing boiled potatoes together with either kale or cabbage and then adding milk, butter, and finely chopped green onions. It is often served with boiled bacon and parsley sauce, a traditional dinner made out of ingredients that all would have been available in Irish homes in the past because many families would have grown their own vegetables and kept a pig. In America, Irish immigrants often substituted corn beef for the bacon because it was easier to find, some then bringing this variation back to Ireland with them so that it is now considered typically Irish as well.

Mayonnaise

Origin: France

Date: 1589

Type: Cold sauce

✦ **CULTURAL**

✦ SOCIAL

✦ COMMERCIAL

✦ POLITICAL

✦ **MILITARY**

At its most basic, mayonnaise is a sauce made by whisking oil and egg yolk briskly together, usually with a splash of vinegar and a pinch of salt, to form an emulsion, a blend of two liquids that would not otherwise mix. It is now so widely available in jars and tubes from supermarkets and used to embellish so many everyday foods that it can be easy to forget that it was originally one of the classic sauces of French cuisine.

THE SOURCE OF MAYONNAISE

According to its name, mayonnaise should be associated with a place called Mayon in the same way as Béarnaise sauce is related to the region of Béarn in the southwest of France; Hollandaise sauce was named after a similar recipe for a sauce from the Netherlands. No similar associations exist for mayonnaise: there are no regions of France or any towns called Mayon, leading to suggestions that the name was adapted from the city of Mahon in Spain, the capital of the island of Menorca, and came to France after 1752, when the French expelled the British from the island during the Seven Years War.

Evidence exists to suggest that the name was being used for a sauce in France before 1752, leading to an alternative theory that the name comes from the French region of Mayenne, which is near Le Mans in the northwest of the country, and, in particular, named after Charles of Lorraine, the Duke of Mayenne, a prominent figure in the French Wars of Religion that ripped the country apart in the latter half of the 16th century. The wars were fought between French Catholics and Huguenots, members of the Protestant Reformed Church of France, in a series of conflicts and outbreaks of civil unrest, most famously the St. Bartholomew's Day Massacre in Paris in 1572 in which Catholic mobs murdered thousands of Huguenots in Paris and at numerous other locations around the country.

Mayonnaise — one of the sauces which serve the French in place of a state religion.

Ambrose Bierce (1842–1913)

The Duke of Mayenne was a military leader of the Catholic League, and commanded the Catholic forces at the Battle of Arques in September 1589, fought against the forces of King Henry IV, who had ascended to the throne of France a few weeks previously despite being a Protestant, but was then forced to fight a war over the course of the next four years to establish his legitimacy to rule. The town of Arques, now called Arques-la-Bataille, was a strategically important port on the northwest coast of France and had been occupied by Henry. Mayenne was attempting to recapture the town, but, so the story goes, before going into battle he insisted on finishing his meal, said to have been cold chicken with a sauce — the one that would later be named after him.

CHARLES MAYENNE
The Duke of Mayenne, a true Frenchman, finished his lunch before fighting the Battle of Arques.

The battle was fought from September 15th to September 29th and both sides suffered heavy casualties. Mayenne's forces significantly outnumbered those of Henry and the duke appeared to be gaining the upper hand when a force of English soldiers arrived to reinforce the king, sent across the channel by Queen Elizabeth and bringing with them heavy guns that turned the tide of the fighting. The Catholic forces retreated, handing the victory to Henry, who would go on to defeat Mayenne again at the Battle of Ivry in the following year and then besiege Paris. The Catholic forces in the city held out and the fighting in this phase of the war only came to an end in 1593, when Henry reached a truce agreement with Mayenne and converted to Catholicism, having been advised that the French people would never accept a Protestant king.

Like every other story to do with the origin of foods for which there is no actual direct evidence, this one needs to be treated with a certain amount of skepticism. And, let's be honest, even if mayonnaise played any role at all in the Battle of Arques, it is stretching the truth to suggest that it had anything other than a minor impact on the history of the French Wars of Religion. Nevertheless, the sauce we now call mayonnaise is one of the few items of haute cuisine to have expanded beyond its aristocratic origins to be enjoyed by the man and woman in the street. And it still goes very well with cold chicken.

HELLMANN'S

✦

In 1905, Richard Hellmann began selling jars of his wife's mayonnaise from the delicatessen he ran on Columbus Avenue, New York City. It proved to be so successful that he opened a mayonnaise factory in 1912 and then, in 1932, sold the business to Best Foods, a San Francisco-based producer of mayonnaise. Rather than combine the two businesses, the company continued to sell Hellmann's on the East Coast and the identical Best Foods mayo west of the Rockies. The world is similarly split between the two brands, now owned by the Anglo-Dutch multinational Unilever, so in Britain you can eat Hellmann's mayonnaise and in Australia the same thing is called Best Foods mayonnaise.

Rendang

Origin: Sumatra

Date: By the 16th century

Type: Dry and spicy meat dish

+ **CULTURAL**
+ **SOCIAL**
+ COMMERCIAL
+ POLITICAL
+ MILITARY

Rendang is now associated with the cuisines of Indonesia, Malaysia, and Singapore and can be found on restaurant menus all over the world. It originally comes from the highlands of West Sumatra and it is a traditional dish made by the Minangkabau people to celebrate religious festivals and weddings. It has spread along with the people as they have followed the cultural practice of *merantau*, in which young men are encouraged to move away from their home territory.

FROM PADANG

The Indonesian city of Padang is on the west coast of Sumatra, facing the Indian Ocean, and it is the regional capital of the province where the Minangkabau people live. During the 16th century, the city began to develop into a commercial port, its merchants becoming particularly associated with dealing in gold, which was mined in the interior of the island, and with the spice trade, so that links were established with other cities in the region and with Portuguese and Dutch merchants. The *merantau* tradition meant that young men from the Minangkabau highlands not only traveled to Padang to become merchants, but were prepared to move much further afield, establishing communities in those cities with which they had trading relationships. Because of the way rendang is cooked, it can keep for several weeks in the tropical climate of the region, making it an ideal food to take on long journeys, so, as the Minangkabau migrated, they took rendang with them and introduced it to numerous other communities.

The traditional method of making rendang involves cooking beef slowly in coconut milk and a paste of spices, made by grinding red chilies, ginger, galangal, turmeric, and other spices together. It is cooked until almost all of the moisture has evaporated out of the coconut milk, leaving quite a dry dish that is dark brown in color. People who are not used to eating spicy food and who are trying an authentic rendang for the first time can be in for a shock because the sort of spice paste made in West Sumatra contains a seriously large amount of chili. These days, restaurants in Western countries that serve rendang usually adapt the original recipe so that it is not quite so hot, catering to the tastes of their customers, who do not necessarily want to eat food that sets their mouths on fire.

By the 19th century Padang had declined as a trading port after the gold mines had been exhausted and the Dutch colonized what is now Indonesia. The major trading route for spices went through the Strait of Malacca on the eastern side of Sumatra, which became one of the busiest shipping lanes in the world after the British established a trading post at Singapore, but which bypassed Padang. The migrating tradition of the Minangkabau that had seen many young men move away from West Sumatra to work as merchants now continued, but in a different field as they began to open restaurants in Jakarta and in many other cities across the region. Padang restaurants, as they are usually called, are now a common feature in cities across Indonesia and beyond, famous for their Minangkabau food and, in particular, for rendang, which has become one of Indonesia's most recognized dishes.

Minangkabau communities have been established all over Indonesia and the Malay Peninsula, particularly in the Malaysian state of Negeri Sembilan immediately to the south of Kuala Lumpur, where the Minangkabau form the largest ethnic group. In the highlands of West Sumatra, traditional Minangkabau society is matrilineal; that is, the inheritance of property and land is arranged to pass from mother to daughter, a system that is thought to have developed and been maintained because so many Minangkabau men spent most of their time working away from their homes. These days young men leave West Sumatra to go to college and to work in Jakarta, Singapore, or Kuala Lumpur, sending some of their salaries back home to support their families, but the restaurant business still provides employment for many others and, as rendang and other Minangkabau dishes are now eaten around the world as well as in Indonesia and Malaysia, the association between *merantau* and Padang cuisine looks set to continue well into the future.

RIJSTTAFEL

✦

The influence of Padang cuisine can be seen in the Netherlands today in the form of the *rijsttafel*, which literally means "rice table." It is based on nasi padang, the usual way of serving food in Padang restaurants that involves displaying numerous precooked Minangkabau dishes so that customers can choose which ones they want and then pay accordingly. *Rijsttafel* can consist of 40 or more dishes, including rendang and other examples of Padang cuisine, as well as dishes from other parts of Indonesia, such as the fried rice dish *nasi goreng* and *gado-gado*, vegetables in a peanut sauce, reflecting the huge variety of Indonesian food.

Sugar

Origin: New Guinea

Date: 17th century onward

Type: Carbohydrate

+ **CULTURAL**
+ **SOCIAL**
+ **COMMERCIAL**
+ **POLITICAL**
+ MILITARY

REFINED SUGAR
Raw sugarcane (top) can be refined to produce a variety of sugar, including white and brown, in the form of grains, cubes, or crystals.

According to evolutionary biologists, all animals, with the exception of cats, have a sweet tooth. It is an adaptation that developed in the natural world where sweet-tasting foods may not always be readily available, but, when they are found, provide an excellent source of energy. In human beings this desire for sugar can cause health problems when it is abundant, as it is now, whereas in the past it was the driving force behind one of the most shameful episodes in history — the transatlantic slave trade, in which, according to conservative estimates, 15 million Africans were shipped across the ocean, many to work on sugarcane plantations.

WHITE GOLD

Up until the 17th century, sugar was a rare and expensive commodity in Europe. It originally came from Southeast Asia, most likely first domesticated in New Guinea, and had been taken to the New World by Christopher Columbus in 1493 on his second voyage. The Portuguese and Spanish established sugarcane plantations in their New World colonies in the 16th century, followed by the Dutch, but the quantities of sugar arriving in Europe were modest so the price remained out of reach for most people. The burgeoning spice trade developed by the Dutch East India Company from its instigation in 1602 demonstrated that fortunes could be made in commodities and, as England and France began to colonize parts of the Caribbean, where it was apparent that sugarcane would thrive, the potential to develop the region and to make enormous profits had become obvious.

The problem was that, although the land was available, cane cultivation and the process of refining it into sugar were both labor intensive. Attempts were made to use indigenous people to work on the newly established plantations, but in much of the Caribbean their numbers had already been decimated by diseases introduced by European settlers. In the British colony of Barbados, settled in 1627 and one of the first where sugarcane was grown, planation owners had more success in attracting indentured laborers from the British Isles with the offer of a plot of land if a commitment was given to work for five years first. However, the men who arrived were often more interested in enriching themselves than working in the cane plantations and, anyway, were unsuited to the prevailing hot conditions and often succumbed to tropical diseases like malaria.

The Portuguese had already shown how the labor problem could be solved in their Brazilian colony by importing slaves from Africa. If the English and French had any scruples over the morality of using slave labor, it appears to have been easily overcome as slaves began to transform struggling plantations into highly profitable businesses. As well as Barbados, sugarcane plantations began to be established on the other islands in the Lesser Antilles, the English growing cane on St. Kitts and Antigua and the French on St. Lucia, Martinique, and Guadeloupe, the easternmost chain of islands in the Caribbean that faced the Atlantic Ocean and allowed for the shortest passage from West Africa.

Both the English and the French had already established links with West Africa, trading goods made in Europe for gold and ivory, and these links were then extended to include slaves. A triangular trade was developed in which European goods were traded in West Africa for slaves, who were then shipped over to the Caribbean to work on sugarcane plantations in what became known as the Middle Passage. The end product, refined sugar, was then carried back to Europe, allowing the ships involved in the trade to carry a full cargo on each leg of their voyages. The Middle Passage became notorious for the brutal treatment of the slaves involved, packed into ships as tightly as possible so that many died of disease and starvation during the voyages. It has been estimated that of the total 15 million people sold into slavery in West Africa, three million died during the Middle Passage.

> I own I am shock'd at the purchase of slaves,
> and fear those who buy them and sell them are knaves;
> What I hear of their hardships, their tortures, and groans,
> Is almost enough to draw pity from stones.
> I pity them greatly, but I must be mum,
> For how could we do without sugar and rum?
>
> *William Cowper (1731–1800)*

The potential profits to be made from the triangular trade were huge, but required large initial investments. It led to the formation of companies to raise the finance. Some of the institutions that developed as a result of these arrangements are household names today and investments were made by, amongst many others, the British royal family. The trade increased over the course of the 18th century as the demand for sugar in Britain and France soared, at the very least because of the fashion for drinking tea in Britain and coffee in France, sweetened with sugar and often accompanied by sugary cakes. Port cities facing the Atlantic Ocean in both countries grew rich because of their involvement in the trade, including Bristol, Liverpool, Bordeaux, and Nantes, while the sugar plantations spread across much of the Caribbean and onto the mainland of Central and South America.

By 1750, sugar was the most valuable commodity in international trade, accounting for a fifth of all imports into Europe, and almost all of it came from the sugar plantations in the Caribbean. The wealth generated by the trade was instrumental in providing the finance to allow Britain to develop the industries that would make it the most prosperous nation in the world during the 19th century and for London to become the global financial center it remains today.

CANE WORKERS
An image made for a stereoscopic viewer in the late 19th century entitled *Native Cane Growers in Sunny Florida.*

As the price of sugar came down, demand soared, most people apparently prepared to turn a blind eye to the brutality and inhumanity of the methods used to produce it. An abolitionist movement began to develop in the second half of the 18th century, gaining many more supporters as first-hand accounts of the terrible nature of slavery were published, most famously *The Interesting Narrative of the Life of Olaudah Equiano*, written after Equiano had purchased his freedom and settled in England. In Britain, the slave trade was finally outlawed in 1807 and then slavery was abolished completely in 1834, the French following suit in 1844, having abolished and then reinstated slavery on a number of occasions beforehand. By that time sugarcane plantations had been established in a number of other parts of the world and, in Europe, sugar beet was being extensively grown in competition to sugarcane plantations.

RUM AND REVOLUTION

In the late 17th century a different version of the triangular trade in sugar and slaves began to emerge than the one going through Britain and France. American colonists in the port cities of New England such as Boston and Newport, Rhode Island, began to buy molasses, a by-product of sugar refining, from the West Indies to make their own rum rather than import the spirit from the British-owned distillers in the Caribbean. Slave traders then used the American rum as currency in West Africa to buy the slaves they then transported back across the

Atlantic to the sugar plantations. After 1690, New England rum distillers began to buy molasses from French sugar refiners in the Caribbean rather than the British-owned ones because France had imposed a ban on the distilling of rum in their colonies to protect their own brandy makers at home. With no local market, the French refiners were prepared to sell their molasses at less than half the price of the British product, allowing New Englanders to make rum much more cheaply and consequently pay out more of it to buy slaves in West Africa.

In 1733, the British attempted to put a stop to this trade because it was undercutting their own business in West Africa by imposing a duty on molasses imported into New England from the French colonies in the West Indies. The law, known as the Molasses Act, set the duty at a prohibitive 6 pence a gallon, which, if it had been paid, would have ruined the rum distillers and was clearly designed to force them to buy their molasses from British sources, which, in reality, was in short supply because much of it was already being sold to rum makers in the Caribbean. Rather than submit to what was widely thought of as being an unjust duty, the New England rum makers chose instead to smuggle molasses from the French colonies, bribing customs officials when necessary, and in the process establishing a precedence for defying heavy-handed British attempts to impose taxes on their American colonies.

Over the next few decades after the duty was imposed, rum-making actually increased in Boston, the British having given up even trying to collect the duty. The expense incurred by Britain during the French and Indian Wars, fought between the British and French American colonies from 1754 to 1763, led to a further attempt by the British to impose duty on molasses. The British had run up a large public debt to pay for the war and, with the so-called Sugar

BOSTON MOLASSES FLOOD

♦

At about 12:30 in the afternoon of January 15th, 1919, a huge tank containing over 2 million gallons of molasses burst in the North End neighborhood of Boston, unleashing a wave of molasses 40 feet (12 m) high that killed 21 people and was so powerful it buckled the tracks of the nearby elevated railroad. The tank belonged to the Purity Distilling Company, who used the molasses to make industrial alcohol. In a class action brought by local residents, the company initially claimed that anarchists had bombed the tank, but then settled out of court when it emerged that it had been badly constructed and had suffered a catastrophic failure after a sudden build-up of pressure.

I know not why we should blush to confess that molasses was an essential ingredient in American independence.

John Adams, writing in 1818

Act of 1764, were attempting to recoup some of the money. It was set at half the level of the previous duty, but nevertheless was resented in the colonies, opposition to it being directed primarily against the tax having been imposed without consent because the American colonies were not represented in the British parliament, leading to the slogan, "No taxation without representation."

The second act was by no means as severe as the first, even if, on this occasion, it contained provisions to enforce the collection of duty, and it was imposed to raise revenue to cover the cost of a war that had benefitted colonial America as well as Britain. But, having defied the earlier Molasses Act, the Americans were in no mood to have any further taxes imposed on them, which, as well as the Sugar Act, would include those contained in the Stamp Act of 1765, the Townshend Acts of 1767, and the Tea Act of 1773. The protestors who first came together to argue against these taxes would go on to form the core of the movement for American independence, which was only strengthened by the measures taken by Britain in an attempt to enforce the acts.

Brazilian Sugar

✦

Brazil is currently the largest sugarcane grower in the world. As well as producing sugar, Brazil's refineries are designed to distill ethanol from molasses and to burn the residue of crushed cane, known as bagasse, to produce electricity to power the refineries. As a consequence of the oil crisis of the early 1970s, the Brazilian government passed legislation in 1976 to make it mandatory for the fuel used in all light vehicles in Brazil to include ethanol, the amount of which has varied between 10 and 25 percent over the years depending on availability, making the country the largest user of biofuel in the world.

Haiti and Cuba

After the success of the revolution in the French colony of Saint-Domingue in 1804 had established the Republic of Haiti, French sugarcane planters moved to Cuba and Louisiana, where they continued to use slaves in their sugar plantations. Before the revolution, Haiti had been one of the largest sugar producers in the Caribbean, and one of the wealthiest. However, its economy was shattered after the sugar business collapsed, a situation compounded in 1825 when France imposed a huge debt burden on the country by claiming compensation for the losses it had incurred as a consequence of the revolution, threatening to use military force if the Haitians refused to pay. The fragile Haitian economy, already suffering from the loss of its sugar trade, was devastated and never fully recovered, a situation only made worse by a succession of corrupt and oppressive rulers of the country that continued into the modern period.

Whereas Haiti was suffering, the Cuban sugar industry boomed by supplying the expanding market in America. During the American Revolutionary War, the British banned all exports from its Caribbean colonies to America, opening up the market to Cuba, which then benefitted from an increase in production after the influx of planters from Haiti and a further interruption to the Caribbean trade during the war of 1812 between America and Britain. As Cuba was a Spanish colony, it was unaffected by the abolition of slavery in Britain and France and its sugar plantations continued to be worked by slaves until 1886, when the

institution finally came to an end. Over the course of the 19th century, American investors bought up much of the Cuban sugar industry, many consolidating their interests with the formation of the American Sugar Refining Company, which operated a factory in Brooklyn, New York, and by the beginning of the 20th century controlled almost all of the Cuban sugar crop.

The sugar trade was the beginning of a long involvement of American business interests in Cuba, which on a number of occasions appeared to be leading to the annexation of the island. In 1897, American involvement in the Cuban independence movement led to the Spanish–American War, during which America assumed military rule in Cuba. The island became fully independent from Spain in 1898, but the American military did not finally leave until 1903, even then retaining the naval base it had established in Guantánamo Bay. Over the course of the 20th century, American interests diversified away from sugar and came to dominate the economy until relations between the two countries came to an abrupt end with the success of the Cuban Revolution of 1959, led by Fidel Castro, the son of a Cuban sugar planter.

Biltong

Origin: South Africa

Date: 17th century

Type: Cured meat

For people who speak either Dutch or the related Afrikaans, the word biltong goes some way to explaining what it is. It means "rump strip" and refers to cuts of either beef or game that have been flavored with herbs and spices, cured with salt and vinegar, and then wind dried so that they will keep for ages. These days it is often sold as a snack food, but in the past it made up an important part of the diet of the early Dutch colonists of South Africa.

+ **CULTURAL**

+ **SOCIAL**

+ **COMMERCIAL**

+ **POLITICAL**

+ **MILITARY**

THE GREAT TREK

The Dutch East India Company first established a settlement on the tip of the African continent to resupply their ships on voyages to the Far East. The company had no intention of establishing a permanent presence, but Dutch settlers together with significant numbers of Germans and French Huguenots soon began to arrive to found the Cape Colony, bringing with them the technique of curing meat to make biltong that would later prove to be so important. By the middle of the following century, groups of settlers were beginning to move into the interior to escape the authoritarian control of the company, becoming known as Trekboers (*boer* means farmer in Dutch), some establishing farms but many living a nomadic lifestyle as they drove their cattle from one area of pasture to another, in the process developing a culture of independence and self-reliance and a language that began to diverge from the original Dutch, eventually becoming Afrikaans.

TREKBOERS
An illustration from 1804 by Samuel Daniell of a Boer family camping next to their wagon.

The Trekboers were living beyond the borders of the Cape Colony so could not rely on its military garrison for help in the regular armed encounters in which they became involved as they moved into new territory, first with the Khoikhoi people of the Cape region and then, toward the end of the 18th century, with the Xhosa to the northeast, who were themselves under pressure from the expanding Zulu nations. A system of militia service was initiated among

the border farmers that became known as the Boer commandos, each unit attached to their own community and expected to be ready to be called up at all times. The commandos were what would be described in military terms as irregular light cavalry, who were familiar with the territory and were used to living off the land, hunting game and eating the biltong they had previously made and carried with them. It was a lightweight and nutritious type of food and could be eaten on the move when necessary as well as being added to stews and soups, making it almost perfect for military purposes.

By 1795, the Dutch East India Company was in serious decline and the British took the opportunity to occupy the Cape Colony because of its location on the sea route to India. The colony was eventually ceded by the Dutch in 1814 as part of a wider settlement at the end of the Napoleonic Wars and the British began to expand their sphere of influence into the territories where the Boers were living, at first joining with the commandos in the continuing border wars with the Xhosa. Toward the end of the 1830s, a movement among Boer communities began that advocated a mass migration farther into the interior of the African continent. It was a continuation of the tradition of their Trekboer forefathers by heading to the northeast and establishing what would become known as the Boer Republics, including Natal, the Transvaal, and the Orange Free State, which now form the northeastern regions of South Africa.

The exact reasons for the Great Trek, as the migration became known, are not entirely clear, beyond a desire to continue the pioneering heritage and to look for fresh land for cattle-farming. It has been suggested that the Boers were unhappy at coming under British rule, together with a perception that had developed that the British were not interested in continuing with the Xhosa wars, which by that time had been going on for 60 years, instead attempting to introduce measures to promote racial equality and integration as a means of ending the conflict. The British were also moving toward abolishing slavery in the colony at that time, but it would appear unlikely that this would have had any great impact on the Boer communities because few of them owned slaves. For whatever reason, around 12,000 Voortrekkers, as they became known, made the journey, establishing the Boer Republics that would remain independent until the end of the Second Boer War.

THE BOER WAR

After the Boer Republics were formed in the 1850s, the Boer leadership made peace treaties with the neighboring Zulu Kingdom and were largely left to themselves by the British. Everything changed in 1867 with the discovery of diamonds in the Kimberley region and this was followed by gold strikes in the Transvaal. It prompted a huge influx of people from all over the world, including many from the Cape Colony, which led to an increasing level of instability throughout the region. At the same time, the British had adopted an expansionist policy throughout their African territories, which included the desire expressed by Cecil Rhodes, the prime minister of the Cape Colony, for an unbroken chain of British colonies stretching from the Cape to Cairo. It would lead to a situation in which conflict between Britain and the Boer Republics had become almost inevitable and, in 1880, fighting would break out in what would become known as the First Boer War. In the following year, the war was settled by the signing of a truce, but, after the vast scale of the gold deposits discovered in the Boer Republics had become clear, in 1899 a much more protracted and costly conflict ensued.

At a distance of a few inches apart hung these long thin strips, presenting the appearance of so many serpents or skinned eels. They are left so suspended until the hot sun has dried them up to a hard, shrivelled substance, when they are declared in an estable state, and, under the name of biltong, constitute the principal food of the Boers.

Lady Florence Dixie, In the Land of Misfortune *(1882)*

BOER WAR
A photograph from about 1900 of a group of tough-looking commandos, taken during the Second Boer War.

At the start of the Second Boer War, the Boer forces besieged the British garrisons at Ladysmith, Mafeking, and Kimberley, forcing the British to send huge numbers of troops to South Africa to reinforce the British Army units already there. In Britain, the expectation was that, as the Boers were comprehensively outnumbered, the war would be over quickly, but after the British had lifted the sieges the Boer commandos began a campaign of guerrilla warfare that dragged on over the course of two years and showed no signs of stopping. The ability of the Boers to go for weeks on end without supply, living on game and the biltong they carried with them, was in stark contrast to the conventional forces of the British, who required constant resupply. The tenacity and fighting spirit they demonstrated in defending their homeland caused the British to rethink their whole strategy in the war.

It became clear to the British that they could not defeat the guerrilla tactics of the Boers by military means alone, so they began a campaign of counterinsurgency aimed at containment. The British military commander, Lord Kitchener, also adopted a scorched earth policy against Boer farms, destroying crops and livestock, and forcing families into concentration camps where many women and children died of disease and starvation. As a consequence of such brutal tactics, in May 1902 the Boers decided to surrender, accepting the peace terms offered by the British, which brought the fighting to an end. The Boer Republics became part of the British Empire and Britain's territories in the region were amalgamated with the creation of the Union of South Africa, which in 1961 would become independent from Britain as the Republic of South Africa.

These days biltong is widely available at butchers and supermarkets around South Africa and in many parts of the world, particularly where there are large South African communities. It is usually made with beef, but numerous different meats have also been used, and it is often sold in three different types, either wet, medium, or dry, depending on the length of time it has spent drying, which, these days, is usually done in an oven on a low setting rather than in the open air. Wet biltong has only been dried for a day or two, whereas dry biltong may have been in the oven for up to two weeks, by which time it is in a condition where it will last for years.

BILTONG
The traditional method of making biltong involves air-drying the meat after it has been cured.

BOEREWORS

✦

Another South African food that can be traced to Dutch immigration into the Cape Colony is the *boerewors*, which literally means "farmer's sausage." It is made with minced beef flavored with a number of spices, including coriander seed, nutmeg, and cloves. The Dutch sausage *verse worst* is made in exactly the same way, with the exception that it is usually made of pork rather than beef.

A variation is *droëwors*, or "dry sausage," which uses much the same ingredients but is made into a thinner shape and then air-dried so that it will keep for much longer.

Irish Stew

Irish stew is uncomplicated, though none the less tasty for that.

John Lanchester, The Debt to Pleasure

Origin: Ireland

Date: From the 17th century

Type: Meat and vegetable stew

✦ **CULTURAL**

✦ **SOCIAL**

✦ COMMERCIAL

✦ **POLITICAL**

✦ MILITARY

Irish stew may be a straightforward dish, based on lamb, potatoes, onions, and water, but it nevertheless attracts a great deal of debate. It could be argued, for instance, that it is actually either a soup or a broth rather than a stew because nothing is specifically added to it to thicken it beyond the fat from the lamb and the potatoes as they boil down. And endless discussions take place about the place of other ingredients in the stew, with some people insisting that if anything other than the basic four is used then the result is not an authentic Irish stew and others saying that, as it was originally a dish of rural Ireland made from whatever was available, it is acceptable to throw in all sorts of other ingredients, including carrots, parsnips, parsley, and pearl barley. But, whatever the rights and wrongs of different recipes, in the end Irish stew is a way of making dinner out of cheap cuts of lamb, which when cooked slowly with potatoes and other vegetables, tastes great and doesn't cost the earth.

THE CELTIC FRINGE

The way in which Irish stew is made today cannot possibly date back any further than the 17th century because potatoes, one of the core ingredients in every recipe, were not widely grown in Ireland until then. But a similar type of stew has been eaten across the country and in those other parts of the British Isles that have a strong Celtic heritage for a very long time. Dishes like Scotch broth and Lancashire hotpot are

common throughout the western regions — the Celtic fringe as it is sometimes called — and all can be traced back to the Bronze Age, the period when metalworking began and when the technology was available to make the sort of pots that could be hung over an open fire to make a stew.

The oldest Celtic cauldrons found in Ireland date to the 7th century BCE, late in the Bronze Age and only a few centuries before the introduction of more durable iron pots, but this most likely reflects the fact that metal was a precious substance so that, once a cauldron had worn out, it would have been melted down and the metal used again rather than thrown away. Many of the metal artifacts that have survived from the period are those that appear to have been intentionally buried in a hoard or thrown into rivers and lakes, perhaps in a religious ceremony or as a ritual offering, and are usually high-status items such as swords and shields that have been decorated with elaborate designs rather than more everyday items like cooking pots.

The Bronze Age in Ireland is usually said to have begun in about 2500 BCE, when copper was first used and, at some point, tin was then added to it to make bronze. The remarkable skill of Irish craftsmen working in various different metals can be seen in the beautiful examples of gold jewelry found in some of the hoards, so it is reasonable to presume that these people were also more than capable of making cooking pots. An alternative method of boiling meat could have been in what are known in Ireland as *fulacht fiadh*, or burnt mounds, which were pits containing a waterproof trough, either made of stone or lined with clay, which could have been used to boil water by throwing hot stones into them. Fire blackened stones are commonly found at these sites, which occur all over Ireland, suggesting the purpose was to heat water, but it is impossible to know for certain if this was for cooking or for some other reason.

Much of the lowland forest that had formerly covered large parts of Ireland was cleared during the Bronze Age, when a significant rise in popu-

CAWL

✦

Over on the other side of the Irish Sea, the Welsh make cawl, which is pronounced "cowl" and literally means broth. It is much the same as Irish stew, if rather less celebrated, except that in Wales they may add some leeks and usually prefer to boil their potatoes separately and then either add them whole or mash them and then mix them into the broth to thicken it. According to a Welsh proverb attributed to Cattwg the Wise (c. 497–580) — *cystal yfed o'r cawl â bwyta's cig* — it's as good to drink the broth as to eat the meat.

lation occurred, suggesting that the introduction of metalworking had a major impact on farming practices as well as on how food was cooked. An early version of Irish stew, cooked in cauldrons or on a large scale in the pits of the *fulacht fiadh*, could well have been the fuel on which this huge change in the landscape of Ireland was achieved, paving the way for further advances in technology when iron was introduced into the country in about 500 BCE.

The beginning of the Iron Age in Ireland has often been associated with the large-scale arrival of people from continental Europe in what was called the Celtic Invasion. The evidence for such a change can be seen in the adoption of the La Tène style of Celtic art, named after the area of what is now Switzerland, where it originated. However, more recent archaeological and genetic research has shown that the number of people entering Ireland at this time was actually relatively small, even if the impact of the technology they brought with them would be enormous. If this is the case, then the people we know today as the Celts of Ireland, and of Scotland, Wales, and Cornwall, are actually the descendants of those people who were living in the same region during the Bronze Age and, no doubt, for a long time beforehand.

THE CELTIC TIGER

Irish stew has certainly had a long and ancient history in Ireland itself, but it has also had an impact much more recently around the world as well as in Ireland as part of the emergence of a widespread celebration of Irish identity among members of the diaspora that has been embraced by people of many different ethnicities. This phenomenon has been accompanied by a rising sense of self-confidence in Ireland itself, which it is possible to trace back to the visit made to the country in June 1963 by President John F. Kennedy, whose great-grandparents on both sides left Ireland for America during the famine years of the 1840s. Kennedy was the first American president to visit Ireland and the extraordinary reception he received, more befitting a rock star than politician, prompted future presidents to visit the country in search of their own heritage. In May 2011, for instance, President Barack Obama arrived in the country, joking while he sipped the obligatory pint of Guinness that he had come in search of the lost apostrophe, but also visiting Moneygall in County Offaly where one of his great-great-great-grandfathers had been born.

If the most powerful man in the world was keen to demonstrate his Irish lineage, as Kennedy certainly was, then, so the theory goes, everybody else of Irish descent should celebrate their heritage as well. An alternative take on the resurgence of Irish culture would see it as beginning more recently, during the 1990s when the Irish economy began to experience an extended period of growth that saw the country described as the Celtic Tiger, linking it to the emerging tiger economies of South Korea, Taiwan, Singapore, and Hong Kong. The global financial crisis that began in 2008 showed that too much of the preceding boom in the country had been based on unsustainable levels of public debt and a massive property price bubble, leading to an equally spectacular bust and a long period of recession from which the country has struggled to emerge. But by that time the celebration of Irish culture had gone global and the small matter of a financial crisis was hardly likely to stop it.

In truth, there is no one answer to the question of why Irish culture has flowered over the past few decades and, perhaps, it is simply a popular movement that has sprung up with no particular underlying reason among the people of Ireland and the huge Irish diaspora, expressed through events like the St. Patrick's Day parades that now occur in many cities around the world. It might be the feast day of St. Patrick, but for most participants it is more like an excuse for a party in an effort to "paint the town green" and a general celebration of all things Irish than it is an observance of a religious festival. And what better way could there be of celebrating your Celtic heritage, even if you don't have any, than a pint of the black stuff and a bowl of Irish stew on St. Patrick's Day?

The Devil returned to Hell by two,
And he stay'd at home till five,
When he dined on some homicides done in ragoût,
With a rebel or so in an Irish stew.

Lord Byron, The Devil's Drive

ST. PATRICK'S DAY
Three men get into the spirit of the thing at a St. Patrick's Day parade in New York.

Tea

Wouldn't it be dreadful to live in a country where they didn't have tea?

Noël Coward

Origin: China

Date: From the 17th century onward

Type: Oriental infusion

+ **CULTURAL**
+ **SOCIAL**
+ **COMMERCIAL**
+ **POLITICAL**
+ **MILITARY**

For what is a delicate infusion of the leaves of *Camellia sinensis*, a small tree native to the border regions of China and India, tea has had an enormous influence on the course of history. It has been involved in wars and revolutions, in the development of global trade and financial systems, and in the establishment of the British Empire, the largest in history where, it was said, the sun never set because of its worldwide span or, to put it another way, in which it was always teatime somewhere.

A VERY BRITISH DRINK

The British may now be associated around the world with tea, but it was almost completely unknown in the country before the mid 17th century and was most probably introduced by either the Portuguese or the Dutch, who at that time had more developed trade links with China. One of the first accounts of drinking tea in England was written by the diarist Samuel Pepys, who described trying it for the first time in 1660, which was about the time when it first began to appear in the coffeehouses of London. The tea he sampled had probably been supplied from Lisbon or Amsterdam because the East India Company, which had been granted a monopoly on trade with the East Indies as part of its charter, had not yet started to import any into England.

Catherine of Braganza, the daughter of King John IV of Portugal, is often credited with introducing tea into England because she brought some with her when she came to the country in 1662 to marry King Charles II, who had been restored to the throne two years previously, but, as is demonstrated by Pepys, it was already available in the country before she arrived, if not very common. In truth, Catherine's preference for tea may have influenced members of her royal court and others in high society, but it probably did not extend a great deal further. Tea remained prohibitively expensive for most people and, as Catherine was not held in regard because of her Catholic faith, it appears unlikely that many people outside of royal circles would have chosen to copy her tastes.

Tea-drinking did not really take off in England and the rest of Britain until the turn of the 18th century, when it began to become more affordable for a wider section of society as a consequence of the increasing presence of the East India Company in trade with China. Over the course of the next 50 years, tea spread throughout British society, perhaps simply because it had become fashionable, but also because of the influence of the East India Company, which engaged in what we would now call a marketing campaign to promote the product they were importing in ever-increasing quantities. The habit of drinking tea with milk and sugar, a practice that most probably horrified the Chinese, put a particularly British stamp on it and, as well as boosting the trade conducted by the East India Company with China, the rise in the amount of tea being drunk in Britain led to an increase in both the demand for sugar from the West Indies and in the transatlantic slave trade to supply the necessary labor in the sugarcane fields. The interconnected and international nature of this trade was one of the driving forces behind the rise of London as the commercial and financial capital of the world and provided a model for the globalization of today.

THE BOSTON TEA PARTY

✦

On the night of December 16th, 1773, American protestors calling themselves the Sons of Liberty boarded four East India Company ships and threw the tea they were carrying into Boston Harbor. It was a protest against the imposition of taxes by the British government on its American colonies without consulting them and, in particular, against the Tea Act, which allowed the company exclusive right to import tea directly to America from China. The harsh response by the British government to the protest provoked further unrest in the colonies which, over the course of the next two years, escalated into the American Revolutionary War.

EAST INDIA HOUSE
The headquarters of the East India Company in Leadenhall Street, London, demolished in 1860 after the company was dissolved.

Earl Grey Tea

✦

Black tea flavored with the essential oil of the citrus fruit bergamot was named after Charles Grey, the Second Earl Grey, who was the prime minister of Britain from 1830 to 1834. His administration was responsible for the Reform Act of 1832, one of the most important in British constitutional history, along with the abolition of slavery in the British Empire and the removal of the Chinese trade monopoly previously enjoyed by the East India Company. One theory of how the tea came to be named after the Earl suggests that it was first specially blended for him because the acidity of the bergamot countered the hardness of the water on his Northumberland estate.

The rise in tea-drinking in Britain was in large part driven by women, who were at the time largely excluded from the all-male environment of the coffeehouse. Fashionable hostesses began throwing tea parties and, as part of what was becoming the ritual of afternoon tea, bought expensive porcelain teapots and crockery that were also imported by the East India Company from China. The trade in fine china, as it became known, went hand in hand with the tea trade because the porcelain was imported into Britain on the same ships that carried the tea, acting as ballast for an otherwise lightweight cargo. The demand for tea services and other types of porcelain encouraged by the availability of goods from China was one of the main reasons behind the enlargement of the pottery business in Britain, which began in the early 1760s when Josiah Wedgwood began to introduce new methods into pottery-making in Stoke-on-Trent in order to improve the quality of his products to compete with those coming from China. It was an early example of the sort of factory system of manufacturing that would become integral to the Industrial Revolution, which transformed first British society and, as the new industrial methods were taken up elsewhere, played a role in creating what we might now describe as the modern world.

Tea and Opium

As the tea trade began to expand in the 18th century, the Chinese maintained a policy of not allowing any foreigners into the interior of the country to buy tea directly from the growers, preferring instead to keep their monopoly on the business by only selling tea to Europeans at trading posts established on the coast of Canton, now Guangdong, in the south of the country. Chinese merchant houses, known as the Hongs, controlled the supply chain to the coast from the mountains of southern China where the tea was grown, preventing Europeans from discovering anything about the tea plant or its cultivation so that some of the European merchants buying from them were not even aware that green and black tea both came from the same plant.

As well as keeping the source of tea secret, the Chinese would only accept payment from the East India Company in gold or silver bullion and, as there was little demand in China for any goods from the outside world, the company had no way of generating income from the Chinese by way of a two-way trade. This resulted in a balance of trade heavily in favor of the Chinese, draining the reserves of the company and forcing it to look for ways of reducing the deficit. It was one of the main reasons for attempts by the company to expand its territorial possessions in India and, in particular, in the state of Bengal, where it engaged in a war against the French East India Company and local Indian leaders, particularly the Nawab of Bengal, in an attempt to fully colonize the region. The victory won in 1757 at the Battle of Plassey, in which the company's forces were commanded by Robert Clive, who would become known as Clive of India, effectively secured Bengal for Britain and, when put together with the company's other possessions on the subcontinent, made the British the major power in India.

In capturing Bengal, the East India Company gained a monopoly on the Indian opium trade and, over the course of the next 50 years, this would be used to finance their commercial dealings in India and, in particular, the tea trade with China. Opium smoking was widespread in China at the time and, even though it was illegal to import it into the country, the ban was weakly enforced. The East India Company developed a complex financial mechanism in order to get around Chinese law which, put simply, involved selling the opium produced in Bengal to third-party traders in Calcutta (now Kolkata), who then smuggled it into China and either then handed the revenue, no doubt minus their cut, to the company offices in the country or used it to buy tea for the company.

The questionable morality of engaging in what we would now describe as drug trafficking and money laundering does not appear to have unduly troubled either the East India Company or the British

Afterwards I did send for a cup of tee (a China drink) of which I never had drank before.

From the entry in the diary of Samuel Pepys for Tuesday, September 25th, 1660

CLIVE OF INDIA
Robert Clive meeting the Nawab of Bengal after the Battle of Plassey in an oil painting (c.1760) by Francis Hayman.

government, even if both attempted to keep at least some distance between themselves and the actual traders. But it was certainly highly lucrative, and by 1800 the East India Company was contributing 10 percent of the entire tax revenue of Britain, a source of finance that made a major contribution to the enlargement of the British Empire and the development of the Royal Navy over the course of the 18th century. The power of the navy was demonstrated in 1805 at the Battle of Trafalgar when the British forces commanded by Admiral Horatio Nelson defeated a combined fleet of French and Spanish ships, a victory allowing Britain to gain a position of unchallenged naval supremacy that it maintained over the course of the following hundred years, a period when Britain really did rule the waves.

> **A hardened and shameless tea-drinker, who has for twenty years diluted his meals with only the infusion of this fascinating plant, whose kettle scarcely has time to cool, who with tea amuses the evening, with tea solaces the midnights, and with tea welcomes the morning.**
>
> *Dr. Johnson's definition of himself.*

With the tea trade now being financed by the proceeds of opium trafficking, the Chinese experienced a rapid decline in the amount of silver bullion coming into the country, causing serious economic problems that were further compounded by rising levels of opium addiction across the country. Attempts by the Chinese to limit the opium trade were prevented by the British and would eventually lead to the two Opium Wars of the mid-19th century, both of which ended in comprehensive defeats for the Chinese because of British military superiority. The First Opium War, fought from 1839 to 1842, resulted in China being forced to cede Hong Kong to Britain and to open up more of its ports to foreign trade, whereas after the second, fought between 1856 and

OPIUM WAR
Nemesis (1843) by Edward Duncan, showing the Royal Navy's first iron-hulled warship destroying Chinese junks during the First Opium War.

1860, further commercial concessions were made by China and the opium trade was legalized in the country.

The Opium Wars led to a long period of foreign intervention in Chinese affairs and were also partly responsible for serious political instability and social unrest in the country. The "century of humiliation," as this period of Chinese history is sometimes called, included the devastating Taiping Rebellion of the 1860s in southern China and the Boxer Rebellion toward the end of that century in which protests in rural areas against the role of foreign powers in China, which included the opium trade, spread to Beijing in 1900 and were supported by elements in the Chinese government and army. The Boxers and Chinese army began a siege of the Legation Quarter, a walled-off area of the city where most foreign nationals were accommodated, prompting the despatch of a combined European, American, and Japanese military force to the city. The siege was broken after 55 days by this combined force, which effectively brought the rebellion to an end, but the inherent weaknesses of the Chinese government had been exposed and, in 1912, a revolution established the Republic of China, bringing over 2,000 years of imperial rule in the country to an end.

TEA CLIPPERS
✦

The tea clippers were three-masted square-rigged sailing ships built between 1840 and 1869, designed to be used in the opium and tea trades, where speed was as important as cargo-carrying capacity. Unofficial races were held between ships competing to be the first to bring China's new season tea crop to London. The opening of the Suez Canal in 1869, which could only be used by steam ships, cut the journey time in half and made the clippers obsolete. One of the last to be built was the *Cutty Sark*, which was also one of the fastest; it is now in dry dock in Greenwich, having been extensively restored after a fire in 2007 that almost destroyed it.

INDIAN TEA

In the late 18th century the East India Company began to look for ways of breaking the Chinese monopoly on the supply of tea. It proved a difficult task because Chinese secrecy over tea cultivation meant that little knowledge of the plants existed outside of that country. Initially little progress was made, despite the research carried out at the Royal Botanic Gardens at Kew in London and, after it was established by the East India Company in 1787, in the botanic gardens in Calcutta. The incentive for the company to grow tea in India was reduced in 1813 when it lost its monopoly on trade between the subcontinent and Britain, but 20 years later, when its monopoly on Chinese trade was also removed, it renewed its attempts to cultivate its own tea,

particularly after tea trees were found to be growing wild in the valley
of the Brahmaputra River in Assam, the region of southeastern India
that borders China and Burma.

The tea plants from Assam were slightly different from those in
China, with a broader leaf more suited to making black tea than green
tea, and it was classified as a particular variety called *Camellia sinensis
assamica*. A selective breeding program with Chinese tea plants produced a variety of Assam tea suitable for cultivation and, from 1835,
tea estates, or tea gardens as they were often called, began to be established, mostly in the Brahmaputra valley in the northeast of the region.
The first of these gardens, the Chabua Tea Estate, continues to grow
tea today; the current owners, Amalgamated Plantations, part of the
huge Tata Group multinational, describe their product as being "golden
tippy teas with liquors that are flavoury, having clonal character."
"Golden tippy" refers to the characteristic color of the tips of leaves
from the second flush, the regrowth on tea bushes after the first picking,
which makes the highest quality black tea; "clonal character" means
that the tea comes from bushes grown from cuttings of a particular
hybrid rather than from seed to maintain the quality of the original.

From these beginnings, numerous British tea-planters began to
develop estates in Assam, at first bringing Chinese laborers in to do the
work but gradually taking on Indian indentured workers. With the
end of the East India Company monopoly, the tea trade became much
more competitive, allowing British merchants to buy from other traders in India or directly from the estates. Tea estates began to spring up
in other parts of India as well, in Darjeeling in the Himalayan foothills
of West Bengal and in the Nilgiri region of the Western Ghats in

southern India, and by the turn of the 20th century India was producing more tea than China.

The East India Company got into financial difficulties after the removal of its monopolies, a situation compounded by corruption and financial mismanagement. The end of company rule in India came after the Indian Rebellion of 1857, which had begun with mutinies of sepoys, Indian soldiers in the company's army stationed in Meerut, a city in the state of Uttar Pradesh, and spread through much of India as large-scale protests against the company's rule occurred. After the rebellion had been put down the following year, the British government came to the conclusion that leaving the jewel in the crown of its colonial assets in the hands of a private company, even one behaving as if it was a nation state, could no longer be justified. The company was dissolved and India came under the direct rule of the British crown, the beginning of the period known as the British Raj.

Under British rule in India, the tea trade was predominantly an export business, even if attempts were made to encourage tea-drinking among Indians as well as in the expatriate British community. Tea breaks were introduced into the workplace and *char wallahs*, tea sellers, were allowed to ply their trade across the extensive Indian railway network. Yet it would not be until after independence in 1947 that tea-drinking started to become more widespread, perhaps because it began to lose its association with the country's former colonial rulers. One of the driving forces behind this change was a promotional campaign carried out by the Tea Board of India after it was formed in 1953 in an attempt to encourage an internal market as a way of insulating the tea trade from the potential for volatility in the world market. The success of this campaign is shown in recent figures stating that 70 percent of Indian tea is now consumed within the country, even if the increase is probably as much a consequence of the Indian people finding their own way of drinking tea, much as the British had done in the 18th century. One of the most popular styles is masala chai, spiced tea, made by brewing black tea with spices such as cardamom, ginger, and cinnamon, a drink that has now spread far beyond the subcontinent.

MASALA CHAI
A cup of masala chai, shown with some of the spices used, including cinnamon, cloves, nutmeg, and star anise.

Hardtack

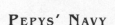

Origin: British Royal Navy

Date: 1660s

Type: Twice-cooked biscuit

Until the development of canned foods in the 19th century, and then refrigeration in the 20th, the staple food for soldiers on military campaigns and sailors on long sea voyages was hardtack, also known as ship's biscuit, a thick and solid cracker simply made from flour and water that has been twice-cooked, making it almost indestructible.

PEPYS' NAVY

Hardtack was one of the three staples of British Royal Navy rations, along with salted meat, either beef or pork, and beer, until the late 19th century. It still forms part of navy stores today, even if it is only now used as an emergency food rather than routinely issued. Records from the period of the Spanish Armada in 1588 show that the standard daily issue to seamen was one pound of biscuit, one pound of salt beef, and a gallon of beer, which would have been augmented with fresh produce at the start of voyages but would then become the sole source of nourishment once these provisions had run out.

Up until the mid 17th century, the supply of rations to the navy was carried out in a haphazard manner, open to all sorts of abuses that included the supply of rotten food, which, when put together with the beer often going off, rats getting into the beef, and weevils infecting the hardtack, made for serious problems with discontent among seamen over the poor quality of food they were given. In July 1660, six months after he began the diary for which he is known today, Samuel Pepys was appointed to the position of Clerk of the Acts on the Navy Board, the body responsible for the administration of the navy, including the provision of supplies, or victualing as it was known. He appears to have benefitted from the patronage of Sir Edward Montagu, a distant relative who was an admiral in the navy and who had commanded the fleet that had brought the

Sea-bisket is a sort of bread much dried by passing the oven twice to make it keep for sea service.
Encyclopaedia Britannica *(1773)*

restored King Charles II back to England from exile in Europe in May of that year. At about the same time as Pepys was awarded his position, Montagu was ennobled as the Earl of Sandwich, a title that would later provide the name for another type of food when the Earl's great-great-grandson supposedly ordered a slice of meat between two slices of bread so that he could eat without interrupting the game of cards he was playing.

Pepys kept his diary for 10 years, covering a remarkable period of English history that, as an insider, he was well placed to observe. As well as the restoration of Charles II, he wrote about the Second Anglo-Dutch War (1665–67), and both the Great Plague of London (1665–66) and the Great Fire of London (1666), while at the same time livening up his accounts with details of his personal life that included arguments with his wife and the affairs he was having with other women. He was also critical of the men holding senior positions in the Royal Navy and Navy Board, opinions he would not have been free to express in his job, but which now give us an idea of the high level of incompetence of the navy's administrators.

In 1665, Pepys proposed a system to centralize the provision of victuals for the navy as a means of reducing the amount of corruption involved and to attempt to make the method of purchase more efficient. The Navy Board accepted his proposal, appointing him to a senior position on its Victualling Commission to oversee the changes, which included requiring each ship's purser, the officer in charge of providing provisions, to produce complete accounts for their purchases. Overall, the reforms instituted by Pepys would prove to be some of the most important in the history of the Royal Navy, beginning the process of creating a professional fighting force that would later go on to dominate the seas.

LOBSCOUSE

✦

Lobscouse is a type of stew originally made by sailors from Liverpool with salt beef and vegetables thickened with crumbled hardtack. Its popularity with the people of the city, sailors or otherwise, led to them becoming known as "Scousers," and it is still cooked there, even if with fresh meat and minus the hardtack. The Norwegian dish *lapskaus* is much the same, while *labskaus*, eaten in the north German port cities of Hamburg, Bremen, and Lübeck, is made from corned beef mashed together with potatoes, onions, and beets, often served with a pickled herring and a fried egg.

The war with the Dutch, fought at sea and in a number of overseas colonies, relied on the navy; and it was not going well. One of a number of conflicts between the two nations over the course of the 17th and 18th centuries, it had broken out over attempts by both countries to gain control of the crucial trade routes to the East and the New World. It had become apparent that the superior administration and training of the Dutch Navy had given them the edge over the English.

The outbreak of the Great Plague in London, which had begun in April 1665 and reached its peak over the course of the summer, caused the English further problems, leading to the death of an estimated 100,000 people, 15 percent of the population of the city. This was compounded in the following year by the Great Fire, which is not thought to have led to any great loss of life but destroyed almost a third of the houses in the city. It started on the night of September 2nd, 1666, in the bakery of Thomas Farriner in Pudding Lane, who was at the time engaged in making ship's biscuits for the navy, and then spread rapidly out from there, burning for four days. Pepys lived a short distance from Pudding Lane and may have been acquainted with Farriner through his work with the Victualling Commission, although he does not say as much in his diary, which otherwise contains a first-hand account of the progress of the fire.

Englishmen, and more especially seamen, love their bellies above anything else, and therefore it must always be remembered in the management of the victualling of the Navy that to make any abatement from them in the quantity or agreeableness of the victuals is to discourage and provoke them in the tenderest point and will sooner render them disgusted with the King's service than any one other hardship that can be put upon them.
Samuel Pepys (1633–1703)

In the aftermath of the fire, recriminations began over its cause and the failure of the authorities to deal with it before it had got out of hand. The truth is that it was almost certainly accidentally started in the bakery, perhaps as a consequence of Farriner leaving the embers of the oven fire burning overnight to continue the process of drying the biscuits he was making. But, if this was the case, he largely escaped any form of censure, public anger being directed against various groups of foreigners, particularly the French, who were held responsible despite a complete absence of evidence to implicate them in any wrongdoing. Others saw it as a reprisal attack by the Dutch for the Holmes's Bonfire, an attack mounted by the Royal Navy two weeks previously using fire ships to set light to a fleet of Dutch merchant ships in a dockyard on the coast of the Netherlands, which resulted in an inferno that spread to a nearby town.

Early in the following year, 1667, it had become clear to the English that they were not going to win the war with the Dutch and they decided to enter into peace negotiations. Charles could no longer afford to keep the whole of the English fleet at sea by this time and much of it was laid up in the naval dockyards at Chatham on the River Medway. In June, while peace negotiations were continuing, the Dutch mounted an attack on the ships in Chatham Dockyard, breaking through the defenses and using marines to capture the English gun emplacements protecting the ships, then using fire ships to destroy the majority of them.

The Raid on the Medway, or the Battle of Chatham as it is sometimes called, would prove to be one of the worst defeats in the history of the Royal Navy. Pepys recorded that he thought it would lead to a revolution in England and to the end of the reign of Charles II, and, although this did not occur, it did lead to the English accepting the

THE MEDWAY
An oil painting from 1669 of the Raid on the Medway during the Second Anglo-Dutch War by the Dutch artist Jan van Leyden.

peace terms offered by the Dutch without any further argument. It also made clear the need to completely overhaul the navy in order for England to be able to compete with the Dutch, a policy that was pursued along the lines Pepys had originally suggested.

In regularizing the way in which the navy was administered, Pepys laid the foundation for the modern Royal Navy, but one problem the changes his new methods of victualing ships had not solved was the regular occurrence of scurvy among crews on long voyages, a problem that limited the time a ship could spend at sea. We now know that a diet based on hardtack, salted meat, and beer did not contain enough vitamin C and that scurvy is a consequence of this nutritional deficiency, but it would be more than a hundred years after Pepys' day before a solution was found. It simply involved adding lemon juice to the rum ration given to sailors, a practice first proposed by the Scottish physician Gilbert Blane in 1779 but not formally adopted by the navy until 1795, showing that its administration was by no means perfect despite the reforms begun by Pepys. It proved easier for the navy to use limes

HARDTACK MAKER
An engraved illustration of a machine to make hardtack from *The Industrial Encyclopedia* (1875) by E. O. Lami.

sourced from British colonies in the Caribbean rather than lemons, which is said to be the source of the derogatory nickname of "Limeys" sometimes used for the British by Americans, originally applied to British sailors and then extended to include everybody else.

CRACKERS

Some of the biscuit makers that would later become household names in Britain first began in business baking hardtack for the navy. One of the best known was Huntley & Palmers, founded in Reading, Berkshire in 1822, which made a huge range of cookies as well as crackers. Over the course of the 19th century, the company became one of the first internationally known brand names and at its height at the turn of the 20th century it operated the largest biscuit factory in the world in Reading, which employed 5,000 people and transported materials around the site on its own railway. Tins of Huntley & Palmers biscuits were exported all over the British Empire and beyond, in their day becoming a symbol of Britain's global reach in a similar way to how Coca-Cola is sometimes considered to represent American power now.

Huntley & Palmers continued to grow in the early 20th century, supplying biscuits to the British Army during the First and Second World Wars, but then began to struggle in the years of austerity that followed the end of the Second World War, as if the fortunes of the company were tied to those of the British Empire as a whole. Nevertheless, its tins of cookies and crackers remained an essential part of the Christmas experience for many British families until the 1970s, by which time Huntley & Palmers had become part of Associated Biscuits, a group that also included Jacob's and Peek Freans, two of Huntley & Palmers' former rivals. The brand name was discontinued in the 1980s and the factory in Reading gradually demolished over the course of the decade. By that time, much of the site was made up of disused and dilapidated factory buildings and warehouses, but the large office block dating from 1937 with its art deco frontage on Kings Road should perhaps have been preserved, if only as a reminder of the long association between Huntley & Palmers and what used to be known as the Biscuit Town.

BISCUIT TIN
A Huntley & Palmers biscuit tin from 1904 in the shape of an India table. This one is now in the Victoria and Albert Museum in London.

Gin

Origin: Dutch Republic
and Flanders

Date: 17th century

Type: Grain-based spirit

+ CULTURAL
+ **SOCIAL**
+ **COMMERCIAL**
+ **POLITICAL**
+ **MILITARY**

Gin has had an influence on the history of England and the British Empire since it was first brought to the country in the mid-17th century by mercenary soldiers returning from the Thirty Years War in central Europe. By the beginning of the 18th century, it had become the drink of the masses, creating the so-called "gin craze," bouts of public drunkenness that caused a burst of moral outrage in the country and that required five Acts of Parliament to be passed before a semblance of sobriety was regained.

GENEVER

In Britain, gin from the Netherlands is still sometimes known as Geneva gin, even though it has no connection to the Swiss city, rather being named after the Dutch word for juniper, *genever*, which at some point became abbreviated in English to gin. It is often said to have been invented by the Dutch physician Franciscus Sylvius (1614–74) by flavoring the spirit obtained from distilling grain alcohol with juniper berries and extracts from other plants which, in the gin trade, are known as botanicals and can include lemon peel, cinnamon, and cloves. In truth, evidence suggests that, long before Sylvius came up with his version, juniper-flavored spirit was being made in the Dutch Republic and Flanders, where it was originally sold for its medicinal properties, which were, it was claimed, capable of curing just about any ailment.

**Martial William drank
Geneva, yet no Age could ever boast
A braver prince than He.**

*Alexander Blunt (1729) — the pen name
of the gin distiller Elias Bockett*

Even if such claims were a little wide of the mark, genever became a popular drink in the Low Countries. Though it had arrived in Britain after the end of the Thirty Years War in 1648, it only began to become popular following the restoration of the monarchy in 1660. After the success of the parliamentary forces led by Oliver Cromwell in the English Civil War, King Charles I was deposed in 1649 and then executed. From that time on, his son, the future Charles II, lived in exile in Europe, including periods in the Dutch Republic staying with his sister Mary, who was married to William II, Prince of Orange. While there,

Charles appears to have acquired a taste for genever. When he returned to England following the political chaos that ensued after the death of Cromwell, it became fashionable in high society to drink the spirit favored by the newly restored king.

The popularity of genever, which was also known as Hollands, was seriously dented by the two wars fought by England and the Dutch Republic between 1665 and 1674, both a consequence of commercial competition over trade in the Far East and New World, but also because Charles was attempting to restore his nephew, William III, Prince of Orange, to the throne of the Dutch Republic. A wave of anti-Dutch feeling swept across England, so drinking genever would hardly have been the patriotic thing to do even if by that time it was being distilled in England and was called gin.

WILLIAM III
The Prince of Orange became joint monarch of England together with his wife, Mary, after the Glorious Revolution of 1688.

THE GLORIOUS REVOLUTION

James II ascended to the English throne after the death of his brother Charles II in 1685, despite having converted to Catholicism on marrying his second wife, the devote Catholic Mary of Modena. The perception among Protestant noble-men in the royal court was that James was showing favor to Catholics, compounded in 1687 when he issued the Declaration of Indulgence, granting much wider religious freedom to Catholics than had previously been the case. Matters came to a head in June of the following year with the birth of James' first son, also called James, opening the prospect of a Catholic dynasty ruling England for the foreseeable future. A group of Protestants, known as the Immortal Seven and made up of six noblemen and a bishop, wrote to William III in the Dutch Republic inviting him to bring an army to England to oust James and saying that, if he did, he would have the support of much of the English nobility.

As if the situation was not confusing enough, William was married to James' eldest daughter from his first marriage, also called Mary, giving his claim to the throne some legitimacy even if the line of succession was clear. On November 5th, William landed with an army at Torbay in Devon, initially taking up defensive positions in the expectation that anti-Catholic feeling in England would lead to the collapse of the monarchy without a fight. With his support draining away, and having famously been abandoned by the Duke of Marlborough, James fled the country for France in December, leaving the throne to William, who was crowned as joint monarch along with his wife Mary in the following year.

THE GIN CRAZE

Two of the most important Acts of Parliament in British constitutional history were passed during the reign of William and Mary, both of which remain on the statute books today, even if they have each been amended over the years. The Bill of Rights Act of 1689 established a constitutional monarchy in which Parliament, rather than the king or queen, was the ultimate seat of power and the 1701 Act of Settlement sorted out the line of succession of the monarchy to ensure it remained Protestant. In between, another Act of Parliament was passed that was hardly of such constitutional importance, but that would have the unintended consequence of unleashing the gin craze, a period of binge-drinking that gripped London and a number of other English cities during the first half of the 18th century.

The Act, passed by the English Parliament in 1690, lowered the duty on spirit distilled from English grain while raising it on all other spirits and beer, together with allowing anybody to distill spirits as long as they bought an inexpensive license and gave notice to the local excise man. It was no coincidence that this new law was enacted shortly after William and a coalition of European states, the Grand Alliance, had entered into a war against France because its main purposes was to discourage the consumption of French brandy, while, at the same time, propping up the English grain market. The popularity of gin was already on the rise as a consequence of the ascendency of a Dutch monarch to the English throne, so, now that the law promoted the sale of English gin over French brandy, distilleries began to open all over the country, often producing cheap versions of the spirit flavored with turpentine rather than juniper, making it an affordable drink for the masses.

By the turn of the 18th century, sales of gin had shot up, especially because women had joined men in the gin shops for the first time, leading to the spirit becoming known as Madame Geneva or, as it is still sometimes

JUNIPER SPIRIT
The label from a bottle of Dutch genever, named as "Genièvre," the French word for juniper.

called today, mother's ruin. Over the course of the next 50 years, consumption continued to rise in London, as did incidences of public drunkenness, crime, and prostitution. It is difficult to distinguish now exactly how much the gin-drinking was responsible for these social problems as opposed to being a symptom of the high levels of poverty and social deprivation that had grown up in the extensive slums of London during this period. Whether it was the availability of cheap gin or if it was poor people seeking the oblivion of drunkenness to avoid the harsh reality of their lives, the public perception of a breakdown in social order led to an episode of moral outrage among the righteous and demands that the government clamp down on the sale of gin.

Many Members of Parliament at that time were landowners who benefitted from the increase in the grain market brought about by rising sales of gin. Together with others who were also making money from the craze, the distillers and merchants, they obstructed any government action that attempted to deal with the problem. It was not until 1729 that the government finally took steps to control gin consumption by raising the taxes on it and making it illegal for distillers to sell it to unlicensed gin shops. The legislation was the first of five so-called Gin Acts; the first four were entirely ineffective and give the impression more of being an attempt by the government to appease the moral crusaders without damaging the interests of the landowning classes.

Between the first act and the fourth act, passed in 1743, gin consumption actually went up in London, the consequences of which were illustrated in William Hogarth's 1751 engraving *Gin Lane*. It depicts a scene of drunken debauchery on the streets of London in which a

LONDON DRY GIN

♦

The most common type of gin available today is London dry gin, even if there is only one gin distillery actually left in the city. It was first made after 1830, following the invention of the column still, which produces a purer spirit than is possible by using the older pot still. Column-distilled gin has a cleaner taste and, as it does not need sweetening, unlike many of its predecessors, it is described as being dry, a quality that makes it ideal for the basis of such cocktails as the Martini and the Tom Collins.

A perfect Martini should be made by filling a glass with gin then waving it in the general direction of Italy.

Noël Coward

gin-soaked and disheveled mother is shown dropping her child to its death while attempting to take snuff. Hogarth's companion piece to this apocalyptic engraving was *Beer Street* and, in stark contrast, it shows healthy and happy men and women enjoying tankards of ale, presumably after a hard day's work, sitting in front of a pub as other people go about their business in an orderly fashion. The message was not subtle and, no doubt, was not intended to be; gin-drinking caused all the evils of society while a beer or two didn't do anybody any harm.

The last of the Gin Acts, which came into force in 1751, was a more determined attempt to restrict the sale of the spirit and, over the course of the following decade, consumption began to fall away. An increase in the price of grain following poor harvests in the mid-1750s may have had as much effect in curbing the habit as the new law, forcing the poor to spend more on buying food as well as pushing up the price of gin, but, however it happened, by the end of the decade, the craze that had lasted more than 50 years had finally come to an end.

GIN LANE
William Hogarth's engraving from 1751 showing the disastrous social consequences of the Gin Craze.

IMPERIAL GIN

By the middle of the 19th century gin had been transformed from mother's ruin into the drink of choice across the British Empire. The addition of Indian tonic water allowed Victorian colonial gentlemen to relax in the British club with a large G & T after a long day administrating some far-flung outpost on the empire, equipped with the ready-made excuse, if one was needed, that the tonic contained quinine, then the only known treatment for malaria. Quinine was isolated from the bark of the South American cinchona tree in 1820 by the addition of a dilute solution of sulfuric acid, giving quinine sulfate, a white powder that could then be dissolved in water. The only problem was that quinine sulfate has a very bitter taste, so dissolving it in a sweetened tonic water and then adding gin made taking the malaria treatment a much happier experience. Lemon, it turns out, helps quinine to dissolve, resulting in the gin and tonic with a slice of lemon.

It might be stretching the truth to suggest that the gin and tonic has changed the course of history because, after all, it was the bark of the cinchona tree that actually made the difference and the gin was only really involved, if we are being honest, because it made a great drink.

JUNIPER BERRIES

✦

Juniper berries are not actually berries at all, but the fleshy seed cones of the small evergreen tree. They have been used as a flavoring in cooking and in herbal remedies for thousands of years, including in Egypt, where the remains of berries were found in Tutankhamun's tomb. Dried berries are most commonly used in gin-distilling and are crushed before being added to pure grain spirit to ensure that the flavor infuses into the liquid, which is then usually redistilled so that the resulting gin is colorless and clear.

Nevertheless, the gin and tonic is now enjoyed around the world, including in many places where no cases of malaria have ever been recorded. In any event, quinine has largely been replaced by other treatments these days, even if a vaccine for a disease that, according to the World Health Organization, is responsible for about 660 million deaths a year, has so far eluded medical science. Should the day come when researchers develop an effective vaccine, then that will certainly change the course of history.

Vindaloo

If jealousy was the vindaloo of love, I'd imagined her tongue burning.

Hanif Kureishi, Something to Tell You

Origin: Goa

Date: 16th century

Type: Hot curry

+ **CULTURAL**

+ **SOCIAL**

+ COMMERCIAL

+ **POLITICAL**

+ MILITARY

The ridiculously hot curry vindaloo, now a regular feature on the menus of Indian restaurants everywhere, except possibly in India, is eaten by those brave or foolhardy enough to order a dish packed with red chilies and it is usually served alongside several pints of lager. Its path to global recognition can be traced back to the Indian restaurants of Britain, many run by people of Bangladeshi origin, then back further to India, specifically to the state of Goa in the southwest of the country and the influence of the Portuguese in that region.

PORTUGUESE GOA

As well as a lot of chili, the modern version of vindaloo often includes vinegar and potatoes, the two ingredients that are often said to have provided it with its name; *aloo* meaning potato in both the Hindi and Urdu languages. In fact, the name is a corruption of *carne de vinha e alhos*, which means "meat with wine and garlic" in Portuguese, a dish usually made with pork and introduced into the Portuguese colonial enclaves around the coast of India during the 16th century. The Portuguese explorer Vasco da Gama had landed in Calicut on the Malabar coast, to the south of Goa, in 1498 and within a few years trading links between India and Portugal were established, followed by permanent Portuguese settlements in a number of locations. In 1510, the Portuguese defeated the Islamic Bijapur Sultanate of Yusuf Adil Shah, who controlled Goa at that time, establishing the capital of the Portuguese Empire in India in the city founded by the sultanate on the northern bank of the Mandovi River estuary and now known as Old Goa.

As well as the recipes for *carne de vinha e alhos* and other dishes, the Portuguese also brought some of the vegetables they had discovered in the New World, including potatoes and tomatoes, together with the spice that would go on to have an enormous impact on Indian cuisine across the whole subcontinent — the chili pepper. As wine had to be imported from Portugal, palm vinegar became a common substitute in those recipes that required it, together with the addition of vegetables, Indian spices, and, of course, chili, although not in anything like the quantity used in a modern vindaloo.

Beginning in the late 16th century, the Portuguese built numerous churches in Old Goa, including the Cathedral, which remains the largest Christian place of worship in India today, and the Basilica of Bom Jesus, a particularly fine example of baroque religious architecture. A significant number of the local inhabitants of Goa converted to Catholicism, also beginning to eat both pork and beef in what was otherwise a largely vegetarian society, as much of peninsular India still is today, and one in which cows were sacred to Hindus and pork proscribed in the Islamic faith. It would lead to colonial Portuguese using Christian Goans as cooks and, for exactly the same reasons, to the British taking them on as well, particularly after the British peacefully occupied Goa in 1797 as a consequence of the French Revolutionary Wars.

The East India Company was at the time involved in a conflict with the Kingdom of Mysore, ruled by the Tipu Sultan, also known as the Tiger of Mysore, a staunch ally of the French who, under the overall command of Napoleon Bonaparte, were threating British interests across the subcontinent. Britain and Portugal held long-standing treaty alliances and were both in conflict with the French, leading to an agreement for Britain to occupy and protect Goa, which was then returned to Portugal after Napoleon's final defeat in 1815 at the Battle of Waterloo. The British may not have stayed in Goa for very long, but they not only took their Goan chefs with them when they left, but also a taste for what was now being called vindaloo.

RED CHILIES
The chili was probably first introduced to India by the Portuguese in Goa, before spreading across the subcontinent.

GOING FOR A CURRY

Indian food has a long history in Britain as a consequence of the colonial connection between the two countries begun by the East India Company in the 17th century and then continued after 1857 by the British Raj. On returning from colonial service, many British ex-patriates retained their fondness for the spicy food they had encountered, sometimes bringing their Goan chefs back to Britain with them to cook the particular hybrid of British and Indian food they had become accustomed to in India. The main courses of these meals were called curry, as they had been by the British in India, but it was not a name widely used by Indians themselves, either then or now, who for the most part refer to each separate dish by its specific name rather than as a generic type of food.

After the Second World War communities of people from the Indian subcontinent began to develop in British cities, especially after 1947 as a consequence of the violence and chaos that accompanied the partition of India during independence. In the East End of London, particularly around Brick Lane, a thriving community developed consisting mostly of Bangladeshi people from Sylhet, the region of northeastern Bangladesh that borders Assam. People from this region were well known as boatmen on the Surma River and had been employed by the British to carry tea from Assam to Calcutta and then as seamen in the ships taking the tea to London. The Brick Lane community originally grew up as lodging houses for Sylhet seamen because it was close to the docks where the tea was landed and then began to expand as some people stayed in Britain to work in the garment and textile trades prevalent in that part of London.

BRICK LANE
Street sign of Brick Lane in London in both English and Bengali. A large Bangladeshi community still lives in the area.

Another common form of employment was in the restaurant business, particularly when it began to expand in the 1960s, Brick Lane in particular becoming famous for its many restaurants, as it still is today. The Bangladesh Liberation War, fought against Pakistan in 1971, resulted in the displacement of millions of people and a flood of refugees, leading to an increase in immigration to Britain. People from Sylhet who arrived in the country often already had connections in the catering trade and, as curry was becoming increasingly popular, Indian restaurants run by Bangladeshis from Sylhet began to open across the country so that there are now estimated to be 10,000 in total.

The nature of British alcohol licensing laws has contributed to the popularity of curry and the spread of curry houses, as they are often called. Regulations first introduced during the First World War in an attempt to reduce drinking among workers in munitions factories were retained after the war, requiring pubs to close at eleven o'clock at night, while restaurants with an alcohol license could remain open until much later. In the 1970s curry houses took advantage of these laws to stay open late, giving people who were not inclined to go home at eleven o'clock somewhere else to go after the pubs closed. The laws were subsequently relaxed to allow pubs to open later, but by that time "going for a curry" had become something of a social institution across Britain.

The menus in the Indian restaurants of Britain are now much the same everywhere. The food may be cooked by Sylhet chefs but many of the dishes would be unrecognizable to most people from either India, Pakistan, or Bangladesh. The food is a combination of the Anglo-Indian style of the British Raj together with influences from different parts of the subcontinent, particularly that found in the meat-eating Muslim north, together with a few dishes that have been invented in Britain, such as chicken tikka masala and balti. Vindaloo is an ever-present item on all menus and has become part of British culture, famous for being ordered in an alcohol-fueled show of male bravado after a night out in the pub, a display that can later be the cause of some regret.

The British taste for curry has seen a remarkable transformation in a country with a reputation for the blandness of its food, characterized by some as consisting of boiled meat with boiled vegetables, so that now curry is regarded as being almost as much of a national dish as fish and chips. The acceptance of curry, particularly since the 1970s, may have also played a role in a much greater willingness of the British to try foods from many other parts of the world than was previously the case. And once you have eaten a vindaloo and survived, there can be little to fear from any other type of food, no matter what it is.

ROGAN JOSH

◆

One of the few dishes on the menus of British curry houses that is almost the same as it is in India is rogan josh, a dish of lamb or mutton in a red sauce made using the spicy but not intensely hot Kashmiri chili powder. The dish is originally from Kashmir in the northwest of the subcontinent, a region split between India and Pakistan during Partition. It is associated with the Persian style of cuisine introduced during the period of the Mughal Empire, which flourished in northern India from the 16th to the 18th century before it was absorbed into the British Raj in 1857.

A vindaloo that may have started off as a simple stew acquired more and more Indian flavorings over time, and today even the name vindaloo stands for "hot, hot, hot" the world over.

Madhur Jaffrey, Madhur Jaffrey's Ultimate Curry Bible

Apple Pie

Origin: All over the world

Date: 18th century

Type: Fruit in a pastry crust

✦ **CULTURAL**

✦ **SOCIAL**

✦ COMMERCIAL

✦ **POLITICAL**

✦ MILITARY

It could be argued that there is nothing specifically American about apple pie. The apple itself originally comes from Central Asia, in the mountainous regions of Kazakhstan and Kyrgyzstan, and pies of one sort or another have been made throughout history all over the world. Yet there is nowhere else in the world where apple pie is not only so highly appreciated but has come to be associated with what it means to come from that country.

AS AMERICAN AS...

Apple pie arrived in America with some of the first English Puritan colonists who landed in New England in the early 17th century and brought with them the foodstuffs and recipes of their homeland. As well as being present almost from the start of colonial America, an argument can be made that apple pie was involved, albeit peripherally, when the Thirteen Colonies rebelled against British rule during the American Revolutionary War, even if this relies on an extrapolation of the available evidence rather than any direct statements by those people involved. In this interpretation of events, the apple pies made by the Pennsylvanian Dutch are seen as the ones that have been taken to the hearts of the American people rather than those of English colonists because, of course, it was British rule that the revolutionaries were rebelling against.

By the time of the outbreak of the revolution in 1775, the Pennsylvanian Dutch made up about half of the total population of the state, having initially been attracted to emigrate there by the assurances of religious freedom and tolerance made by William Penn, the founder of the Province of Pennsylvania, almost a century before. Many of the immigrants who would become known as

Pie is the food of the heroic. No pie-eating people can ever be permanently vanquished.

From an editorial in The New York Times, *May 3rd, 1902*

the Pennsylvanian Dutch actually came from Germany, the name most likely being an anglicized version of Deutsch, but perhaps also a reminder of the original Dutch colony that had preceeded the English one. The level of immigration prompted by Penn made Philadelphia not only the largest city in Pennsylvania, but also in the Thirteen Colonies of colonial America, which, together with its relatively central location, led to it becoming the location of the First Continental Congress. It was convened on September 5th, 1774, as a meeting of the representatives of 12 of the colonies, Georgia having declined an invitation to attend because it was involved in a border war with Native American tribes and was seeking British help.

The purpose of the meeting was to discuss the response of the colonies to the British government's overbearing reaction to the events of the Boston Tea Party (see page 137), which had involved the introduction of the so-called Coercive Acts, a series of punitive measures taken against the colony of Massachusetts including closing the Port of Boston until compensation had been paid for the lost tea and the removal of self-governing powers to bring the colony under direct British rule. At the Congress, the delegates decided to institute a boycott of British goods and to petition King George III, then to meet again in May of the following year to discuss the results of their actions.

SHOOFLY PIE

✦

Another type of pie associated with the Pennsylvanian Dutch is the shoofly pie, made from a pastry crust filled with molasses and topped with a sugar, butter, and flour crumb. This is the traditional version, known as a "wet bottom" pie. There is also the "dry bottom" pie, in which the crumbs are mixed in with the molasses. It was originally a winter dish, made from ingredients from the store cupboard after apples and any other fillings had run out, and, according to one version of the story at least, it acquired its name because of the need to shoo flies away from it once it had been taken out of the oven.

By the time of the Second Continental Congress, attended by the representatives of all the colonies this time, fighting in the revolution had already broken out and the British had declared the rebels to be traitors, so its function became to act as a de facto government of the colonies, appointing George Washington as the commander in chief of the American forces and then beginning a debate on the issue of full independence from Britain. Much of this debate occurred in the taverns and coffeehouses of Philadelphia rather than in the formal setting of the Congress, where the delegates would no doubt have encountered the sort of apple pies made by the Pennsylvanian

Dutch, famous for their baking skills, even if they would have been unlikely to meet many of the people who actually made the pies because of their religious convictions and opposition to the demon drink.

After intense discussions during which many of the delegates who had initially wanted to remain a British colony came round to the idea of independence, a decision was taken for Thomas Jefferson to draw up the document that would become the Declaration of Independence. The first sentence of its preamble, not much remarked on at the time, would come to stand for the ethos of the new country of America:

> We hold these truths to be self-evident, that all men are created equal, that they are endowed by their Creator with certain unalienable Rights, that among these are Life, Liberty, and the pursuit of Happiness.

The declaration was signed by the men who would become known as the Founding Fathers on July 4th, 1776, and published shortly afterward. From then onward the Congress continued to meet in Philadelphia, moving occasionally to convene elsewhere when the city was threatened by British forces, but returning shortly afterward. In 1777, the Articles of Confederation were ratified, again after a period of intense debate, which after the revolution had been won would lead to the creation of the United States of America and the drafting of its constitution, the Congress itself evolving into the two chambers of the US Congress as it is today, the House of Representatives and the Senate.

THE ALL-AMERICAN PIE

Making an association between apple pie and the foundation of the USA based on the likelihood of the delegates eating Pennsylvanian Dutch pies and then returning to their various states with an idea of it in some way representing the values of the country they were founding is, it must be admitted, a little tenuous. Neither George Washington, John Adams, or Thomas Jefferson, the first three American presidents, made any great speeches extolling the virtues of pie or suggesting that it represented anything in particular to do with America and, in truth, it would not be until the late 19th century that such sentiments were expressed. By that time, America was transforming into an industrial and urban country, leaving its rural and small town roots behind, and the apple pie had become a symbol of the heritage of what was being left behind, perhaps in the hope that the values it represented would not be forgotten as the world moved on.

Home made pies made fresh daily. Children and political discussion encouraged.

Sign in the Bipartisan Cafe, Portland, Oregon, which sells 30 types of pie, including apple

As well as industrializing, America experienced large-scale immigration over the course of the 19th and 20th centuries from many different European countries. The immigrants all brought their own cultures and cuisines with them, everything thrown into the great melting pots of American cities and a blend emerging in which the components were still recognizable but had become individual parts of a distinct American culture. As far as food was concerned, hamburgers may have originally come from Germany and pizza from Italy, but both were taken up by people of all different ethnicities and converted into their own food in a way that would become typically American. But amongst the great variety of national cuisines and individual dishes that now made up American food, apple pie was different. Almost every immigrant group had brought an apple pie of one sort or another with them, whether they came from Britain, Ireland, Germany, Italy, or anywhere else. It was, and still is, the universal food among all the diversity, demonstrating another self-evident truth about America — that everybody loves pie.

SLICE OF PIE
Everybody loves apple pie, including this young lady in a photograph from 1950s America.

American Whiskey

Origin: America

Date: 18th century

Type: Grain spirit

Over the course of the 18th century whiskey gradually replaced rum as the spirit of choice in Britain's American colonies, in part because of the number of Scottish and Irish immigrants who began to arrive, bringing their methods of distilling grains with them, and also because, as the colonies expanded into the interior, the grains needed to make whiskey could be grown at home while molasses to make rum had to be imported. By the time of the revolution in 1775, rum had also taken on associations with the British government and its attempt to impose an import duty on molasses, leading to the homegrown whiskey becoming the preferred drink of the rebels.

THE WHISKEY REBELLION

Following the British surrender at Yorktown on October 19th, 1781, no more serious fighting in the American Revolutionary War would occur, but it would take almost two years for peace negotiations to be concluded. In September 1783, Britain signed the peace agreement, formally recognizing the existence of the United States of America, allowing George Washington, the commander in chief of the American forces, to disband the American army and, to the surprise of many, retire to Mount Vernon, his estate on the banks of the Potomac River in Virginia. He was persuaded, apparently against his will, to return to public life at the Constitutional Convention held in Philadelphia in May 1787, being elected to preside over the convention, which established the Articles of the US Constitution.

One of the Articles made provision for the election of a president, a position held for two terms by Washington before he decided to retire for a second time in 1797, setting a precedent for the number of terms served by American presidents that endures today. Back at Mount Vernon, he began to distill whiskey as a business venture, making a good profit from the first batch, and is said to have been relieved to leave behind him the political world of Philadelphia (Congress had not yet moved to Washington DC, which was under construction at that time). One of the distasteful issues he had dealt with during his presidency had also involved whiskey, on that occasion a dispute over duties imposed on whiskey distillers by the

GEORGE WASHINGTON
The Whiskey Rebellion
(1819), attributed to
Frederick Kemmelmeyer.
It is the only time a
sitting US president has
commanded an army
in the field.

federal government, which had escalated into an armed rebellion, demonstrating that the citizens of the new republic were no keener on paying taxes than they had been under British rule.

The roots of the Whiskey Rebellion, as it became known, were in the need of the federal government to raise revenue after the new US Constitution had been ratified in 1789, giving it the authority to impose taxes that had not been part of the previous Articles of Constitution. As a result, the new government had been constituted with a large national debt to service and no means of doing so, a situation made worse by a sudden increase in the number of counterfeit copper coins in circulation, causing a loss of confidence in the value of copper and in the currency as a whole. In March 1791, Washington's close associate Alexander Hamilton, the Secretary of State for the Treasury, oversaw the passage of the Whiskey Act through Congress, leading to the implementation of a law which, for the first time since the Revolution, levied taxes on American citizens.

The new law proved to be unpopular, as all taxes tend to be. It was seen by some veterans of the revolution as a tax levied by the federal government without the agreement of local state legislatures, leading them to draw comparisons between it and the imposition of taxation under British rule, which had occurred without consulting the colonies. It was not an entirely valid argument, the federal government, after all, being made up of elected representatives of the people, but it raised an important issue concerning the role of central government in America and what the division of power should be between the federal and state governments.

More specific grievances were expressed by those farmers in the western counties of the states who distilled whiskey on a relatively small scale and considered that the real reason for the Whiskey Act was to protect the larger distilling companies in the east from competition. Under the terms of the act, duty could either be paid on the amount of whiskey distilled or as a single flat fee, clearly favoring those larger operations that could afford a one-off payment because, the more whiskey they made, the less tax they paid per gallon. It led to accusations of collusion between Hamilton and the distilling companies, heightening the tension, which was then increased further still as federal government officials appointed by Washington attempted to collect the taxes.

By 1794, some of the protests had turned violent and, in August, reached a peak when more than 6,000 people congregated at Braddock's Field in western Pennsylvania, not far from Pittsburgh, in what appeared to be the beginning of an armed insurrection. Washington sent negotiators to Braddock's Field in an effort to find a solution to the protest, but when no progress was made and when some of the protestors began to demand that the western counties break away from the Union, he called up militias from a number of states in order to put down the insurrection by force if that became necessary. Washington and Hamilton both traveled west to join the militia camp, composed of about 13,000 men, and Washington took charge in what has been described as the only occasion when an American president has commanded an army in the field while in office.

Washington described the insurrection as being a serious test of the US Constitution in which a small number of protestors were attempting to dictate terms to the American people, but in the event, and as he had predicted, a show of overwhelming force caused the crowds to disperse with very little trouble. Nevertheless, the Whiskey Rebellion was the largest insurrection on American soil between the Revolutionary War and the Civil War, which also began as a disagreement between the federal government and a number of states, even if on this occasion the cause of the dispute was slavery rather than whiskey.

PROHIBITION

In some respects, the implementation of Prohibition in America in 1920 was an almost exact opposite to what had occurred during the Whiskey Rebellion. It involved a protest group, in this case the temperance movement, lobbying the federal government in order to achieve its aims and succeeding despite widespread opposition. The motivation behind the movement was largely a religious one that saw almost all the ills of society as being a consequence of alcohol, particularly hard liquors like whiskey, and the momentum toward a ban had grown for several decades before the outbreak of the First World War, which then provided further impetus to the movements as campaigners argued that alcohol was harming the war effort. In the end, legislation intended to curtail drinking while the war was being fought was not passed before the fighting was over, but by that time the Prohibitionists had converted enough members of the US Congress to their cause for the process toward a ban to continue.

Once, during Prohibition, I was forced to live for days on nothing but food and water.
W. C. Fields

The Eighteenth Amendment to the US Constitution was eventually ratified in January 1920, making the manufacture, transport, and sale of all alcoholic beverages illegal, but not consumption of it in the home. It was accompanied by the Volstead Act, which came into force on January 17th and contained the details of how Prohibition was to be enforced as well as defining exactly what was

PROHIBITION BITES
Government agents watch as a barrel of confiscated beer is poured down the drain in New York in about 1921.

being banned. Protests began almost immediately among
people who considered that the federal government had no
business interfering in their lives in such a way and among
those who may have been less ideologically motivated but
nevertheless enjoyed a drink. The law was also thought by some people
to favor wealthy people, who could stock up on alcoholic drinks and hold
parties in their homes, while ordinary people who could not afford such
luxuries were the ones who were losing out.

The ban was effective up to a point, cutting alcohol consumption by
about a half, but it would also create conditions in which many people
would attempt to get around a law they did not support, in effect crim-
inalizing a large proportion of American society, most of whom had
previously been entirely law abiding. It also had the unforeseen consequence of leading to a dramatic rise in organized crime as gangsters
took over the manufacture and distribution operations formerly run by
legitimate companies. A further outcome was that the American public
not only began to tolerate the involvement of criminals in the liquor
trade, but in some cases even began to admire gangsters for providing a
service denied to them by the government. The extent of the criminal-
ity created by the Volstead Act meant that there were not enough
enforcement officers to police it, so bootlegging across America's borders with Canada and Mexico and the distilling of illegal moonshine
became widespread, while speakeasies opened up in cities across America to sell illicitly acquired alcohol.

The role of Prohibition in allowing organized crime to flourish in
America is exemplified by the rise of Al Capone, who began his criminal

AL CAPONE
Capone and the Chicago
Outfit made a fortune
bootlegging alcohol during
Prohibition.

career as a small-time gangster in New York before moving
to Chicago in 1920 to take advantage of the opportunity presented by Prohibition of bootlegging alcohol across the Canadian border. Through a combination of audacity, brutality,
and the corruption of state officials, Capone and his associates,
the Chicago Outfit, came to control the alcohol supply across a
wide area of eastern USA, raking in millions of dollars
and using some of the profit to pay off as many policemen and
politicians as was necessary. Over the course of the 1920s he
amassed enormous personal wealth, making an estimated $100
million from bootlegging in 1925 alone.

During the presidential election campaign of 1932, Franklin D. Roosevelt made the repeal of Prohibition one of the
central tenets of his candidacy so that it became a run-off
between the Democrat "wets" and the Republican "drys."

Roosevelt went on to win a landslide victory in part because of his stance on Prohibition, but also because his opponent, President Herbert Hoover, was widely perceived as having been ineffective in dealing with the disastrous economic situation of the country during what would become known as the Great Depression. On being inaugurated as president in March 1933, Roosevelt immediately began to implement the policies of the New Deal in an effort to get the economy going again and, within a few weeks, had amended the Volstead Act to allow beer to be manufactured and sold. In December of that same year, the Eighteenth Amendment was repealed by the Twenty-first Amendment, bringing the era of Prohibition to an end and giving public finances a significant boost with the tax revenue that began to flow in from the sale of alcohol.

By the time Prohibition was lifted, Capone was in jail after being convicted on charges of tax evasion and was no longer the powerful figure in organized crime he had previously been. But the end of the black market in alcohol was by no means the end of the crime syndicates that had grown up across America, many of which had come under the control of the Sicilian mafia and, even before Prohibition was lifted, had diversified into all sorts of other illegal activity, such as racketeering and loan-sharking, and would later become major players in the drug trade.

The Prohibition era in America only lasted for 13 years but it had an enormous impact on the country that would go on for many years afterward, unleashing a crime wave that, it could be argued, continues in some respects today. Since the Twenty-first Amendment came into law, any further legislation on Prohibition has been left to individual states by the federal government and, while none have enacted laws on a state-wide basis, there remain numerous dry counties across America. One of these is Moore County, Tennessee, the location of the city of Lynchburg and the Jack Daniel's distillery, which means that its Tennessee whiskey can be enjoyed in bars around the world but not in the county where it is made.

THE MANHATTAN

◆

The Manhattan is one of the classic cocktails, made from five parts American whiskey to one of sweet vermouth (or any other ratio, depending on taste), with a few drops of Angostura bitters and garnished with a maraschino cherry. Traditionalists say that it should be made with rye whiskey, but these days bourbon and Tennessee whiskey are commonly used as well and, to tell the truth, after a couple it's hard to spot the difference.

Madeleines

Origin: France

Date: 19th century

Type: Small sponge cake

CULTURAL
+ SOCIAL
+ COMMERCIAL
+ POLITICAL
+ MILITARY

The little sponge cakes called madeleines in France are not at first glance obvious candidates for a food that has changed the course of history and, in truth, no wars have been fought or revolutions begun over them. But these unassuming scallop-shaped cakes have had an enormous impact on the history of literature in France and around the rest of the world after Marcel Proust wrote about them in one of the most celebrated episodes of his major work, *À la recherche du temps perdu*, originally translated into English as *Remembrance of Things Past* and more recently as *In Search of Lost Time*, so that now it would not be unreasonable to say that, once Proust's narrator had encountered a madeleine, the modern novel as we know it today was born.

THE EPISODE OF THE MADELEINE

One of the reasons why the episode of the madeleine has become so widely known is because it occurs toward the start of the first of seven volumes. Many people have embarked on the enormous undertaking of reading the 3,000-page novel, no doubt intending to read it all because of its status as a masterpiece of French literature, but not quite so many have got to the end. But the episode also introduces one of the major themes of the novel, the role of memories in our lives and the way in which these can be triggered by sensory experiences. In this case, the narrator, who is called Marcel and is clearly based on Proust himself, eats a madeleine that he has dipped into his cup of tea and experiences a strange sensation that he at first does not understand until he comes to realize that the particular taste of the tea combined with crumbs of the cake has unlocked hidden memories from his childhood, a period of his life that, he says, he had otherwise left long behind him.

> **No sooner had the warm liquid mixed with the crumbs touched my palate than a shudder ran through me and I stopped, intent upon the extraordinary thing that was happening to me.**
>
> *Marcel Proust*, In Search of Lost Time

This small and apparently insignificant episode eventually leads to a flood of memories, propelling the narrator through multiple narratives that switch between the present and what are sometimes half-remembered past experiences, many of which are prompted by further sensory stimuli. Proust described these episodes as being examples of "involuntary memory," a term now used in psychology for recollections of the past that arise without any deliberate or conscious attempt to remember them. In using such literary techniques as involuntary memories and by exploring the inner emotional lives of his characters, Proust breaks from the formal devices used in the plot-driven novels of the 19th century, pre-empting the later work of modernist writers like James Joyce, and Virginia Woolf, who acknowledged the influence of Proust's writing on her own.

Anybody eating a madeleine today could be forgiven for wondering what all the fuss is about. It is a quite plain little sponge cake, made in the style of a genoise, the type of cake named after the Italian city of Genoa and common in French baking. It is made by what is known as the batter method, which involves beating air into the cake mixture to ensure that the resulting cakes will have a light texture and the mixture is then sometimes flavored with lemon or almond before being baked in trays with scallop-shaped molds pressed into them.

Proust is said to have changed his mind on a number of occasions about the type of cake eaten by his narrator, suggesting that he had not based this particular episode in his novel on an autobiographical detail, even if the setting where many of the recollections take place, the fictional town of Combray, is in part based on the French town of Illiers, where he had spent long periods living as a child. In 1971, the town officially changed its name to Illiers-Combray to mark the centenary of Proust's birth and perhaps also in the event that any Proust enthusiasts who were considering following in the footsteps of the author and needed their memories jogged about his connection to the town.

LAMINGTONS

✦

An Australian may not have much of a reaction to a madeleine, but could possibly experience a Proustian moment over a lamington, a small square of sponge cake that has been coated in chocolate icing and then sprinkled with desiccated coconut. It appears to have been named after Charles Cochrane-Baillie, Lord Lamington, who was the Governor of Queensland from 1896 to 1901, but exactly why it has since achieved such iconic status in Australia is rather more mysterious.

Caviar

Origin: Caspian Sea

Date: 19th century

Type: Cured sturgeon roe

> I heard thee speak me a speech once, but it was never acted, or if it was, not above once; for the play, I remember, pleas'd not the million, 'twas caviare to the general.
>
> *William Shakespeare*, Hamlet

Caviar is the salt-cured roe of any species of sturgeon, but it is most closely associated with the three that inhabit the Caspian Sea: the beluga, ossetra, and sevruga. During the second half of the 19th century caviar from these three fish began to appear in Western Europe in greater quantity and of better quality than had been the case in the past, acquiring an image of being a prestigious and luxury food because of its links with the fabulously wealthy tsars of Russia. This led to a caviar boom that had a devastating impact on the sturgeon from the Caspian and in other parts of the world.

+ **CULTURAL**
+ SOCIAL
+ **COMMERCIAL**
+ POLITICAL
+ MILITARY

THE CAVIAR RUSH

In 1556, the Russian tsar Ivan the Terrible conquered the steppe region to the north of the Caspian Sea, enormously extending the Russian Empire and, as well as capturing the city of Astrakhan in the Volga delta, he acquired the sturgeon fishery on the river. It was the beginning of the link between caviar and imperial Russia that would continue right up to the end of the Romanov Dynasty in 1917 and would come to define their lavish and opulent lifestyles, which were based on the enormous wealth generated by the territorial expansions that continued during the reigns of Peter the Great and Catherine the Great in the 18th century, providing them with apparently inexhaustible natural resources.

Caviar was known outside Russia during this period, but for the most part only by those who had visited the country or as pressed caviar, a compacted and heavily salted version in which the fish eggs have burst, giving the caviar a jam-like consistency. It was the only way caviar could be transported over the huge distances involved in getting it to Europe without it spoiling, the far superior black caviar, which is not pressed and only lightly salt-cured, being too delicate to survive such a long journey. The situation was transformed by the opening of a railway line linking the Volga with the River Don in 1859, which created a route by ship and train from the sturgeon fisheries to the Black Sea into the Mediterranean, a journey made even faster by the introduction of steamships. It allowed for the export of the best caviar, causing a sensation in Paris, and a boom in sales in the city, which, as Paris was the most fashionable city in the world at that time, was repeated across Europe and crossed the Atlantic to America.

A number of different species of sturgeon inhabit the Great Lakes of America and swim up the rivers of both the East and West Coasts, but they were not highly regarded by fishermen until what became known as the Caviar Rush began.

STURGEON FISHING
A huge beluga sturgeon being dragged out of a boat on the Volga River in a French illustration from 1867.

Sturgeon that had previously been all but ignored were fished in the Hudson and Delaware rivers, reaching a peak in the 1880s when, as well as selling to an ever-increasing domestic market, American caviar was exported to Europe, only for some, it is reputed, to be labeled there as Russian caviar and be sent back to America to be sold at a higher price. By the turn of the 20th century, the scale of the fishing had caused a dramatic decline in the sturgeon populations in the rivers and lakes of America, but by that time wealthy Americans had developed a taste for caviar and, as the sales of the home-produced version fell away as controls were placed on fishing, more and more Caspian caviar began to be imported.

The demand from Europe and America for the best quality caviar had the inevitable consequence of overfishing on the Volga, but rather than reduce the pressure on the fish, Volga fishermen began to take sturgeon from the Caspian Sea as well as from the river, leading to a situation where Caspian sturgeon would have become extinct had it not been for the Russian Revolution in 1917 and the subsequent introduction of strict regulations by officials of the Soviet Union. The collapse of the Soviet Union in 1991 would have the opposite result, opening up a black market in caviar that led to extensive poaching on the Caspian Sea. All three of the Caspian sturgeon are now considered to be critically endangered in the wild, particularly the beluga, the most highly sought after, and almost all caviar now being sold comes from farmed fish.

MAKING CAVIAR

✦

To make caviar, the roe must be removed from the sturgeon before it dies, otherwise enzymes in the dead fish will spoil the flavor. The roe is then sieved to separate the eggs from the surrounding membrane and washed to remove any impurities, before being salted and packed into cans which are then stored for up to a year at a temperature slightly below freezing point while the curing process takes place. It is not a complicated process, but it is said to take a caviar maker years to gain the necessary experience to perfect it.

Bananas

Origin: Southeast Asia

Date: 19th century

Type: Fruit

* CULTURAL
* SOCIAL
* **COMMERCIAL**
* **POLITICAL**
* MILITARY

THE TELEGRAPH
The schooner captained by
Lorenzo Dow Baker shown
in 1872 taking on a cargo
of bananas in Jamaica.

At the Centennial Exposition, the World's Fair held in Philadelphia in 1876, Alexander Graham Bell stole the show with one of the first public demonstrations of the telephone, while the Heinz Company unveiled the latest of its 57 varieties, tomato ketchup. In the Horticultural Hall, an unusual plant may not have been causing quite such a stir, but the banana tree, more correctly described in botanical terms as a large herbaceous flowering plant, was provoking curiosity as well, particularly because its exotic fruit was also on sale at 10¢ each.

UNITED FRUIT

The bananas at the exposition were not the first to be seen in America. Small numbers were brought into the country by seamen returning from the Caribbean, including in 1870 by Lorenzo Dow Baker, a ship's captain from Boston. After becoming aware of the potential market in his home port, Baker established a business importing bananas from Jamaica, selling them on the dockside in Boston because the length of the voyage meant that the fruit would not last long before spoiling. He went into partnership with Andrew Preston, a grocery wholesaler, and a group of investors to establish the Boston Fruit Company. By using steamships to bring the fruit in, he cut the journey time from the Caribbean in half. Preston was responsible for introducing a system of refrigerated transport in steamships and railway boxcars, together with cold-storage warehouses, which allowed the company to begin selling bananas over a much larger part of America, the beginnings of the distribution network for the fruit that is in use today.

The Tropical Trading and Transport Company had been set up a few years after Baker began his banana importing business by Minor C. Keith and had become the Boston Fruit Company's main competition. Keith had worked in Costa Rica on the construction of a railway line and, when the government had been unable to continue financing the project, had reached an agreement in which he would be given ownership of a huge quantity of land by the tracks if he finished the railway. He set up extensive banana plantations and imported the fruit to America through New Orleans, but had taken out huge loans in order to do so that, by 1899, caused his business to get into serious financial difficulties. Bradley Palmer, a lawyer working for Henry Preston, devised a merger between the rival companies that would sort out Keith's financial problems and create a new company that could dominate the banana trade in the Caribbean and Central America, while, at the same time, control the distribution system throughout America.

Time flies like an arrow.
Fruit flies like a banana.

Groucho Marx

The new United Fruit Company began to acquire huge tracts of land in Central and South America, establishing banana plantations in, amongst others, Honduras, Guatemala, and Columbia, and taking an 80 percent share of a rapidly increasing banana market in America. The scale of its operations and the low labor costs it incurred in what were then some of the poorest regions of the Americas meant that bananas were not only plentiful, but also cheaper than other fruit, often being half the price of the apples and oranges grown in America. The size of the company and their extensive holdings in relatively underdeveloped countries allowed it to become

BANANA WAREHOUSE
United Fruit Company workers in America in 1948 packing ripe bananas into boxes to be sent out to stores.

very powerful, dictating the conditions under which it operated, which usually involved the payment of little or no tax and having very few restrictions placed on what it could do or on the working conditions it could impose on its employees.

When the countries where it held holdings did not cooperate, United Fruit worked alongside the US government to put pressure on them in order to secure their acceptance of the company's demands, regularly resorting to both hard and soft interventions in the political processes of these countries by the US military, diplomatic, and intelligence services and leading to some states becoming known as "banana republics." One of the most notorious examples came in Guatemala in 1954, when the CIA conducted a covert operation to remove the democratically elected left-wing government of President

Jacobo Árbenz and install a military dictatorship in its place that was more amenable to American, and United Fruit's, interests.

At the time of the *coup d'état* against Árbenz, United Fruit owned more than 40 percent of the arable land in Guatemala, much of it held as an investment asset rather than being cultivated because of the spread of a fungal infection called Panama disease, which had devastated the banana crop in Central America in the previous few years. After winning the presidential election in 1951, Árbenz had instituted a program of land reform aimed at seizing uncultivated land on large estates and giving it to the landless poor.

> **The Guatemalans resented the fact that their nation was, in most respects, little more than a giant, foreign-owned banana plantation.**
>
> *Dan Koeppel*, Banana: The Fate of the Fruit That Changed the World

The owners of the land were to be paid compensation calculated on valuations taken from their tax returns and, since United Fruit hardly paid any tax, the amount they were due to receive for their seized holdings was much less than its true worth.

United Fruit enjoyed very close relations with the US government, to the point where the difference between official government foreign policy in Central America and the interests of the company were almost indistinguishable, so, when the CIA's role in the coup in Guatemala was later revealed, the agency was accused of working in the sole interests of United Fruit. It claimed the coup had been orchestrated as part of its overall anti-communist agenda in Central America and attempted to demonstrate that the Árbenz government was little more than a puppet state of the Soviet Union, but the evidence it presented to support this claim was not overly convincing.

BANANA PLANTATION
Aerial photograph taken in 1953 of a United Fruit banana plantation in Guatemala, showing the living quarters for workers.

The coup led to a long period of military dictatorship in Guatemala, which only came to an end in 1991, and the continuation of a civil war that had begun in 1944 and went on until a peace settlement was finally achieved in 1996. United Fruit has undergone a number of name changes over the course of the past few decades, but retains extensive holdings in Central and South America and is still the largest player in the banana market in the world, these days selling the fruit under the brand name of Chiquita.

THE CAVENDISH

The banana is by a long way the best-selling fruit in the world today, estimated to be the fourth most valuable cultivated crop of any description, after rice, wheat, and corn. Across the tropical regions of the world, many different varieties are grown, mostly on a small scale and for local consumption, while the commercial market is dominated by a single variety called the Cavendish. The advantage of planting only one variety is that, once a crop has been picked, the fruits ripen together at a predictable rate so the distributors and retailers know exactly how long they have to sell their produce before it starts to go bad. The downside is that all Cavendish bananas are genetically identical, the plants being propagated by vegetative means so they are effectively clones, making them vulnerable to disease, particularly when grown in extensive monocrops, as they are on plantations.

Up until the 1950s, commercially grown bananas were almost all of a different variety, known as the Gros Michel, which proved to be highly susceptible to Panama disease. It wiped out crops across the world, making the continuing use of Gros Michel unviable, and it was replaced by the Cavendish because it showed a much greater degree of resistance to the disease. In recent years the Cavendish has come under threat from a different fungal disease called Black Sigatoka, which is spreading through the banana-producing nations and has the potential to have the same devastating effect on the Cavendish as Panama disease did on the Gros Michel. Research on developing a resistant strain of the Cavendish and attempts to breed a new resistant variety have so far failed to find a suitable replacement, which must meet commercial criteria as well as not being affected by either Panama disease or Black Sigatoka. Until a solution to this problem is found, the possibility exists of commercial banana-growing as we know it today coming to an end.

GROWING BANANAS
Bunches of immature Cavendish bananas growing in the flower of a tree in Brazil.

DOLE

✦

United Fruit, now Chiquita, has been the largest commercial company involved in the banana trade since it was formed in 1899, but there have also been others. Today, the second largest is the Dole Food Company, a huge American multinational that began trading in Hawaiian pineapples in the 19th century and in the 1960s acquired the Standard Fruit Company, United Fruit's main competitor, which was originally set up in 1924 and was involved in the banana business in a number of Central American countries.

Corned Beef

Origin: South America

Date: 19th century

Type: Canned salt-cured beef

Corned beef got its name from the grains of salt, known as "corns," that were used to cure the cooked and ground meat before it was pressed and canned. In America, the name is also used for joints of beef, usually brisket, that have been cooked in brine, called salt beef in Britain. In this chapter we concentrate on the canned version that became an essential part of the rations of the British Army from the Boer War to the Second World War.

FRAY BENTOS

In Britain, the vast majority of people would most likely associate the name Fray Bentos with a brand of corned beef and meat pies rather than a town in Uruguay. It is actually a port on the Uruguay River, which forms the border between Uruguay and Argentina and opens out into the estuary of the River Plate. The location would prove to be a good one for the Liebig's Extract of Meat Company after it decided to set up a meat-packing factory in the town in 1863 because the River Plate cuts into the huge area of open grassland, the pampas, where extensive cattle ranches known as *estancias* had been established.

Until industrial canning and refrigeration methods were developed in the later 19th century, the cattle on these *estancias* were primarily raised for their hides, much of the meat going to waste. It provided Liebig's with a large resource of very cheap beef that was initially used to make meat extract using an industrial method developed by the German chemist and founder of the company Justus von Liebig. In 1873, the company installed a canning plant and began to produce corned beef, most of which, in common with the meat extract, was exported to Europe, and then in 1899 a dried version of the meat extract that would become known as Oxo in Britain.

By 1900, Liebig's factory in Fray Bentos was the largest meat-packing enterprise in South America, attracting immigrants from all over the world and leading to cattle ranching becoming one of Uruguay's most important businesses. A company town was built along the banks of the river, including a

hospital and school as well as houses for the workers in the factory, which became known as Barrio Anglo (English Town) after Liebig's was bought by the Vestey Brothers in 1924 and the name of the company changed to Frigorífico Anglo del Uruguay, or El Anglo for short. William and Edmund Vestey were originally from Liverpool and had made their fortunes importing meat into Britain, operating their own shipping company, the Blue Star Line, and buying ranches in South America. Their company had developed a business relationship with Liebig's to supply fresh meat as well as corned beef to the British Army and Navy during the First World War, using their own fleet of refrigerated ships to transport the meat across the Atlantic. Over the course of the war they also became involved in a number of meat-packing businesses in America and Canada as well as in South America. Supplying meat to the British public as well as to the military proved to be highly lucrative, but it came with serious risks, chief among them the threat of attack from German U-boats as the ships carrying the meat crossed the Atlantic Ocean.

**All men will get two biscuits each,
I'm sure you're tired of bread,
I'm sorry there's no turkey
but there's Bully Beef instead.**

From Christmas Day on the Somme *by Leslie Rub,
an Australian soldier who died in 1917 during
the Third Battle of Ypres.*

BULLY BEEF

Over the course of the 19th century, the population of Britain grew by more than four times, from about nine million in 1801 to over 40 million by the end of the century. By that time, almost half of the country's food was being imported, including most of the wheat to make bread from America and Canada as well as large quantities of meat and other

HOT RATIONS
British soldiers eating their rations in October 1916 during the Battle of Ancre Heights, part of the Somme offensive.

foodstuffs. The situation was similar in Germany, the population of the country having increased from about 40 million at its unification in 1871 to 65 million at the outbreak of the First World War. During peacetime, it was not difficult for both countries to import as much food as was required, but once the war had broken out there was the additional problem of keeping the armed services fed as well as the civilian population. The situation became more serious

by 1915, by which time a stalemate of static trench warfare had developed on the Western Front in France and Belgium. It had become apparent that the war would be both long and involve armies composed of millions of men, all of whom would have to be fed. "Bully beef," as the soldiers of the British Army called corned beef, was issued as part of standard rations and also made up a part of the iron rations carried by each soldier in case they became isolated during a battle. Corned beef was almost ideal for this purpose; it did not go bad quickly and was packed in durable cans, allowing soldiers to eat it straight out of the can if necessary. Over the course of the war, Britain imported huge quantities of it, the largest supplier being the Fray Bentos factory in Uruguay, but it was also sourced from other operations in Brazil and Argentina, with a significant amount coming from America and Canada as well.

THE SUPPLY WAR

As soon as war was declared in September 1914, the Royal Navy imposed a blockade on the major German ports on the North Sea and Baltic Sea coasts to cut off Germany's supply lines. The superiority of the Royal Navy's surface fleet meant that the Germany Navy could not break the blockade or carry out a surface campaign against shipping carrying cargo to Britain. In the years leading up to the war, Germany had begun to develop its submarine fleet and in February 1915, once it had become obvious that the war would not be over quickly, it responded to the blockade on its ports by declaring unrestricted submarine warfare in the North Atlantic against cargo vessels of any nationality.

THE LUSITANIA
A painting of the sinking of the *Lusitania* by a German U-boat, which caused outrage in Britain and America.

It was an attempt to stop, or at least restrict, war materials and food supplies crossing the Atlantic to Britain and involved Germany's U-boats attacking vessels in the declared war zone without warning. In May 1915, a U-boat torpedoed and sank the *Lusitania*, a British-owned ocean liner, off the coast of Ireland with the loss of 1,198 lives, 128 of whom were American citizens. The *Lusitania* had also been carrying a cargo of munitions, which technically made it a legitimate target, but the sinking and loss of life caused outrage in Britain and America. President Woodrow Wilson resisted calls for an immediate American declaration of war against Germany, but after an exchange of terse diplomatic messages between the two countries, he made it clear that he would regard any further attacks against American citizens or shipping as being "deliberately unfriendly."

In early 1916, the Germans suspended their campaign of unrestricted submarine warfare because of the very real fear that it would provoke the Americans into joining the war on the side of the Allies, but they continued with the covert operations they had initiated within America itself, in which secret agents attempted to sabotage factories producing war materials and the transport network used to carry cargo to Britain. In 1914, Franz von Papen, the German military attaché in Washington, had recruited agents to carry out an attack on the Welland Canal, the Canadian waterway linking Lake Erie with Lake Ontario that was used by ships carrying goods produced in the factories of the industrial cities in the north of America, including the meat-packers Armour & Company, a major supplier of corned beef to the British Army. The plan was aborted before being carried out, but was revealed to the British after Horst von der Goltz, one of the secret agents involved, was captured by the British in 1915 on a spying mission in London and offered the choice of talking or facing the firing squad.

The British sent von der Goltz back to America in 1916 for trial on charges of sabotage, allowing him to talk to an American reporter on the voyage across the Atlantic so that details of German secret missions in the country would

GERMAN MENACE
A US Navy recruiting poster from 1917 showing an evil Germany wading through a sea of dead bodies.

SPAM

✦

In the Second World War, tins of Spam joined corned beef in the rations of British soldiers. It was made by George A. Hormel & Company in Austin, Minnesota, as it still is today, and transported across the Atlantic Ocean in merchant ships that were formed into convoys and protected from U-boat attack by naval ships. It was the beginning of a love–hate relationship between the British and the tins of chopped spiced ham that continues today, even if Spam fritters, deep-fried battered Spam, are not as popular now as they used to be.

become public. Stories of German "dyna-miters" filled the pages of the newspapers so that when an enormous explosion ripped through the railroad yards on Black Tom Island in New York Harbor, where explosives were being stored prior to being shipped to Britain, it was immediately assumed to be the work of German agents. The subsequent investigation established that the fires that had caused the explosion were started deliberately, but could not determine who was responsible, even if suspicions of German involvement remained.

As well as targeting the USA, German agents were also working in South America, attempting to sabotage ships carrying supplies that were sailing out of ports along the eastern coast of the continent. One of the most successful was Fritz Duquesne, an Afrikaner who had fought against the British during the Boer War and whose mother and sister had both died as a consequence of the scorched earth policy the British had adopted toward the end of that war. He was implicated in the sinking of at least 15 ships, even if it is difficult to know for certain exactly which acts of sabotage were his work. The method he employed was to pose as a mining engineer in order to stow what he described as mineral samples in the holds of ships that were actually bombs timed to go off after the ships had left harbor.

At the beginning of February 1917, the Germans decided to renew their campaign of unrestricted submarine warfare, gambling that, even if America was provoked into declaring war, by the time it was prepared to actually fight Britain would have run out of supplies and would at the very least be forced to negotiate a peace settlement before the huge potential of America in both manpower and industrial capacity could affect the course of the war. As German U-boats began to sink commercial vessels again, President Wilson immediately severed diplomatic relations with Germany.

A few weeks later the British passed on the contents of a telegram they had intercepted and decoded that had been sent by the German foreign minister Arthur Zimmermann to the German ambassador in

Mexico. The Zimmermann Telegram, as it is now known, contained a German offer to the Mexican government of a military alliance that would, in the event of America entering the war, entail German support for Mexico to regain those territories it had lost to America over the course of the 19th century if the Mexicans undertook to attack America as a means of forcing it to keep its armed forces at home rather than sending them to Europe. The Mexicans ignored the German offer, having no intention of attacking their much more powerful neighbor, but after the details were leaked to the press in America it caused outrage, which, when taken together with the increasing number of ships being sunk in the Atlantic by U-boats, was an important influence on public opinion and on the subsequent decision taken on April 6th, 1917, of the US government to declare war on Germany.

A succession of U-boat attacks on Brazilian merchant ships carrying goods either to America or to Britain resulted in a Brazilian declaration of war against Germany a few months after the Americans. The main contribution made to the Allied war effort was in providing naval ships to help escort convoys of merchant ships across the Atlantic. After it had been adopted in June 1917, the convoy system proved to be an effective measure in countering the German U-boat campaign, which did not succeed in preventing sufficient supplies from reaching Britain. Soldiers in Allied trenches continued to receive their rations, including the cans of bully beef from the other side of the Atlantic, while German rations began to diminish in 1917 and 1918, contributing to the lowering of morale that is said by some military historians to have occurred in the summer of 1918 and been an important factor in bringing the war to an end.

BOVRIL

✦

Johnston's Fluid Beef, as Bovril was originally called, is a meat extract first made by John Lawson Johnston in the 1870s after he won a contract to supply the French Army. During the First World War, it became a staple of the British Army, when it was used to make an instant version of beef tea by simply adding hot water. After the war, the drink would become an institution for many spectators at soccer matches, as it still is today, drunk for the same reason as it had been in the trenches; to keep out the winter chills.

Jaffa Orange

Origin: Near the city of Jaffa

Date: By the mid-19th century

Type: Fruit

✦ CULTURAL

✦ SOCIAL

✦ **COMMERCIAL**

✦ **POLITICAL**

✦ MILITARY

In the arcane world of cricket terminology, "bowling a Jaffa" means that the bowler has sent down an unplayable delivery. The ball may not actually get the batsman out, but if he survives it is considered to be more a result of luck than judgment. The use of the name of a particular type of orange to signify a great piece of bowling is thought to have arisen because Jaffas were considered to be the best oranges available to buy. It also gives a hint of the history between Britain and the city of Jaffa, the place where the oranges come from, which at one time was in the Ottoman province of Southern Syria, then part of British Mandatory Palestine and has, since 1948, been in the State of Israel.

THE SHAMOUTI

Orange-growing was introduced to the region around the ancient city of Jaffa at some time after the Arab invasion of the Levantine territory of the Byzantine Empire in the 7th century. Oranges were originally a bitter fruit, grown for their essential oils and as a flavoring, and more recently to make marmalade. The sweet orange did not appear until about the 15th century. By the 1850s, Arab growers had established the particular variety of sweet orange, the Shamouti, which would later be given the commercial name of Jaffa after the city from where it was exported. As well as having a good flavor, the Shamouti had a relatively thick skin that protected it while it was being transported and was almost seedless, making it the perfect fruit for the export market, and from about 1870 onward the trade to European countries expanded.

By that time, the city of Jaffa, in common with many other port cities around the Mediterranean, had a cosmopolitan culture, comprising significant communities of Christians and Jews as well as Muslims. The prosperity that had developed as a result of the orange trade and other commercial activities conducted through the port attracted many more people to the city, leading to its expansion and, in the 1880s, to the establishment of a Jewish suburb to the north of the old city that would become Tel Aviv. By this time, an increasing number of Jewish immigrants were arriving at the port of Jaffa from different parts of the world, including Ashkenazi Jews from Russia and Eastern Europe who were escaping persecution and had, to an extent at least, been inspired by the rise of Zionism, the movement to establish a Jewish homeland.

THE BRITISH MANDATE

Jaffa had been within the Ottoman Empire since it had been captured from the Mamluk Sultanate of Egypt in 1516 and would remain part of the empire for 400 years. During the First World War, the Ottomans sided with the Central Powers of Germany and Austria–Hungary, which would lead to a disastrous attempt by British and French forces to invade the Gallipoli Peninsula to the west of Constantinople, as Istanbul was then called, and British support for the Arab Revolt in the Arabian Peninsula made famous by the exploits of Lawrence of Arabia.

In 1915 the British also began a campaign against Ottoman possessions in Palestine and by November 1917 had pushed the Ottoman Army back as far as Jaffa, capturing the strategically important Jaffa–Jerusalem railway before going on to take the city. Jerusalem fell in December and the British force, made up of Indian, Australian, and New Zealand divisions as well as British, would eventually take Damascus in October of the following year so that, by the end of the war, they had occupied much of the Ottoman Empire with the exception of Turkey.

Over the course of the war, Britain had entered into a number of different and contradictory commitments concerning what would happen to the territories of the Ottoman Empire in the event of its dissolution at the end ofthe war. As a means of encouraging the Arab Revolt, they had given assurances of support to Hussein bin Ali, the Sharif of Mecca, over the creation of an independent Arab state after the war centered on Damascus and, at least as it was understood by Hussein, including all of Syria, Iraq, and Palestine as well as Arabia. At the same time as these assurances were being made, the British and French were holding secret negotiations to establish how they would divide up the region between themselves.

OLD JAFFA
Market at Jaffa (1877) by Gustav Bauernfeind, a noted German orientalist artist of Jewish origin.

Surrounding Jaffa are the orange gardens for which it is justly extolled, and which are a considerable source of wealth to the owners.

Captain R. W. Stewart in a survey for the Palestine Exploration Fund dated 1872

JAFFA CAKES

✦

In 1927, the British cookie maker McVitie's released the Jaffa Cake, which had a base of sponge cake with orange-flavored jelly on top, coated in chocolate. The debate about whether they are cakes or cookies continues today, even though it was legally settled in 1991 by a court ruling that determined that, in the eyes of the law, they are cakes. The case arose because in Britain the sales tax VAT applies to cookies but not to cakes and the decision of the court on Jaffa Cakes is now taken as being the benchmark for the dividing line between the two.

The Sykes–Picot Agreement was signed in May 1916 and was named after Sir Mark Sykes and François Georges-Picot, who had led the negotiations for Britain and France respectively. It divided the Ottoman territories into "spheres of influence" between the two countries, leaving only the arid interior of the Syrian desert and the Arabian Peninsula to become an independent Arab state, while Britain controlled the stretch of the Mediterranean coastline that included Jaffa. To complicate the issue even further, in November 1917 the British foreign secretary Arthur Balfour wrote a letter to Lord Rothschild, a prominent member of the Jewish community in Britain, which stated that, "His Majesty's government view with favor the establishment in Palestine of a national home for the Jewish people." The Balfour Declaration, as it is now known, did not go as far as a commitment by the British to found a Jewish state in Palestine and was probably issued as a means of securing support among the Jewish diaspora around the world for the British war effort and for its intention to take control of Palestine after the war, but it nevertheless came to be regarded as one of the founding documents of the State of Israel.

The British remained in Palestine after the end of the First World War and began the process of formalizing control of the region in the Treaty of Sèvres, the peace settlement signed in 1920 between the Allies and the defeated Ottoman Empire. Britain then obtained a mandate from the League of Nations in 1922, giving their presence legitimacy under international law. With Zionists encouraged by the Balfour Declaration, Jewish immigration into Mandatory Palestine increased considerably, many settling in Tel Aviv having landed in the port of Jaffa. As the British would do in many of their colonial territories, they encouraged the development of the export of agricultural produce to boost the economy and during this period the Jaffa orange was one of the principal items of trade.

Despite friction between the Jewish and Arab communities that sporadically erupted into violence, both were involved in the cultivation and marketing of oranges and regularly worked together.

In common with every aspect of the conflict between Israelis and Palestinians, the extent to which the orange business was enlarged by people from one community or the other is controversial today, but it would certainly appear that Jewish settlers contributed toward improving the agricultural productivity of the region and would later extend the area under cultivation by developing irrigation methods in more arid zones. It is equally clear that Arabs had established productive farming methods themselves and the later Israeli claims that they were converting a barren wilderness into agricultural land, "making the desert bloom" as it was described, are not completely accurate either.

Over the course of the Second World War and in its aftermath, many more Jewish people arrived in Mandatory Palestine, both as refugees escaping persecution and as survivors of the Holocaust. The influx of people heightened tensions between Arabs and Jews, which escalated into a civil war in 1947 and, when the British announced their intentions to leave in the following year, the new State of Israel was declared. The First Arab–Israeli War broke out almost immediately afterward, fought between what had become the army of Israel and a coalition of forces made up of the Palestinians and soldiers from the surrounding Arab countries.

The events of that war form the background to the bitterness and division that exists in the region today. One of the most controversial aspects of the war was the exodus of Palestinian people, who were either forced to flee or left voluntarily, depending on which viewpoint is being expressed, to refugee camps outside Israel, leaving their homes and almost everything they possessed behind. In Jaffa, only about 4,000 Palestinians remained after a ceasefire in the war was declared in 1949 out of perhaps 60,000 Muslim inhabitants of the city before the war

ORANGE PACKERS
Jewish workers in British Mandatory Palestine in c.1933, packing Jaffa oranges for export.

had started. From then onward, the orange business was continued by Israelis, the export of fruit to Britain and other European countries providing the fledgling state with much-needed revenue. These days, Israel has a diversified economy in which agricultural produce plays a relatively minor role, but even though the export of oranges has declined in recent years, citrus fruit is still the country's largest agricultural export.

American Buffalo

Origin: The Great Plains of America

Date: 19th century

Type: Large mammal

+ **CULTURAL**
+ **SOCIAL**
+ **COMMERCIAL**
+ **POLITICAL**
+ MILITARY

By 1890, the huge herds of buffalo, or American bison as the animal is more correctly called, that had inhabited the Great Plains of America in numbers of up to 60 million had been brought to the point of extinction. A few hundred animals remained in scattered populations, a situation that had arisen for a combination of reasons over the course of the 19th century. This had been exacerbated in the 1870s by political decisions not to take measures to protect the remaining animals after the decline had become apparent as a means of undermining, or "pacifying" as it was sometimes called, the Native American tribes of the Plains.

BUFFALO CULTURES

Buffalo and humans had coexisted on the Great Plains for thousands of years. The sheer number of animals meant that those killed by hunting made little difference to the overall numbers even after the introduction of the horse, which was brought to the American continent by the Spanish in the 16th century and allowed Native Americans to hunt more effectively. But no external market existed for buffalo hides or meat until the 19th century, so there was little incentive to hunt more than was necessary for food, shelter, and clothing. The cultures that developed on the plains were by no means static or unchanging; tribes migrated from one region to another, technologies evolved and were adopted from outside sources. The Lakota people, one of the tribes of the Great Sioux Nation now most associated with the buffalo culture, had migrated onto the Great Plains in about 1650 and came to rely heavily on the buffalo by the 1730s, when the neighboring Cheyenne introduced them to the horse.

The status of the land in which the Lakota and the other tribes on the Great Plains lived changed in 1803 when the title to it was sold by Napoleon Bonaparte to America for the bargain price of $15 million in the Louisiana Purchase. The full extent of the land involved was not known at the time, but it included all of the territory west of the Mississippi up to the Rocky Mountains, encompassing almost the entire extent of the Great Plains and including the Black Hills where

Historically the buffalo had more influence on man than all other Plains animals combined. It was life, food, raiment, and shelter to the Indians. The buffalo and the Plains Indians lived together, and together passed away.

Walter Prescott Webb, The Great Plains *(1931)*

HUNTING BUFFALO
A watercolor by Alfred Jacob Miller (1810–74) showing a rather exaggerated scene of buffalo being driven over a cliff.

the Lakota had settled, now on the border between the states of South Dakota and Wyoming. Needless to say, nobody involved in the purchase thought to consult the people who were already living across the entire territory, but it would be the beginning of the opening up of the West to settlers and in less than a hundred years would result in the buffalo cultures coming to an end.

THE LAKOTA

After the Louisiana Purchase, expeditions began to travel through the newly acquired territory to map its extent and assess the potential for settlement. The first of these, and now the most famous, was led by Meriwether Lewis and William Clark and encountered the Lakota while crossing the Great Plains. It led to a tense standoff but no actual fighting before the expedition continued westward to make the first crossing of the North American continent. It would lead to the opening up of the Oregon Trail. As well as wagon trains of settlers, an increasing number of traders and fur trappers began to pass through Lakota territory, leading to numerous violent confrontations between the two groups. The California Gold Rush of 1848 only increased the problem, resulting in the establishment of Fort Laramie by the US Army in Lakota territory in an effort to protect the wagon trains.

In 1851, the US government negotiated the Treaty of Fort Laramie with the Lakota, Cheyenne, and other Native American tribes living

along the Oregon Trail, guaranteeing the sovereignty of their territory in exchange for allowing safe passage through it for wagon trains. The government and US Army did little to uphold their part of the treaty, failing to restrict settlers in the region so that what had begun as a trickle turned into a flood after the end of the Civil War in 1865 and, despite another treaty in 1868 to establish the Great Sioux Reservation, grew even more when gold was discovered in the Black Hills. It would be the major cause of the Great Sioux War of 1876, in which a band of about 2,000 Lakota warriors led by Sitting Bull and Crazy Horse were joined by members of other Sioux tribes, together with Cheyenne and Arapaho, after the government issued a proclamation that any Native Americans living off the reservations would be considered as "hostiles."

The Battle of the Little Bighorn was fought on June 25th and 26th, 1876, and resulted in the deaths of George Armstrong Custer and 267 US soldiers serving under him. It was a major defeat for the US Army and prompted the despatch of many more soldiers to the Black Hills region to begin a campaign of continuous harassment of those warriors who were not living in the reservation in an effort to deny them the resources they needed to survive. It took nearly two years for the policy to succeed, but with buffalo numbers severely depleted and few other resources available to them, by April 1877, most of the hostile tribes had surrendered and had been moved onto reservations where they were dependent on government supplies for food.

YELLOWSTONE

✦

Yellowstone National Park, the first protected area of its kind in the world, was created in 1872, the necessary legislation signed by President Ulysses S. Grant. About 20 buffalo had survived in the region that would become the park and were later joined by a further 20 from the captive herd that had been established by the Texas rancher Charles Goodnight. These formed the basis of the Yellowstone Park bison herd, which is currently composed of about 3,500 individuals, making it the largest herd on publicly owned land in America.

TO THE BRINK AND BACK

The buffalo had been in serious trouble for several decades before the Great Sioux War had broken out. A severe and prolonged drought in the Great Plains between 1840 and 1865 had depleted the herds while increasingly the grassland on the plains was being converted to farmland so that many of those that had not already been shot by ranchers contracted diseases spread by cattle. Demand for hides led to an increase in hunting by both European settlers and Native Americans and the advance of the railroads not only allowed for the improved transportation of the hides, and later for buffalo bones to be ground down into fertilizer, but increased the hunting pressure as the railroad companies employed hunters to shoot buffalo in an attempt to prevent accidents between them and trains.

William Cody, who would become famous as Buffalo Bill in the touring Wild West shows of the period, began his commercial hunting career shooting buffalo to provide meat for a railway company and then, along with many others, continued to decimate what was left of the herds for the hides, usually leaving the meat to rot because there was little demand for it. By 1874 it was clear that the buffalo was in serious danger, but attempts to protect it through legislation in the US Congress were vetoed by President Ulysses S. Grant because of advice he had received from General William T. Sherman, the commander in chief of the US Army, and General Philip Sheridan, who commanded the US forces who were conducting the campaign against the tribes of the Great Plains, both of whom advocated the elimination of the buffalo as a means of pacifying those who refused to move to reservations.

BUFFALO BILL
A studio portrait of William Cody from 1892, by which time the buffalo was almost extinct.

By the 1890s, and with the buffalo on the brink of extinction, some states began to introduce measures to restrict hunting, while a number of private individuals started breeding programs on ranches that would eventually form the basis of the wild herds and domestic animals of today. In recent years there has been a surge of interest in keeping domestic buffalo that has seen the numbers rise to about half a million, helped by a rising market for the meat because it has a lower cholesterol level than beef. About 30,000 buffalo inhabit national parks and other protected areas across the country and there are a few living in the wild outside these areas, mostly those that have migrated out of the parks. It may be impossible to envisage the return of enormous herds of buffalo to the Great Plains, or a resurgence of the Native American culture that grew up alongside them, but at least the buffalo's future appears to be secure for now, which, considering how close to the edge it came, must be regarded as a great success.

Let them kill, skin, and sell until the buffalo is exterminated, as it is the only way to bring lasting peace and allow civilization to advance.

General Philip Sheridan, speaking in 1874

Coca-Cola

Coca-Cola. Delicious! Refreshing! Exhilarating! Invigorating!

The first advertisement for Coca-Cola in the Atlanta Journal, *May 29th, 1886*

Origin: America

Date: 1886

Type: Soft drink

* CULTURAL
* SOCIAL
* **COMMERCIAL**
* POLITICAL
* *MILITARY*

Coca-Cola is currently available to buy in over 200 countries around the world, more than there are members of the United Nations, and since Burma lifted a ban on it in 2012, it is only now prohibited in Cuba and North Korea, even if it is apparently possible to buy it in both if you know the right people. Those two countries are long-standing opponents of the American government, demonstrating the close association that has developed between Coke and the USA.

THE REAL THING

In 2013, the brand consultancy Interbrand caused a minor stir in certain circles when it published its annual rankings of Best Global Brand. For the first time in the 14-year history of the rankings, Coca-Cola was not placed at number one, beaten by both Apple and Google. This slide down the chart was not caused by any problems at the Coca-Cola Company, the value of its brand having increased to a reported $79 billion, but was rather caused by advances in the other two companies to push them ahead. Coke won the consolation prize of remaining the most recognizable brand name in the world and, given the nature of the businesses of its two rivals, it would not be any great surprise to see it make a comeback in the chart in the near future. Apple and Google both rely on constant innovation to keep them ahead of their competitors in the volatile markets of high-tech electronics and Internet services, whereas Coke has largely stayed the same for over a hundred years and only runs into trouble if it tries to change.

The origins of Coca-Cola would not necessarily lead anybody to think that it would become a brand with such a wide global reach. It was first developed in 1886 by the pharmacist John Pemberton in Atlanta, Georgia, who was actually attempting to make a patent medicine rather than a soft drink. In the previous year he had come up with Pemberton's French Wine Coca by mixing wine with extracts from coca leaves from South America, kola nuts from West Africa, and damiana, a shrub from Texas reputed to be an aphrodisiac. Pemberton made all sorts of claims about the properties of his patent medicine, including that it could

cure morphine addiction, a problem he had experienced himself during the Civil War after he had been wounded and taken morphine as a pain-killer. Considering that his medicine contained alcohol, cocaine from the coca leaf, and caffeine from the kola nut and the damiana, it was certainly going to have an effect on those people who drank it, even if it was hard to know exactly what that might be.

The adoption of temperance legislation restricting the sale of alcohol in Atlanta in 1886 prompted Pemberton to begin experimenting with a version of his patent medicine using carbonated water rather than wine and reducing the bitterness of the other ingredients by adding sugar. Once he had perfected the recipe, he sold what had now been named Coca-Cola after the main two ingredients as a concentrated syrup to pharmacies, many of which had soda fountains because of the supposed health benefits of drinking carbonated water. As the popularity of the drink began to rise, Pemberton entered into a number of different business arrangements to manufacture and market his invention, leaving a confused situation about who owned what after he died in 1888 from stomach cancer.

The confusion was sorted out by Asa Chandler, another pharmacist and maker of patent medicines from Atlanta, who bought out everybody who had a stake in Coca-Cola and set about transforming it into a nationwide drink, reorientating it as a soft drink rather than a tonic so that it would appeal to everybody, not just to people who were ill, and also removing the cocaine, even

CHRISTMAS COKE

✦

The story that the Coca-Cola Company created the modern image of Santa Claus by dressing him in the company colors of red and white for an advertising campaign in 1931 is not entirely true. Coke's Christmas advertisements certainly used a red and white Santa that year, but by then the image had already existed for at least 20 years and it was most likely simply borrowed by the company because it appealed to children, allowing them to market Coke to kids without actually depicting any children drinking a product that contained caffeine.

if other extracts from the coca leaf remained. After some initial reluctance, in 1899 he also agreed to a deal with a bottling company, selling them the syrup and, in the process, increasing sales enormously because Coke became available in grocery stores as well as pharmacies and could be drunk anywhere. From that point onward, and together with plenty of advertising and marketing, Coca-Cola has never looked back, rapidly spreading across America and then, as a consequence of the Second World War, around the world as well.

TASTES LIKE HOME

Prohibition in America between 1920 and 1933 boosted sales of Coke, but even when the ban on alcohol was repealed sales of the soft drink continued to rise. By that time it had become an all-American product to go with hamburgers and hot dogs, an egalitarian drink enjoyed by everybody up to and including the president. It was also bought by the US Army because it was a nonalcoholic drink that soldiers from all ranks liked and it would be this association that would transform Coca-Cola from an American drink into a global brand.

When America entered the Second World War after the Japanese attack on Pearl Harbor on December 7th, 1941, Robert W. Woodruff, the president of the Coca-Cola Company at the time, who had close links to the American military, gave an undertaking that, "every man in uniform gets a bottle of Coca-Cola for 5¢, wherever he is and whatever it costs the company." In line with the usual company practice of supplying Coke as syrup rather than in bottles, Coca-Cola began to establish temporary bottling plants in large American military bases around the world and installed soda fountains where that was not practicable. The Coca-Cola employees who accompanied the military wherever they went were given the status of Technical Observers and the work they did was considered vital to America's war effort by many senior military commanders because of its impact on morale. One of those who recognized the value of Coca-Cola was General Dwight D. Eisenhower, the supreme commander of the Allied forces in Europe, who was responsible for the planning and implementation of Operation Overlord, the code name given to the Allied invasion of Normandy and the subsequent liberation of Western Europe and invasion of Germany.

Coca-Cola's Technical Observers arrived in Britain together with US soldiers as the build-up for the Normandy landings was underway and then followed behind the American forces as they fought across Europe. Much the same occurred in all the other parts of the world where US military personnel were stationed, which, over the course of the war and its immediate aftermath, would encompass numerous countries that had fought on either side during the war. As the American military withdrew and post-war reconstruction began to transform the economies of many of these war-torn countries, Coca-Cola's bottling plants were transferred to civilian ownership, giving the company facilities to exploit new markets around the world.

The close association between Coca-Cola and the American military and its worldwide availability has seen Coke being thought of as an icon of the free world or a symbol of American economic and cultural imperialism, depending on the viewpoint of the observer. This image prevented the company from becoming established in the Soviet Union or in any of the other countries behind the Iron Curtain until after the Berlin Wall came down in 1989 and the Soviet Union collapsed in 1991, at which point Coke, along with other Western brands and consumer products, suddenly became symbols of freedom from oppression.

More recently, Coke has been seen to represent American global dominance and the rise of predatory capitalism and mass-market consumerism. But however clever the advertising and marketing campaigns may be, it remains hard to sell a product that people do not want to buy. An ice-cold Coke, on the other hand, is a refreshing drink and lots of people really do love it. Whatever associations it may have with America, good or bad, that has been the key to its success.

NEW COKE

◆

In 1985, the Coca-Cola Company made one of the few marketing mistakes it has made in its history when it introduced New Coke, presumably having forgotten that old adage of not trying to fix something if it isn't broken. Market research had suggested that people preferred a sweeter cola to Coke and its only serious rival, Pepsi, which is sweeter, had been gaining ground since the introduction of its "Pepsi Challenge" marketing campaign. A consumer backlash caused the company to have a rethink, bringing back the old recipe as Coke Classic after three months with the sugar now replaced by high-fructose corn syrup and, in the process, gaining a huge amount of free publicity.

COKE IN WARTIME
An advertising poster from 1944. Wherever American servicemen went, the Coca-Cola Company followed.

Hamburger

Origin: Somewhere in America

Date: late 19th century

Type: Ground beef in a bun

+ CULTURAL

+ SOCIAL

+ COMMERCIAL

+ POLITICAL

+ MILITARY

In the summer of 2013, McDonald's announced it was opening its first restaurant in Ho Chi Minh City, Vietnam, which means that it now operates in 120 countries around the world. The enormous success of the company and of other American fast food sellers has been described by some as being a sign of the democratization of food, and yet, at one time or another, McDonald's has been blamed for almost all the ills of modern society. Opinions may differ, but what is not in doubt is that the hamburger, ground beef in a bread bun, has become a global phenomenon, eaten by millions, each buying their own little piece of American culture without having to spend a fortune to get it.

THE HOME OF THE HAMBURGER

In common with many aspects of popular culture, there are conflicting accounts of the origin of the hamburger. Numerous cities across America claim to be "the home of the hamburger," among others Athens, Texas, and New Haven, Connecticut. A different version of the story suggests that it arrived in America along with German immigrants at some point during the 19th century. In the absence of any clear documentary evidence to support one version of the story ahead of any of the others, all that can be said with certainty is that Hamburg steak existed as a dish in America from about the 1830s, most likely first made by German immigrants before becoming more widely adopted. It was made from chopped or ground beef, served on a plate with gravy rather than as a sandwich, and, like those other European imports, meat loaf and meatballs, it made use of cheap cuts to provide an inexpensive meal.

Later in the 19th century, America went through a rapid period of industrialization and population growth, in which cities expanded and many factories and businesses began to operate around the clock. In true American entrepreneurial spirit, the opportunity to make a few dollars by feeding these workers was quickly taken

Do you know what they call a Quarter Pounder with Cheese in Paris?

The character Vincent Vega, in Pulp Fiction

up by people operating lunch carts, which enabled them to sell food from any location where there were likely to be hungry customers. The food was either pre-prepared or could be cooked quickly and had to be convenient for people to eat standing up and at any time of day or night. By the 1870s, frankfurters were being sold in a bread bun, acquiring the name of hot dogs (see page 94), and it would not have been a great leap for anybody running a lunch cart, or, as time went on, one of the larger lunch wagons, to put a beef patty between two pieces of bread and call it a Hamburg steak sandwich or simply a hamburger.

WHITE CASTLES AND GOLDEN ARCHES

As the number of cars increased on American streets, cities began to pass laws to restrict the number of lunch carts and wagons to ease congestion, forcing those purveyors of hamburgers who wanted to stay in business to open restaurants. In 1921 the first White Tower restaurant opened in Wichita, Kansas, in a distinctive building modeled on the castle-like Chicago Water Tower. The owners set high standards of cleanliness, unlike many of their competitors, while keeping prices low by adopting a production line system to make hamburgers, not unlike the system developed by Henry Ford in his car factories. Success led to more outlets in other cities, making White Tower, which is still going in America today, the first chain of hamburger restaurants.

HOMESTYLE
Metal sign of the type seen across America before the Golden Arches of McDonald's took over.

Beef was rationed in America in the Second World War and many hamburger outlets attempted to make up for the reduced quantity of meat they were able to offer by adding French fries, which, it turned out, went so well with the hamburgers that, when rationing came to an end after the war, the fries remained on most menus. Add a Coke or a shake and the result is the sort of all-American meal we are still eating today. But what really made the hamburger take off was the explosion of American culture in the 1950s, when the era of rock and roll and Elvis Presley caused a seismic shift in society and newly affluent Americans could watch it all on TV. The excitement generated by Elvis was not

SALISBURY STEAK

✦

In 1888, Dr James H. Salisbury published a recipe for a chopped beef patty that he claimed could form part of a healthy low carbohydrate diet. He suggested flavoring the cooked patty with salt, pepper, and other condiments like Worcestershire sauce or mustard. The Salisbury steak, which, by any other name, is a hamburger without the bun, first began to appear regularly on restaurant menus during the First World War, when customers preferred to buy food that didn't sound as if it came from Germany. The dish remains popular in America today, where it is often served with mashed potatoes and gravy.

lost on young people in other parts of the world and, together with Hollywood movies, American TV shows, American clothes, and, of course, hamburger and fries, that young and vibrant culture began to spread.

Meanwhile, in San Bernardino, California, Dick and Mac McDonald had been perfecting their hamburger restaurant, refining the model established by White Castle and introducing a system of self-service that dispensed with the need for waitresses or carhops. In 1953, they began to franchise the business and its success caught the attention of Ray Kroc, who sold Dick and Mac the mixers they used for making shakes. Kroc became the franchise agent for the chain and, by 1960, had grown it to over a hundred restaurants. Disagreements with the McDonald brothers, who appear to have been satisfied with the success they had already achieved, led to Kroc buying them out for $2.7 million in the following year. By that time he had already introduced the Golden Arches, now one of the most recognized brand symbols in the world, and, with control of the McDonald Corporation, as it now was, embarked on a huge program of expansion, backed up with vigorous advertising campaigns. It was highly ambitious and faced serious competition from other chains such as Burger King and Wendy's, but Kroc's policies of appealing to families and, in particular, to children paid off; McDonald's soon established itself as the leader in the field.

LE BIG MAC

The attraction of American culture combined with some clever marketing strategies allowed McDonald's to begin expanding overseas in the 1970s, beginning in Europe and then into the Far East and others parts of the world. In 1979, the first McDonald's opened in France and, much to many people's surprise, proved to be popular. Needless to say, not everybody in the birthplace of haute cuisine was delighted by what they described as the Americanization of French culture. In one famous incident in 1999, the sheep farmer and producer of Roquefort cheese José

THE BIG MAC INDEX

✦

In 1986, *The Economist* newspaper, on what must have been a slow day in the business world, came up with a method of comparing the purchasing power of different currencies based on the price of a Big Mac. Divide the dollar price of a Big Mac in America, say, by the equivalent price in pounds sterling in Britain, then multiply by the exchange rate and the figure you end up with gives a rough indication of the relative value of the currencies, showing if one is overvalued against the other. It's hardly foolproof, but, as *The Economist* noted, it is more digestible than most economic theory.

Bové led a protest against the building of a new McDonald's in Millau, near where he farmed in the South of France, by demolishing the restaurant with his tractor.

Some of the protests aimed at McDonald's have really been directed at the idea of globalization and at America in general, the Golden Arches being treated as if they were a symbol of American power rather than a marketing tool to sell Big Macs. But, over the years, McDonald's has been accused of specific failings and has been investigated by a number of journalists and TV documentary makers. Complaints against it have ranged from accusations of treating its staff badly and contributing to rising levels of obesity to damaging the environment through its use of polystyrene packaging and buying its beef from suppliers who have used inhumane methods of production. The bad publicity McDonald's received after it sued members of Greenpeace in London for producing and distributing a leaflet listing many of these accusations in what became known as the McLibel trial appears to have caused it to rethink how it handles criticism. Rather than adopt the sledgehammer approach favored by many multinational companies, in which the threat of legal action is used to intimidate protestors, McDonald's has begun to engage with its critics in a positive way in an attempt to resolve the issues raised. This new approach has, for instance, led to the company providing nutritional information on the food it sells and to the introduction of salads onto its menus.

Cynics might suggest that McDonald's has changed its approach for commercial reasons rather than through any newfound sense of social responsibility, but, even if they are right, at least the company has been prepared to move with the times. The prosperity it has achieved, after all, was founded on wide-ranging social changes that have seen those millions of people who were attracted to American culture buying into it by, amongst other things, eating hamburger and fries. If McDonald's loses the essence of what has attracted so many people to it in the first place, then its customers will vote with their feet and either buy their hamburgers elsewhere or get something else to eat instead. And that, in itself, is an example of the sort of competition and freedom of choice on which the American dream was built.

CHINESE BURGERS
McDonald's in the southern Chinese city of Guangzhou, which, apart from the Chinese lettering, could be anywhere in the world.

It is the Americans who have managed to crown minced beef as hamburger, and to send it round the world so that even the fussy French have taken to *le bœuf haché, le hambourgaire.*
Julia Child (1912–2004)

Anzac Biscuits

Origin: Australia and
New Zealand

Date: 1915

Type: Oatmeal cookie

Anzac Biscuits (oatmeal cookies) are made today by commercial companies and home-bakers in Australia and New Zealand to be sold both before Anzac Day on April 25th and at events on the day itself to raise money for veterans charities. Anzac Day is a day of remembrance for servicemen and -women of the two countries who died in war and is held on the anniversary of the day when the soldiers of the Australian and New Zealand Army Corps first went into action in the Gallipoli campaign of the First World War.

+ *CULTURAL*

+ SOCIAL

+ COMMERCIAL

+ POLITICAL

+ *MILITARY*

GALLIPOLI

In August 1914, when the First World War began, Australia and New Zealand were both self-governing dominions within the British Empire and decided to contribute a joint force to fight as part of the British Army. It was called the Australian and New Zealand Army Corps, or ANZAC for short, an acronym that would become attached to the soldiers themselves because it was used as a stencil to mark supplies destined for them. The first contingent of soldiers was due to arrive in Britain in December 1914, but was then diverted to Egypt to train because it was thought that the climate would be more suitable and they were joined there by the rest of the corps over the next few months.

The original intention was for the Anzacs to be sent to the Western Front, which, by the time they had arrived in Egypt, had become a stalemate of trench warfare. The British began to consider a number of plans to widen the war away from the Western Front, including one vigorously promoted by Winston Churchill, then the First Lord of the Admiralty, for a naval attack on the Dardanelles, the narrow waterway that, together with the Sea of Marmara and the Bosphorus, connects the Mediterranean Sea with the Black Sea and separates European and Asiatic Turkey. The aim was to force through the narrowest parts of the straits of the Dardanelles that were protected by Turkish gun emplacements on the Gallipoli Peninsula into the Sea of Marmara, from where it would be possible to capture Constantinople, the capital of the Ottoman Empire, in order to knock the ally of Germany and Austria–Hungary out of the war and to open up another front in the war in southern Europe.

A naval force of British and French ships began the attack in February 1915, launching the main attempt to force the straits on March 18th and, initially at least, it appeared likely to succeed. Ten ships entered the Sea of Marmara, but then six of them hit mines, causing three to sink. The naval commander of the squadron ordered a withdrawal and, much to Churchill's annoyance, refused to renew the attack in the following days. In Britain, it was decided to call off the naval attack and to mount a combined navy and army operation in which soldiers would be landed on the Gallipoli Peninsula to capture the Turkish gun emplacements and then advance on Constantinople while minesweepers were sent through the straits, followed by naval ships.

The Anzacs were still training in Egypt, "getting a suntan" as they described it, and were included in the plans for the landings because they were the divisions of the British Army then stationed the closest to the Gallipoli Peninsula. Over the course of the following month while the operation was being planned, the Turkish Army had time to prepare defenses. It was commanded by the German general Liman von Sanders and the officer in charge of the reserves, which would play a decisive role in the Turkish defense, was Lieutenant Colonel Mustapha Kemal, who would later become the first president of Turkey and known as Atatürk, the Father of the Turks.

It should be noted that approvals for the word "Anzac" to be used on biscuit products have been given provided that the product generally conforms to the traditional recipe and shape, and is not used in association with the word "cookies," with its non-Australian overtones.

From a statement by the Australian Government's Department of Veterans' Affairs

THE TRADITIONAL ANZAC BISCUIT

◆

Anzac Biscuits are traditionally made from rolled oats, desiccated coconut, plain flour, butter, golden syrup, bicarbonate of soda, and water. No eggs or any other ingredients that might reduce the shelf life of the cookies are included, which may originally have been a measure taken to ensure they did not go bad when they were sent to Anzac soldiers stationed on the other side of the world. The Australian and New Zealand governments have both passed laws to regulate the use of the name "Anzac" by commercial companies, ensuring that the cookies remain the same and that profits go to charity.

The landing began at dawn on the morning of April 25th with the Anzacs coming ashore in a cove on the western side of the Gallipoli Peninsula (now known as Anzac Cove after its name was officially changed by the Turkish government in 1985), while the British landed on five beaches around Cape Helles on the tip of the peninsula and the French mounted a diversionary attack on the Asiatic side of the Dardanelles. The Turkish defenders were spread out around the coast, covering what they thought would be the most likely landing grounds, so that some of the British and Anzacs encountered heavy resistance while others landed almost unopposed.

The plan was for the British to move along the peninsula while the Anzacs crossed it to prevent supplies from reaching the Turkish forces and to sever their communications, and then for the two to join together to take the plateau in the center of the peninsula, from where the Turkish gun emplacements could be attacked from the rear. After the Anzacs had got ashore successfully and begun to move inland, hand-to-hand fighting began in the difficult terrain of the interior, made up of steep-sided hills cut with deep ravines. The situation quickly became confused and, with no effective communications, the attack began to stall. At this point, Kemal brought the Turkish reserves into action, issuing an order to them which would become famous in Turkey and began, "I do not order you to fight, I order you to die."

The intervention of the Turkish reserves prevented the Anzacs from advancing onto the central plateau of the peninsula, an action that would make Kemal a hero in Turkey because it most probably prevented the Turkish Army from losing the battle. But with the British encountering similar difficulties, and despite the success of the landings, both they and the Anzacs were forced to dig in and fight on from difficult positions while the Turks continued to hold the high ground. Rather than break the stalemate in the war, the attack at Gallipoli had only succeeded in creating another line of trenches, this time in Turkey.

Over the course of the next few months, both sides mounted attacks against their opponent's trenches, which were protected by barbed wire and covered by machine gun posts, incurring large numbers of casualties for very little gain. The heat and flies made living conditions difficult and led to numerous cases of dysentery, or the Gallipoli gallop as it was called by the Anzacs. In August, the British mounted further landings at Suvla Bay, to the north of the Anzac positions. At the same time, the Anzacs attacked the Turkish trenches to keep them occupied while the British were coming ashore. The first of these attacks was the Battle of Lone Pine, beginning on August 6th and continuing over the course of the next three days. It involved some of the fiercest fighting of the whole campaign, in which the Turkish trenches were captured, but with the British unable to advance inland from Suvla Bay, all that had been achieved was to extend the lines of trenches without any real change in the overall situation.

The British and Anzacs remained on the Gallipoli Peninsula until December, when the order was given for a withdrawal after senior military commanders and politicians in London finally were forced to concede that the campaign had been a failure, a conclusion that had been apparent for some considerable time. The operation to take what was by then 120,000 men off the peninsula was conducted in an exemplary way, the only really successful part of a campaign that had cost the lives of 44,000 Allied servicemen, including 8,700 Australians and 2,700 New Zealanders.

From Gallipoli, the Anzacs returned to Egypt, where the corps was enlarged and would go on to fight in further campaigns against the Ottoman Empire in Palestine and the Middle East and on the Western Front, where Anzac divisions fought in all of the major battles conducted by the British Army, including at the Somme and Passchendaele. The baptism of fire that the soldiers underwent at Gallipoli and their involvement in some of the worst and most costly battles ever fought in any theater of the war had a profound impact on people at home in Australia and New Zealand, and it has been described as being the moment when both countries first came together as nations, when both began to regard their relationship with Britain as part of their colonial past and not their future, and when separate national identities began to emerge.

ANZAC ACTION
Australian troops attacking a Turkish position shortly before the Allied withdrawal from the Gallipoli Peninsula.

REMEMBRANCE

The first day of the Gallipoli campaign was marked on April 25th, 1916, by people in Australia and New Zealand and by soldiers serving abroad. As well as ceremonial marches and religious services being held to commemorate those soldiers who had been killed, fundraising events were organized to raise money for the wounded. One way of raising money was to make home-baked cakes and cookies to sell and this was most probably the start of the tradition of making Anzac Biscuits that continues today. It has been suggested that the cookies were also sent out to the Anzacs who were stationed abroad by their families and, although there is very little evidence to show that this happened, the nature of the cookies themselves suggests that they were baked to a recipe that would allow them to keep for several months without going bad, so they would survive the long journey from Australia and New Zealand to the Western Front in France and Belgium or wherever else the Anzacs were stationed.

A certain amount of confusion has arisen over the difference between Anzac Biscuits and the hardtack that formed part of the standard rations of the British Army during the First World War and was sometimes also known as the army biscuit. The Anzacs came up with a variety of names for hardtack, most of which were jokes referring to the fact that it was so hard soldiers were known to break their teeth trying to eat it. One of these names was "the Anzac wafer," comparing the solid blocks of hardtack to light and crisp wafer cookies or, perhaps, suggesting that the Anzacs were tough enough to eat hardtack as if it was wafer. But, whatever names were used, the families of Anzac soldiers certainly sent parcels of food to them and, if they were baking a particular type of cookie for Anzac Day, then surely they would have included some in their parcels.

After the war was over, the traditions of remembrance and commemoration followed today began to take shape and April 25th was declared a public holiday in both Australia and New Zealand. Anzac Day begins with a dawn service, held to coincide with the landings at Anzac Cove, which involves formal acts of remembrance such as the laying of wreaths at war memorials. Later in the day, further religious services and acts of commemoration take place, followed by military parades through towns and cities. On some occasions in the past, these parades have proved controversial, being regarded by some as glorifying war rather than as a way of remembering the sacrifices of the past. This was particularly the case during the Vietnam War, in which both Australia and New Zealand participated, when anti-war protests were held on Anzac Day.

In more recent times, there has been something of a resurgence of interests in the Anzacs of the First World War and, in particular, their role in the Gallipoli campaign. The reasons for this are not entirely clear, but it could be because, as the war has receded further into history, it has become more apparent that to remember the people killed in war, whether in the First World War or those wars that came after, and to acknowledge the men and women who came home from those wars, does not amount to a show of support for war. Some of the events held to mark Anzac Day these days, it must be admitted, have become more like national celebrations and less like commemorations of the dead, but, nonetheless, people from all ages and from across all sections of society still come together to mark the occasion in one way or another. The continuing tradition of baking and buying Anzac Biscuits to raise money for veterans charities provides a tangible connection with the past and, even though it is impossible to know what it was really like for the men in the trenches of Gallipoli or for their families at home, we can at least remember them in this way.

GUNFIRE BREAKFAST

✦

One of the traditions of Anzac Day is for military personnel who have taken part in the dawn service, and, no doubt, some civilians as well, to have a gunfire breakfast. This is simply a cup of coffee with a shot of rum in it, of the type often drunk by Anzac soldiers before the start of a battle in the First World War. Other traditions include wearing a sprig of rosemary, which grows wild on the Gallipoli Peninsula, and to play two-up, a gambling game popular with soldiers in the trenches that involved betting on the outcome of the toss of two coins.

Birds Eye Frozen Fish

Origin: America

Date: 1915

Type: Quick frozen fish

✦ CULTURAL

✦ *SOCIAL*

✦ *COMMERCIAL*

✦ POLITICAL

✦ MILITARY

Clarence Birdseye may sound like a name invented by advertising executives, but the man really existed and the research he conducted in methods of freezing fish and other foodstuffs would go on to have a huge impact on the food industry and the way in which many of us eat today. The methods he developed would, for instance, later enable Swanson to develop its TV Dinner range of frozen foods and, although some of the technology may have changed over the years, most of the food in the frozen sections of supermarkets today was prepared in a way Birdseye would have recognized.

FROM BIRDSEYE TO BIRDS EYE

Freezing food as a means of preserving it has a long history, going back hundreds of years before Clarence Birdseye became interested in it. But it was not widely used because, for one thing, home freezers did not become available to buy until after the Second World War, but also because of the very noticeable deterioration in the quality of food after it was frozen, caused by the formation of large ice crystals within the food during the freezing process that damaged the structures of its cells.

> Quick freezing was conceived, born, and nourished on a strange combination of ingenuity, stick-to-itiveness, sweat, and good luck.
>
> *Clarence Birdseye (1886–1956)*

Birdseye came across the solution to this problem at some point around 1915, while he was in Labrador in northeast Canada, even though he did not go to the region with that purpose in mind. He was actually engaged in fur trapping, living for long periods in a remote cabin with his wife and young son and often eating fish and game he caught himself. During the winter months, when temperatures in Labrador can drop down to −58°F (−50°C), Birdseye was shown by Inuit fishermen the technique of ice-fishing, which involved drilling a hole through the ice and casting fishing lines down into the water beneath. He observed how the fish that were caught froze almost instantly in the subzero temperatures when they were pulled out of the water. When the fish that had been frozen so quickly in the winter were thawed out to eat, Birdseye found that the flesh was firmer and the fish retained their flavor much better than those frozen more slowly at other times of the year because only

ICE FISHING
An Inuit woman catching fish through a hole in the ice of a frozen lake.

small ice crystals had formed in the flesh, which did not damage the cells.

By 1917, Birdseye and his family had moved back to America and he began experimenting with different methods of freezing fish and other foodstuffs quickly to emulate what he had seen in Labrador. It would take him until 1924 to develop a process that worked, which involved cooling two metal plates to a temperature of –40°F (–40°C) with calcium chloride brine and then pressing the fish between these plates. From that starting point, he constructed a freezer unit that consisted of a double belt of hollow tubes filled with cold brine so that fish or other foodstuffs could be passed through it. It would form the basis of what he would later call his "quick freezing" method and it would become the beginnings of the frozen food industry.

Birdseye began his own company, the General Seafood Corporation, and opened a freezing plant in Gloucester, Massachusetts, in 1925, but the business did not initially do that well because stores did not have freezers to sell his products from and hardly any potential customers had a freezer at home either. Despite such obvious drawbacks, Birdseye persisted with his business, a stubbornness that might now be described as far-sighted but was more likely regarded as being, at best, eccentric at the time. In 1929, Birdseye's frozen fish was eaten by Marjorie Merriweather Post, a wealthy heiress whose father had started the Postum Cereal Company. It would lead to Birdseye selling his company and the patents he had taken out on his quick freezing method to Postum for a staggering $22 million, which changed its name to the General Food Company and would later begin selling frozen food under the Birds Eye brand.

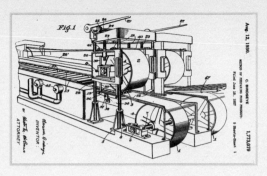

QUICK FREEZING
A diagram submitted by Clarence Birdseye to the US Patent Office in 1930 of a machine to quick freeze fish.

BIRDS EYE FISH FINGERS

✦

One of Clarence Birdseye's numerous experiments led to the herring savory, a type of breaded fish stick. In the early 1950s, herring was plentiful in Britain and Birds Eye's British division began to conduct market research with herring savories, testing them against what was thought a blander version made from cod. Everybody who tried them preferred the cod sticks to the herring, leading to the birth of the fish finger, a name adopted in Britain because "fish sticks," as they are known everywhere else, was already in use for another fish product.

Swanson TV Dinner

Origin: America

Date: 1953

Type: Convenience food

In 1953, C. A. Swanson and Sons, a food-manufacturing company based in Omaha, Nebraska, experimented with a new product line, producing 5,000 trays containing precooked frozen turkey dinners with gravy, mashed potatoes, and peas. It was not the first complete frozen meal to be sold in America, but by describing it as a TV Dinner and through an extensive advertising campaign, Swanson and Sons had launched the first one that tapped into what would prove to be an enormous market for ready meals. In doing so, they reflected the social changes that were transforming American society in the post-war years.

SWANSON NIGHT

The success of the Swanson TV Dinner, which is said to have sold 10 million turkey dinners in its first full year of production alone, was in part due to the price of only 98¢ and the convenience. It came in an aluminum tray, divided up into compartments for each constituent of the dinner, and it could be put in the oven straight from the freezer. The tray served as a plate and could be thrown away after the meal was finished, leaving only a knife and fork to wash up. But, whether by luck or judgment, Swanson also introduced it at exactly the right moment. The early 1950s has been described as the beginning of a golden age in American capitalism, a time when the American economy was surging forward and when there was almost full employment, with more women going out to work than had ever done in the past.

By 1953, 33 million American households owned a TV and popular shows like *I Love Lucy* were watched by all the family, clustered in front of the TV with their dinner on a tray. The episode "Lucy Goes to Hospital," which first aired in January 1953, attracted an enormous audience, getting a rating of over 70, the figure giving the percentage of all households with TVs who were watching, still one

How to catch the early early show with an easy easy dinner. Swanson TV Brand Dinner, the oven-quick meal that tastes home-cooked.

From a Swanson advertisement in 1955

of the highest ratings ever achieved in America. As well as owning TVs, people could buy refrigerators for their kitchens for the first time that had large freezer compartments rather than small ice boxes, technology that had been invented years previously but only became widely available after the end of the Second World War. So, rather than buy food fresh every few days, busy people could choose to stock up on frozen food and, when they bought Swan-son TV Dinners, they could simply throw it in the oven, wait 25 minutes, and then sit in front of their favorite TV show while they ate it.

FAMILY LIFE
A photograph from 1958 of an American family watching TV.

Swanson stopped using the label TV Dinner for their frozen meals in the early 1960s, apparently thinking that it was preventing people from eating their products at other times of the day when they were not watching TV. But the name stuck and the concept was picked up around the world as people in other countries began to follow the social trends set in America. An increasing number of families in which both parents work, together with more one-parent families and people choosing to live on their own, has meant that the TV dinner, whatever it may be called around the world, has gone from strength to strength, particularly since the development of the microwave oven and the advent of chilled meals rather than frozen ones, which may not keep so long but usually retain a better flavor of the original ingredients. And then there are all the rest of us who are not especially busy or short of time, but are too lazy to go shopping or to cook anything beyond turning the microwave on, preferring instead to veg out on the sofa watching whatever is on TV and eating one of the enormous range of prepared foods it is now possible to buy.

A SWANSON MYTH

✦

The often repeated story that Swanson invented TV Dinners when they got stuck with tons of unsold turkeys after Thanksgiving is, like many other stories about the origins of food, a myth, invented by a Swanson salesman. The real story, as far as it is possible to tell, appears to be a little more mundane. A Swanson employee noticed the type of meals being served on airplanes, which were precooked, frozen, and in trays, thought it was a good idea, and decided to try replicating it. It's not very exciting, but it's probably true.

Campbell's Soup

Origin: USA

Date: 1962

Type: Canned soup

The Campbell Soup Company of Camden, New Jersey, is, by any measure, a very successful company. It has been going since 1869 and now sells its products around the world, but it would be difficult to justify including its soup in this book if one of the great American artists of the 20th century had not been inspired by the cans the soup came in to create work which, if it did not change the course of history, would certainly change the history of art.

✦ **CULTURAL**

✦ SOCIAL

✦ **COMMERCIAL**

✦ POLITICAL

✦ MILITARY

WARHOL'S CANS

The design of Campbell's soup cans has not changed very much since 1898, with the exception of the addition of an image of the gold medal the company was awarded in 1900 at the Universal Exposition held in Paris that year. The distinctive red and white bands, now familiar to its customers across the world, were first adopted because one of the company's executives liked the strip worn by the Cornell University football team, in particular the color of their shirts, which is known as carnelian red. Over the first half of the 20th century, the company grew to become one of the largest food manufacturers in the world and in the 1950s expanded its range to include a variety of other foods, even if it would remain best known for the soups in the red and white cans, as it still is today.

At that time, Andy Warhol was a successful commercial artist, working on illustrations for magazines and advertisements and designing record sleeves, and he had held a number of exhibitions of his fine art in New York. In the spring of 1962, he began to work on the project that would make his name as an artist; individual paintings of all of the 32 varieties of soup Campbell's were then making. The reason why he chose Campbell's soup cans is unclear. His own comments on the matter shed little light on the subject because he appears to have treated interviews as opportunities for performance art. From what we can tell, Warhol had seen the work of Roy Lichtenstein, whose paintings based on popular cartoon strips were being exhibited in New York at the time, and, having been working on similar ideas himself, asked friends for other ideas so that his artworks would not look like those already done by Lichtenstein. One of the suggestions was to paint Campbell's soup cans, which appears to have struck a chord with him, perhaps, as he would later say, because he had the soup for lunch every day himself.

WARHOL'S SOUP
The original 32 canvases
of *Campbell's Soup Cans*
as they are now displayed
at the Museum of Modern
Art in New York.

Once Warhol had found his subject, he is said to have asked an assistant to go to the store and buy one of every variety of the soup, then produced a silkscreen print of a general image of a Campbell's can onto which he handpainted the names of the different varieties. The finished paintings were then exhibited at a solo gallery show in Los Angeles, the first time his work had been seen on the West Coast. In the gallery, the 32 paintings were placed side by side on a shelf going around a room and the exhibition provoked intense public and media comment. The reaction was by no means all positive and Warhol's work was not the first to make use of an image of an everyday object, but it can nevertheless be seen as being the moment when pop art, and the use of repetitive images from popular culture, from TV or advertising, began to be taken seriously as an art form.

All 32 of the original paintings are now in the Museum of Modern Art in New York, recognized today as one of the great works of the pop art movement and an iconic image of America in the 20th century. Warhol continued to produce works featuring the soup cans, which could have been a comment on the mass-produced nature of modern culture, in which the image is more important than the content, or it could have been simply because he liked to paint soup cans. The Campbell Soup Company may have been a little suspicious of Warhol's intentions at first, but would come to embrace his work, particularly because it did no harm to their sales figures. The company has even produced special editions of their soup cans based on some of the later multicolored designs Warhol produced, perhaps acknowledging that, thanks to him, their cans have now had more than 50 years of fame.

I used to drink it. I used to have the same lunch every day, for 20 years, I guess, the same thing over and over again.

Andy Warhol, speaking about Campbell's Soup

Starbucks Coffee

Origin: Seattle

Date: 1971

Type: Coffee shop coffee

Starbucks represents something beyond a cup of coffee.

Howard Schultz, CEO of Starbucks

PIKE PLACE
The interior of the Starbucks in Pike Place Market, Seattle, in 1977. It originally only sold coffee beans.

During the height of the global economic crisis that began in 2008, Boris Johnson, the Mayor of London, suggested that, the ways things were going, all we would end up doing was selling each other cups of coffee. He was probably joking, it's not always easy to tell, but if anybody was going to give it a try it would be the people of Seattle, where coffee culture is king and, as the hometown of Starbucks, the city has been responsible for exporting lattes and macchiatos to the rest of the world.

COFFEE COUNTRY

Coffee is an American obsession, beginning with the birth of the nation when the founding fathers met in the coffeehouses of Philadelphia to discuss and argue over the Declaration of Independence in 1776 and, after victory over the British in the Revolutionary War in 1783, to agree on the US Constitution. Tea may have been popular beforehand, but its association with the taxes imposed on the American colonies before the revolution and the control the British exercised on the tea trade from China and then later from India did it no favors in the newly constituted country. Coffee was also easier to import from the plantations where it was grown in Brazil and Central America, particularly after America's acquisition of New Orleans in 1812 as part of the Louisiana Purchase. Not only was the port city perfectly placed to import goods from the south, but it controlled trade on the Mississippi River as well, so that coffee spread into the interior as America expanded westward. The war of 1812 with Britain further distanced America from British

tea-drinking habits and, with tea imports prevented for the three-year duration of the war, coffee took a hold on the country that has never been broken.

If it is possible to explain why America is a coffee-drinking country in general, the reasons why Seattle in particular has become such a center of coffee shop culture are rather harder to elucidate. There are more coffee shops in the city per head than in anywhere else in America, beating such coffee towns as New York and Boston by a clear distance. Beyond suggesting that the people of Seattle just like coffee, it is by no means clear why this should be the case, but it is perhaps less surprising that Starbucks, which emerged out of this competitive environment, should go on to do so well elsewhere. It began in 1971 as a coffee roaster and retailer in Pike Place Market, but did not begin to expand as a coffee shop business until the company was taken over by one of its former employees, Howard Schultz, who remains the chairman and executive officer today. He began a rapid phase of expansion, taking the model established of the Starbucks coffee shops in Seattle to other cities in America before going international, opening the company's first coffee shop in Tokyo in 1996 and then following that with one in London two years later.

Starbucks now has over 20,000 coffee shops spread across six continents, more than 10 times as many as the second largest coffeehouse chain, the Britain-based Costa Coffee. The company has clearly found a huge market for its style of coffee shop and the coffee it sells, which is based on the Italian style of espresso, but its success is also due to the strong business model on which it has been based and an aggressive policy of expansion. But the company could not have become so successful without providing a service that its customers want and are prepared to pay for, in the process changing coffee culture around the world, both through its own coffee shops and its numerous imitators, providing the rest of us with a slice of the Seattle coffee scene.

FORBIDDEN STARBUCKS
A Starbucks opened in the Forbidden City in Beijing in 2000, but proved controversial. It closed in 2007.

ESPRESSO
◆

Espresso coffee provides the base from which lattes, Americanos, mochas, and all the other varieties found in thousands of coffee shops around the world are made. It is a style of coffee developed in Italy, where the first espresso machines were made at the beginning of the 20th century, and it is made by forcing almost boiling water through ground coffee beans at a high pressure. As well as some of the coffee dissolving in the hot water, the process creates a suspension of coffee solids, which is why espresso coffee is so thick compared to coffees produced by other methods.

Powdered Milk

Origin: America and other parts of the world

Date: 1990s onward

Type: Dry milk

+ CULTURAL
+ *SOCIAL*
+ *COMMERCIAL*
+ *POLITICAL*
+ MILITARY

The North American Free Trade Agreement (NAFTA) was signed by the United States, Canada, and Mexico in 1994, creating a free trade zone across the continent. It has mostly had a positive impact, promoting economic growth in all three countries, but it has created some problems as well. The trade in powered milk, or non-fat dry milk as it is also known, is one example. Powdered milk was first developed in the 19th century and became a valuable commodity because it keeps for longer and is easier to transport than liquid milk. But the removal of trade barriers under NAFTA led to the dumping of American powered milk in Mexico, disrupting the market and driving many Mexican dairy farmers out of business.

DUMPED MILK

Commodity dumping occurs when developed countries that subsidize their agricultural sector, such as America and the countries of the European Union, sell agricultural goods such as powdered milk to less developed countries at below the price of production. This can arise because the payment of subsidies often leads to overproduction as farmers receive a guaranteed price for everything, so they continue to produce more and more even after the market has become saturated. In a free market situation, where no subsidy payments are made, this imbalance would correct itself because the market price of the over-supplied goods would drop and some farmers would then turn to other more profitable crops. Where the price they receive has been fixed by the subsidy payments, they can then afford to sell the overproduced goods at less than market value and it is in the interests of the government of these countries for those goods to be exported otherwise it would bring the domestic market down further. This can often result in export subsidies being paid by governments as well as production subsidies to ensure that the oversupply is sold abroad, as has been the case with powdered milk in America.

One way for countries to prevent the dumping of agricultural commodities from other countries that subsidize their farming is to impose import tariffs, which ensure that the imported goods are not sold for less than the locally produced ones. The problem faced by Mexico's dairy farmers after 1994 was that, under the terms of NAFTA, all tariffs on goods traded between Mexico and America in either direction were removed, but the agricultural subsidy paid by the American government to its dairy farmers stayed in place. The agreement contained provisions for the gradual removal of tariffs on some agricultural goods, including powdered milk, but this proved insufficient protection for smaller dairy farmers in Mexico, who found that the market for their milk was now saturated with imports sold at a price below what it cost for them to produce milk themselves. It caused many to go out of business and, when put together with similar experiences in the markets for other agricultural goods, would result, it has been estimated, in over two million Mexican farm workers leaving the land since NAFTA began.

By 2008, the last of the Mexican tariffs on powdered milk was removed and there was a doubling in the quantity that was imported from America. Most of this was probably used in the food-manufacturing industry, and some of the products made then exported back to America, but nevertheless it had a devastating impact on the market for fresh milk as well. One of the consequences of the high levels of unemployment in rural areas has been a movement to cities, but also an increase in emigration to America, both legally and illegally. There is no way of knowing for certain, but it could also be argued that the increase in rural poverty and landlessness that has occurred in Mexico has contributed to the rise in drug trafficking in the country over the course of the past few decades and the subsequent drug war in the country that has resulted in the deaths of tens of thousands of people.

We don't want to come to the city and we don't want to emigrate to the United States. But people have no money.

Alberto Gómez Flores, Mexican representative of La Vía Campesina, which campaigns for the rights of small farmers and landless rural people

THE ZAPATISTA UPRISING

✦

On January 1st, 1994, the day NAFTA came into force, the Zapatista Army of National Liberation, a far-left revolutionary organization from the southern Mexican state of Chiapas, declared war on the Mexican state. The war only lasted a matter of days before a ceasefire was brokered and the Zapatistas have subsequently moderated their approach to protest. But they have continued to argue that the livelihoods of poor farmers in Chiapas, many of whom are of Mayan ethnicity, have been devastated by NAFTA because they cannot compete with the flood of subsidized food imported into Mexico from America.

NAFTA SIGNING
Mexican President Carlos Salinas, US President George Bush, and Prime Minister Brian Mulroney of Canada look on as NAFTA is signed.

Golden Rice

This Rice Could Save a Million Kids a Year.
Cover headline from Time *magazine on July 31st, 2000*

Origin: Switzerland and Germany

Date: 2000

Type: Genetically modified rice

+ CULTURAL
+ *SOCIAL*
+ COMMERCIAL
+ *POLITICAL*
+ MILITARY

Rice has been intimately involved in human history for thousands of years and is a staple food in the diet of more than two billion people around the world today. There are numerous ways in which it can be said to have changed the course of history, but this final chapter concentrates on one, the development of golden rice, which has not yet had an impact but has the potential to save millions of lives, even if it is currently controversial because it has been developed using the techniques of genetic modification (GM).

A GM DILEMMA

The World Health Organization has identified malnutrition as the most serious threat to public health around the world and, as well as an overall shortage of food, this also includes the deficiencies of nutritional elements that form an essential part of our diet. One of the most serious of these is vitamin A deficiency, which is particularly prevalent among young children and pregnant women and can cause blindness and weaken the immune system. About 200 million people around the world, mostly in Southeast Asia and Africa, are affected by this condition and, in one study published in 2005, it was found that it was responsible for the deaths of 600,000 children under the age of five every year as well as causing numerous health problems during growth and development that could have serious consequences in later life.

In 2000, a team of scientists led by Professor Ingo Potrykus of the Institute of Plant Sciences in Zurich and Professor Peter Beyer of the University of Freiburg in Germany developed a new variety of rice that contained beta-carotene in its grains, which being an orange pigment, gave them a golden yellow color. The compound is converted into vitamin A after it has been ingested and occurs naturally in many fruits and vegetables, particularly carrots, sweet potatoes, and squashes, which are orange and yellow as a consequence of containing high amounts of beta-carotene. But it does not occur in grains of rice, leading to some of the highest incidences of the deficiency in parts of the world where rice is the staple crop and in particular in Southeast Asia.

The deficiency can be addressed as a public health issue by, for instance, distributing vitamin supplements and instituting educational programs to advise on how to reduce the risks. It can also be reduced by the adoption of more long-term measures to alleviate poverty so that people can afford to eat a more varied diet that includes sufficient foods containing the vitamin. Golden rice could also be a part of the solution because it would provide vitamin A in the staple food of most people's diet in the region, but despite field trials that have shown no environmental drawbacks to its cultivation, it has yet to be grown beyond experimental research stations, primarily because of concerns raised over the use of genetic modification to introduce genes into the rice, some obtained from daffodils, so that it produces beta-carotene.

Golden rice represents the first use of genetic modification technology that addresses a particular health problem and it has been made freely available, other genetically modified plants having been developed by commercial companies primarily for profit. This has presented organizations that campaign against the use of genetic modification with the dilemma of whether they should continue to oppose the use of the technology in all circumstances, even when it offers the potential to alleviate a serious health problem. Some of the arguments made by protestors against the widespread cultivation of golden rice have relied on the distortion of the facts, often concentrating on the perception of the dangers of the technology, which, in this case, have been shown to be negligible or nonexistent and have caused unnecessary delays in the adoption of the rice. Others have raised legitimate questions about whether this is the right way to address the deficiency and if it represents the best use of resources, which might be better spent on tackling poverty, the underlying causes of the problem.

Beyond the immediate and pressing concerns of vitamin A deficiency, golden rice also shows that the food we eat has the potential to influence our lives in the future as much as it has done in the past. It has yet to change the course of history, and may never do, but it could also play a significant part in reducing malnutrition and, whatever opinions people hold about the rights and wrongs of the way food is produced today, that can surely not be a bad thing.

BETA-CAROTENE
Carrots are orange because of the beta-carotene they contain, which is also why they are good for the eyes.

ORANGE SWEET POTATOES

✦

Vitamin A deficiency has been a significant health problem in parts of Africa for many years and, as first reported in 2012 in Uganda, the development of the orange sweet potato, which is rich in beta-carotene, may prove to be one way of addressing it. Unlike golden rice, the orange sweet potato has been produced using conventional plant-breeding techniques to increase the quantity of beta-carotene it contains, a procedure not possible with rice because it does not contain any in the first place, and ongoing trials being conducted in Uganda and Mozambique have seen a significant reduction in the symptoms of the deficiency.

Further Reading

Brillat-Savarin, Jean Anthelme (1972, first published in 1829) *The Physiology of Taste*, New York: Knopf

Brissenden, Rosemary (1996) *South East Asian Food*, London: Penguin

Coe, Sophie D. and Michael D. (1996) *The True History of Chocolate*, London: Thames & Hudson

Collingham, Lizzie (2005) *Curry: A Biography*, London: Chatto & Windus

Colquhoun, Kate (2008) *Taste: The Story of Britain through its Cooking*, London: Bloomsbury

Dalby, Andrew (2003) *Food in the Ancient World from A to Z*, London: Routledge

David, Elizabeth (1960) *French Provincial Cooking*, London: Michael Joseph

Davidson, Alan (1999) *The Oxford Companion to Food*, Oxford: Oxford University Press

Flandrin, Jean-Louis and Massimo Montanari (1999) *Food: A Culinary History from Antiquity to the Present*, New York: Columbia University Press

Fletcher, Nichola (2010) *Caviar: A Global History*, London: Reaktion Books

Freedman, Paul, ed. (2007) *Food: The History of Taste*, London: Thames & Hudson

Hom, Ken (1990) *The Taste of China*, London: Pavilion Books

Hyman, Clarissa (2013) *Oranges: A Global History*, London: Reaktion Books

Jaffrey, Madhur (2003) *Madhur Jaffrey's Ultimate Curry Bible*, London: Ebury Press

Keay, John (2005) *The Spice Route: A History*, London: John Murray

Kiple, Kenneth F. and Kriemhild Coneè Ornelas, eds. (2000) *The Cambridge World History of Food (Vol. 1 & 2)*, Cambridge: Cambridge University Press

Koeppel, Dan (2008) *Banana: The Fate of the Fruit That Changed the World*, New York: Hudson Street Press

Kurlansky, Mark (2013) *Birdseye: The Adventures of a Curious Man*, New York: Broadway Books

Lanchester, John (1996) *The Debt to Pleasure*, London: Picador

LeBor, Adam (2006) *City of Oranges: Arabs and Jews in Jaffa*, London: Bloomsbury

Luard, Elisabeth (1986) *European Peasant Cookery*, London: Bantam Press

McGee, Harold (2004) *McGee on Food and Cooking: An Encyclopedia of Kitchen Science, History and Culture*, London: Hodder & Stoughton

McGovern, Patrick F. (2009) *Uncorking the Past: The Quest for Wine, Beer, and Other Alcoholic Beverages*, Berkeley, CA: University of California Press

Millstone, Erik and Tim Lang (2004) *The Atlas of Food: Who Eats What, Where, and Why*, Brighton: Earthscan

Newman, Kara (2013) *The Secret Financial Life of Food: From Commodities Markets to Supermarkets*, New York: Columbia University Press

O'Connell, Sanjida (2004) *Sugar: The Grass that Changed the World*, London: Virgin Books

Parker, Philip, ed. (2012) *The Great Trade Routes: A History of Cargoes and Commerce Over Land and Sea*, London: Conway

Pendergrast, Mark (1993) *For God, Country and Coca-Cola: The Unauthorized History of the Great American Soft Drink and the Company that Makes It*, London: Weidenfeld & Nicholson

Pilcher, Jeffrey M., ed. (2012) *The Oxford Handbook of Food History*, Oxford: Oxford University Press

Pollan, Michael (2013) *Cooked: A Natural History of Transformation*, London: Allen Lane

Pollan, Michael (2006) *The Omnivore's Dilemma: The search for a perfect meal in a fast-food world*, London: Bloomsbury

Reader, John (2008) *Propitious Esculent: The Potato in World History*, London: William Heinemann

Rubel, William (2011) *Bread: A Global History*, London: Reaktion Books

Shephard, Sue (2000) *Pickled, Potted and Canned: The Story of Food Preserving*, London: Headline

Smith, Andrew F. (2008) *Hamburger: A Global History*, London: Reaktion Books

Standage, Tom (2007) *A History of the World in Six Glasses*, London: Atlantic Books

Standage, Tom (2009) *An Edible History of Humanity*, London: Atlantic Books

Tannahill, Reay (1988) *Food in History* (Revised Edition), London: Penguin Books

Toussaint-Samat, Maguelonne (1992) *A History of Food*, Oxford: Blackwell

Warner, Jessica (2003) *Craze: Gin and Debauchery in the Age of Reason*, London: Profile Books

Wrangham, Richard (2009) *Catching Fire: How Cooking Made Us Human*, London: Profile Books

Useful Websites:

British Nutrition Foundation: *www.nutrition.org.uk*

Official site of the town of Castelnaudary: *www.ville-castelnaudary.fr*

Coca-Cola: *www.coca-cola.com*

Consultative Group on International Agricultural Research (CGIAR): *www.cgiar.org*

Department for Environment, Food and Rural Affairs (UK): *www.gov.uk/government/organisations/department-for-environment-food-rural-affairs*

Fairtrade Foundation: *www.fairtrade.org.uk*

Food and Agriculture Organization of the United Nations: *www.fao.org*

The Golden Rice Project: *www.goldenrice.org*

Green & Black's Chocolate: *www.greenandblacks.co.uk*

The Hereford Cattle Society: *www.herefordcattle.org*

International Olive Council: *www.internationaloliveoil.org*

The International Rice Research Institute: *www.irri.org*

Marine Stewardship Council: *www.msc.org*

Pilsner Urquell: *www.pilsnerurquell.com*

La Société des Caves de Roquefort: *www.roquefort-societe.com*

Starbucks Coffee Company: *www.starbucks.com*

Theo Chocolate: *www.theochocolate.com*

UK Tea Council: *www.tea.co.uk*

UNESCO: *www.unesco.org*

US Food and Drug Administration: *www.fda.gov*

The Washington Banana Museum: *www.bananamuseum.com*

World Health Organization: *www.who.org*

World Trade Organization: *www.wto.org*

Index

Credits